Praise for *Democracy and the N*

"Ramos' work is impressive for its breadth and refreshing for its focus on tangible solutions and opportunities at a time that is dominated by expressions of concern about the growing litany of problems we all see before us."

—Anthony D. Romero, Executive Director,
American Civil Liberties Union

"Henry Ramos doesn't merely envision a new, more equitable, inclusive economy, supported by truly representative democracy. He shows us how to get there."

—Jared Bernstein, Ph.D. and former Chief Economist
and Economic Advisor to Vice President Joe Biden

"Ramos offers a compelling vision of how we can create a more equitable and inclusive economy by building on real life examples and proven practices that are showing us the way; in doing so, he reveals that the future we wish for is already here—should we choose to act."

—Deborah Frieze, Founder and President, Boston Impact Initiative

"This book is necessary reading for all seeking to live in a world infused with equity and justice. Getting there requires work. Fortunately, Henry A. J. Ramos has provided us with the blueprint for action."

—Angela Glover Blackwell, Founder in Residence, PolicyLink

"Every now and then a book appears that gives us a new perspective on our situation and flips a switch so we see new possibilities for our future. *Democracy and the Next American Economy* is one of those works."

—Susan Henderson, Executive Director,
Disability Rights Education and Defense Fund

"Ramos offers a strong case for a new and different kind of way to advance democracy and prosperity-sharing based on real life examples from all across the nation."

—Saru Jayaraman, Co-Founder and Co-Director,
Restaurant Opportunities Centers (ROC) United

"Henry A. J. Ramos has assembled a must-read book for all people who want a more inclusive and sustainable political economy that is better for people and the planet."
—Cristina Jiménez, Co-Founder and
Executive Director, United We Dream

"Democracy and the Next American Economy should be required reading for all Americans who are troubled by our current path and seeking tangible alternatives."
—Zachary Norris, Executive Director, Ella Baker Center

"Inspiration is important—but so is a roadmap. With this book, Ramos offers a practical pathway to a better way forward, using proven and promising innovations from regions and cities across the land to connect the dots."
—Manuel Pastor, Director, Program on Environmental
and Regional Equity, University of Southern California

"Henry Ramos approaches his research like any good organizer: he gathers people and ideas and creates a synthesis that is greater than the individual parts."
—Felicia J. Wong, President and CEO, Roosevelt Institute

DEMOCRACY
WHERE
AND THE
PROSPERITY
NEXT AMERICAN
MEETS JUSTICE
ECONOMY

DEMOCRACY
WHERE
AND THE
PROSPERITY
NEXT AMERICAN
MEETS JUSTICE
ECONOMY

HENRY A. J. RAMOS

Foreword by Anthony D. Romero
Executive Director of the American Civil Liberties Union

Arte Público Press
Houston, Texas

This volume is made possible in part through a major grant from the Marguerite Casey Foundation, as well as generous individual contributions from Dr. Michelle Cale, Shirley Fredricks, Sergio Garcia and Amelia Gonzalez, Linda Gebroe, Robert L. McKay, Feisal Nanji and Gretchen Sandler. We are grateful for their support.

Recovering the past, creating the future

Arte Público Press
University of Houston
4902 Gulf Fwy, Bldg 19, Rm 100
Houston, Texas 77204-2004

Cover design by Mora Des¡gns

Names: Ramos, Henry A. J., 1959- author.
Title: Democracy and the next American economy : where prosperity meets justice / Henry A.J. Ramos ; foreword by Anthony D. Romero.
Description: Houston, TX : Arte Público Press, [2019]
Identifiers: LCCN 2018053265 (print) I LCCN 2018060163 (ebook) I ISBN 9781518505706 (epub) I ISBN 9781518505713 (kindle) I ISBN 9781518505720 (pdf) I ISBN 9781558858763 (alk. paper)
Subjects: LCSH: Democracy—United States. I Democracy—Economic aspects—United States. I Polarization (Social sciences)—United States. I Income distribution—United States. I Violence—United States. I Social justice—United States. I United States—Economic conditions—21st century.
Classification: LCC JK1726 (ebook) I LCC JK1726 .R36 2019 (print) I DDC 330.973—dc23
LC record available at https://lccn.loc.gov/2018053265

19 20 21   4 3 2 1

This book is dedicated to the everyday men, women, and young people of America who have struggled and sacrificed over the centuries to advance freedom, democracy, opportunity, justice, community, kindness, joy, and beauty.

Contents

Every moment is an organizing opportunity, every person a potential activist, every minute a chance to change the world.

—Dolores Huerta

Preface

We must trust our own thinking. Trust where we're going.
And get the job done.

— Wilma Mankiller

In the pages that follow, I offer both a critique of current trends in American political economy as well as a call to action and a peek into a select sampling of alternative emerging practices that, properly attended to and scaled, would do much to put America and the world on a more just and sustainable path. Presently, the topics covered here are of interest across the US political and intellectual landscape. There is no shortage of loud and enthusiastic voices entering the fray with varying ideas and opinions about what is happening in the current moment. There are fewer pundits offering more concrete and proven (or at least highly promising) alternatives. This book is my humble attempt to contribute to the discourse from a progressive perspective through analysis of the issues, but also with an eye to lifting up models of innovation that are showing us the way to a future of living democracy, economic restoration and environmental sustainability.

I come to the conversation with a healthy degree of reluctance and regret. Frankly, I wish it were not necessary to offer this contribution to the present discourse. I would have much preferred for national and global events over the past several years to take us in another, better direction, one that would have inspired a greater sense of purpose and continuing progress from a human and ecological point of view. But with the Fall 2016 election of Donald J. Trump to serve as the United

States' 45th president, and subsequent events, it has proven impossible for me not to make an impassioned plea for another pathway to the future. In the current context, it is vital for all forward-looking American civic leaders, intellectuals, artists, workers, youth, immigrants and others with strong opposition to the path we are on as a nation to actively express their concerns and proposals for a better way. What follows is my personal response to this imperative, first and foremost as a progressive American and, second, as a Latino American. On both fronts, the impulse to pen this work came during the very early stages of the 2016 Republican presidential primary, following Donald Trump's announcement of his intention to seek the presidency.

In Trump's very first statement as a candidate, he disparaged Mexican immigrants as drug dealers, criminals and rapists. Soon thereafter he had one of North America's most prestigious Latino journalists, Jorge Ramos of the Univision Television Network, a naturalized US citizen from Mexico, physically removed from an Iowa press conference for asking uncomfortable questions about the candidate's positions on immigration issues. Soon after that, Trump went on record arguing that a California federal district court judge, Gonzalo P. Curiel, a Mexican American who was slated to hear cases related to alleged wrongdoing by Trump University and the Trump administration's authority to build a new wall separating the US and Mexico, was unsuited to preside over these cases owing to his Mexican heritage. Trump later went on to publicly chastise San Juan, Puerto Rico's mayor, Carmen Yulín Cruz Soto, after Hurricane Maria, accusing her of "poor leadership" (following her criticism of Trump's lackluster response to the crisis) and implying that the people of the devastated island were not doing enough to help themselves. And, most recently, in May 2018, he used the word "animals" to refer to the undocumented individuals being repatriated along the US southern border by ICE under the administration's crack down on immigrants. These irresponsible assertions and actions were sadly matched by comparably objectionable and inappropriate comments made by Trump during his first two years in office, relating to African Americans, Muslim Americans, Native Americans, disabled Americans, women, African countries and others.

Trump's public bigotry has been complemented in many instances by reckless policy decisions and proposals, such as withdrawing American support for the Paris Agreement on Global Climate Change, imposing significant new tariffs on China (risking a global trade war), and proposing that we combat mass public school shootings by arming school teachers and administrators. Such irresponsible positions have been met with international concern and a high degree of dismay on the part of Americans all across our nation. Indeed, the entire Trump phenomenon has put all people of conscience and goodwill in a troubled state of mind. And for good reason. The fact that someone like Trump could win the presidency at all suggests something fundamentally new and dangerous has transpired in modern American political and civic culture. Indeed, the kind of vile and divisive behavior exemplified by Trump is entirely unprecedented in American presidential history. To any rational, responsible and reasonable observer, current circumstances underscore that a certain unhinging has taken hold in relation to our national identity and psyche. This is not a safe or necessary situation for America or the world. Rather, it is one that calls for an extremely heightened sense of concern and a redoubling of organized efforts to resist Trumpism's further degradation of American politics and culture.

But the problem is much bigger than merely Trump and the ideology of selfishness and division that his brand of leadership represents. Even more than that, the very nature of our political economy and civic culture has been transformed to such a degree in recent decades that our systems are simply no longer working for most people. Not only are too many of our people being exploited, abused and otherwise left behind in the swirl of trying to achieve or maintain cultural and economic security, but also the expanding machinations of America's modern economy and consumption culture have left growing numbers of Americans feeling vacant and deeply unhappy. With rates of depression, substance abuse and suicide reaching unprecedented levels in recent years, it is hard to deny that all is not well on the home front. Indeed, if asked what they would want the country's social, political and economic agreements to look like if we could start over from scratch, few Americans would support the idea of re-creating our current system. Rather, they would conclude that we badly need a change in course.

This book offers thoughts, ideas and suggestions specifically intended to help advance organized resistance to the misguided trends we currently see in our politics and economic practices, based on the work and thinking of progressive activists and innovators of many diverse backgrounds from all across America. To those who are in the vanguard of change advocacy and thus closest to the work and thinking highlighted here, there will be relatively few headlines in this reading. But for the many progressive Americans across the land, and others, who are deeply concerned and want change but are not situated at the center of gravity in politics and civic decision-making, this book will provide a valuable survey of the issues and a guide to the many ways their voices can be heard in the coming stages of our national journey. This is my main audience and intention in advancing the observations and perspectives that follow. Although the book is extensively researched and referenced throughout (building on highly credible information sources in each instance), there is no pretense that this is a scientific or scholarly work. Nor is there any representation that the leaders and groups included here are the only ones making meaningful change possible in contemporary America. Rather, the work that follows—largely journalistic in approach— offers a broad survey of proven and promising practices in democratic engagement and prosperity-sharing. These models in turn are emblematic of the range of innovative approaches progressive Americans need to champion in order to help make our national political economy more inclusive and responsive to common people.

To achieve these ends, however, will require progressive Americans to pursue and wield political power in unprecedented ways during the coming years. This is an inherent challenge for many on our side of the political spectrum. Often, both liberal leaders and progressive activists have demonstrated their discomfort with acquiring and using power in ways conservatives have not. For example, with only technical electoral college victories after losing the national popular votes in both the elections of 2000 and 2016, Republican presidents have subsequently acted in office as though they were elected with large mandates to enact far-reaching legislative and regulatory changes. In each instance, the resulting policies and actions have compromised our national strength and standing. By contrast, liberals elected to the presidency in 1992-2000 and then again in 2008-2016 have won handily at the polls, only subsequently to act with extreme caution once in office in ways that failed to maximize the advance of more progressive policies.

Given all that is presently at stake in our national political context, progressives simply have to develop a new relationship with power, one that is more enabling than disabling and one that is more suited to winning than losing. At the end of the day, this all boils down to being a matter of faith: faith in our ideas, faith in our positions and faith in each other. It is as the late, great former chief of the Cherokee Nation, Wilma Mankiller once said: "We must trust our own thinking. Trust where we're going. And get the job done." Once we adopt that imperative, once we are able to align our efforts and resources in service to it, and once we cast aside our doubts and differences in ways that harness the full breadth of our humanity and vision, progressive Americans will be able to change the course of our nation, and in the process to change our world. Indeed, this is what it will take to get the job done in the future that awaits us.

In many respects, I am precisely the sort of reporter that conservatives will roundly discount and criticize for my analysis and proposals in this volume. I am a native Californian and a graduate of two of our nation's most prestigious liberal centers of higher learning: the University of California at Berkeley and Harvard University. During my formative studies at these institutions, I was mentored or otherwise taught by the likes of Laura D'Andrea Tyson (dean of the U.C. Berkeley Haas School of Business and former chief economic advisor to President Bill Clinton), Robert Reich (currently a U.C. Berkeley professor of public policy and a former secretary of labor during the Clinton presidency) and John Rawls (the late Harvard professor considered by many to be the most important liberal political philosopher of the twentieth century). I am also a former professional of leading social justice philanthropies, including the Ford Foundation in New York and the charitable grant-making foundation of Levi Strauss & Company in San Francisco. In addition, I am a longstanding member of the ACLU, an activist artist and immigrant rights advocate and a proud former board member of various progressive advocacy organizations, including the Women's Foundation of California and Asian Americans Advancing Justice. All of these markers of my journey place me squarely left of center on the political and ideological spectrum.

However, despite these "credentials," I am otherwise an unlikely individual to advance the perspective and arguments that I do throughout this work. In fact, I was raised in Los Angeles in a solidly conservative Republican household. My family owned a small business and enthusiastically supported Governor Ronald Reagan and other conservative politicians, such as Barry Goldwater, Jr. and John H. Rousselot, with whom my WWII-veteran father worked closely. My first real job was representing Latino armed forces veterans through the American GI Forum, whose leadership was then largely Republican. I was raised—and still pray—in the traditions of the Catholic Church. I live on a ten-acre ranch in a largely conservative rural community. I drive a 1993 Ford F-150 pickup truck and own a shotgun that I am occasionally called to use in order to protect my livestock from encroaching predators. In all of these respects, I simply am not the "liberal" stereotype conservative detractors may want to characterize me as because of the views expressed here.

Their potential attacks and rejoinders are of little consequence to me, because I present my case for needed fundamental change in America not to them but to progressives and to people who believe in the democratic promise. My aim here is precisely to "preach to the choir" in ways that will help those of us on the progressive left to better harmonize our efforts to achieve the change we seek, and that our nation and world badly need. I try to achieve that in part by offering a critique of everything that is not working in our democracy and economy today as a result of the last four decades of conservative-inspired gerrymandering, tax cutting, deregulation and trickle-down economics. But I also attempt to make the case for new and different approaches to solving public problems from a decidedly progressive perspective by providing examples of programs for building power and expressing our voices in order to restore the vitality of our waning democracy and our increasingly unequal economy.

In taking on this ambitious research and writing project, I knew I would need and benefit from much outside help. So I assembled a group of advisors and informants who are leading progressive activists and thought leaders. In addition, I interviewed a number of allied leaders and innovators in civic activism and social investment for their ideas and perspectives. Altogether, more than sixty such indi viduals were my consultants, all of whom are referenced in the Appendix at the end of this volume. Several of the experts interviewed and/or consulted provided especially helpful editorial review and suggestions warranting special recognition here. These include Darrick Hamilton, Scott Nielsen, Carl Palmer, Kathi Pugh, C. M. Samala and Susan Phinney Silver. The collective input and guidance provided by these many diverse sources proved to be essential. But while the inputs and counsel of these leading Americans were essential to the book's completion in its final form, I alone am responsible for any and all conclusions herein that readers may find objectionable or otherwise questionable.

In addition, I have other friends and allies to recognize for their invaluable assistance with the completion of this volume. This includes my publisher, Dr. Nicolás Kanellos of Arte Público Press and his able team of editors and staff, including especially Marina Tristán, Dr. Gabriela Baeza Ventura, Nellie González Robledo and Beatríz Verónica Romero. For some forty years, Arte Público Press has served as the nation's leading producer of Latino-related literary and art publications, as well as educational textbooks and contemporary nonfiction works covering issues of importance to Latino communities, the United States and the Americas in general. It has been my great privilege to be affiliated with the Arte Público Press for now half that time as an author, senior editor and special projects coordinator. I also owe heartfelt gratitude to Frank de Jesús Acosta, my valued research associate for the project and past collaborator on the Arte Público Press Latino Young Men & Boys book series, and Marsha Caldwell, my executive assistant. Both of these individuals have been longtime partners and supporters of my work.

I also wish to recognize the inspiration and example of various leaders and thinkers I once had the honor of collaborating with and learning from, who are no longer with us but whose life works have influenced my thinking and priorities over the years. These include, among others: Evelio Grillo, the long-revered Afro-Cuban Bay Area social worker, activist and writer; Tom Hayden, the late renowned peace activist and California state senator; Dr. Antonia Pantoja, founder of the education and youth empowerment organization ASPIRA; Russell Sakaguchi, the former director of ARCO/BP Foundation; Willie Velásquez, the legendary founder of the Southwest Voter Registration Education Project; and Lynn Walker-Huntley, my late former colleague and mentor at the Ford Foundation who led the organization's civil rights work in the 1980s and 1990s. Leaders and thinkers like these committed their lives and sacrificed greatly for justice in all of its forms over many decades. Their experiences, and the grace and courage with which they faced a lifetime of challenge, should never be forgotten by those who continue to fight now.

Finally, I am particularly indebted to my deceased Mexican grandparents, Jesús and Carmen Rodríguez and Enrique and Josefina Ramos, whose vision and many sacrifices brought them to a successful life in the United States one hundred years ago, making possible all the many gifts that have been bestowed upon their progeny, and especially me. Their hard work, their devout commitment to the teachings and ways of the Catholic Church, and their selflessness in building for the future generations made a lasting impact on my own values and choices, for which I will be forever grateful. Most of all, I am indebted to my beloved wife, Claudia Lenschen Ramos, who for the better part of thirty years has endured my restless pursuit of justice and harmony in our otherwise troubled world, and who has always been there to support me throughout the journey. Without her unwavering and unequivocal support throughout my research and writing, this volume simply would not have been possible.

Henry A. J. Ramos
June 1, 2018

Foreword

These are challenging times for people who believe in democracy, the rule of law, and responsible government in America. They are also challenging times for people and families that are struggling to survive under increasingly unfair and unequal economic circumstances.

America as we know and understand it is a nation based on the ideals of equality, fairness and opportunity. But for a variety of reasons, those ideals remain out of reach for many. We live in an era of growing civic dysfunction, barriers to access, disparities in wealth and public discord. It is a time of heightened intergroup tension, racism and xenophobia, as well as expanding departures from established democratic traditions and growing class divisions.

Somewhat similar circumstances gave rise to the formation of the American Civil Liberties Union (ACLU) nearly 100 years ago, in 1920. At that time, such leading American figures as Roger Baldwin, Helen Keller, Felix Frankfurter and Jane Addams came together to establish the ACLU as a bulwark against arbitrary and unjust overreach by government leaders and agencies relative to the constitutionally guaranteed rights and liberties of the American people.

At the time of the ACLU's formation, just as today, rights and justice in America were being severely denied to many American workers, immigrants, women, and racial and other minority populations. Subsequent eras posed new challenges, including the Japanese American Internment policies of the 1940s, the McCarthy era communist witch hunts of the 1950s, the Vietnam War and Watergate-informed White House excesses of the 1960s and 1970s, "tough on crime" policies of the 1980s and 1990s that led to mass incarceration, and the Patriot Act of 2001 and other post-911 encroachments on civil liberties in the name of national security.

For nearly one hundred years, in these and other contexts, the ACLU has sought to advance American constitutional ideals through a combination of strategic litigation, lobbying, public education and civic activism. We have mobilized our members and allies across the country to defend and expand civil liberties at every opportunity. And we have made a meaningful difference in preserving and protecting the rights and responsibilities of citizenship in the United States of America.

Today, those who support the ACLU's aims, and progressive Americans more generally, are faced with a prevalent policy and power mindset among the nation's ruling elite that is patently antithetical to our core values and beliefs. With each passing day, we see growing evidence that the very nature of the social contract that has successfully guided generation after generation of Americans is being tattered. And it is increasingly self-evident that this shift in national culture and practice is leading us to places that are inconsistent with our essential identity and standing in the world.

While it is true that our nation has always faced the impulse of high-ranking public officials and agencies to abuse their power, our nation has rarely seen a challenge as frontal to our civic integrity as what we have before us today. All of this raises the bar for Americans to challenge and contest our current direction, to organize and join forces with an eye to regaining the best of what we stand for, and to use the courts and other public offices to advocate for the change we seek.

It also compels those of us who share a more progressive view of America's best possibilities to help scale and otherwise accelerate emerging new models in democratic self-governance and economic opportunity that can show us the way to a better future. Henry A. J. Ramos' book, *Democracy and the Next American Economy: Where Prosperity Meets Justice*, is an important contribution to this endeavor. It offers a compelling analysis of our present circumstances and a roadmap to a more promising future based on nascent civic and economic innovations that simultaneously honor the spirit of our nation's founding principles, while portending wholly new modalities for realizing our best potential going forward. Ramos' work is impressive for its breadth and refreshing for its focus on tangible solutions and opportunities at a time that is dominated by expressions of concern about the growing litany of problems we all see before us. His research is heavily informed by extensive inputs from an impressive array of more than fifty leading community, organizational and thought leaders whose work is helping to drive much of progressive America's evolving thinking and action on the issues. Perhaps most compelling about Ramos' offerings is his emphasis on the need for new efforts by progressive leaders to join forces in more lasting and impactful ways than ever before, which he sees as an essential strategy for change at a pivotal moment in history.

Faced with so many extraordinary challenges to our fundamental values, now is not a time to become paralyzed or driven to small thinking or inaction. Ramos does not advocate for change on the margins or in increments. Rather, he is calling for a significant reordering of American politics and economy to meet the imperatives of our nation's formative promises in new and unprecedented ways during the coming generation. The pages that follow are essential reading for our times.

Anthony D. Romero
Executive Director
American Civil Liberties Union
June 2018

Introduction

When people are lost in the wilderness, they move through
predictable stages. The first reaction is to deny they are lost.
— Margaret J. ("Meg") Wheatley
So Far From Home[1]

This book is about encouraging a new and better way forward for
America based on emerging innovations in progressive political and
economic thought, policy and practice. It is intended to help us find
our way forward in a political climate that suggests our nation has lost
its way as the result of pursuing now nearly forty years of policies
designed to put privilege and profit before people and the planet.
Where once our nation was the envy of the world for its robust
democracy and institutional stability, scientific leadership, quality
schools, growing egalitarianism and purposeful global leadership,
today we find ourselves in a notable decline on many of these fronts.[2]

Large US-based global corporations, their board leaders and executives, and those who benefit most directly from their decisions and
power have done well enough in recent years; indeed, the wealthy and
the powerful today have accumulated more for themselves than any
generation of past Americans, save perhaps for those who prevailed in
the prime years of American industrialization, some one hundred years
ago. Yet rather than directing the remarkable wealth our nation has produced in recent times to improvements in the average American's quality of life, the opposite is taking place. It really should not be so.

Despite the current order and direction of things, there are exciting emerging alternatives available to us. These include whole new
modalities in responsible development and investment, sustainable

energy, workplace quality, education, voting, civic participation, and social justice. If properly supported and scaled, they could offer us all a far better way forward. But to realize that potentiality, Americans who care most about our national integrity and future success will have to organize and fight as never before. Indeed, we can and we must do so if our nation is to remain a beacon of hope, opportunity and leadership for its own people and others around the world.

A Nation at Risk

There can be no doubt, much is at stake. All around us there are growing signs that America has lost its moorings. The world's once mightiest democracy and economy finds itself today in a state of domestic upheaval and global decline. Recent growing ideological and political divisions, income and wealth inequality and public violence (often racially, religiously or politically motivated) have marked the most dramatic and challenging moments in the American journey since the late 1960s and early 1970s.[3]

Particularly disturbing have been the renewal of intense racial and religious divisions over a multi-year spate of shootings of unarmed African American citizens by white Americans (mainly police officers), a notable spike in carnage stemming from the mass shootings of innocent civilians in places ranging from concert halls and dance clubs to schools and churches, and a corresponding national increase in anti-Muslim, anti-immigrant, anti-Semitic, and anti-abortion violence (or threats of violence).

Meg Wheatley, a social commentator and systems analyst, assessed the situation in her book *So Far From Home* (2012) as a toxic combination of narcissism, polarization and paranoia that has overtaken American culture and politics in recent years—the net result being a nation separated in cultural, economic and ideological camps that are increasingly dislocated and in conflict. National elections over the past decade have reflected the public's deep partisan and ideological divisions and its ambivalence about the leadership needed to right America's course. In effect, voters in recent elections have decided to split the difference in most cycles by dividing power between the executive and the legislative branches of government.

But under split Republican and Democratic leadership, little progress on economic and social policies has been achieved and partisan wrangling, public anger and frustration have intensified across the political spectrum—starting with the short-lived Occupy Wall Street and Tea Party movements.[4]

Intolerance and Division on the Rise

This toxic combination of factors and forces has unleashed formidable challenges to modern American democracy and global economic leadership, producing a historic lack of public confidence in American institutions[5] and ultimately making possible the recent unlikely election of controversial Republican businessman and political neophyte Donald J. Trump as president of the United States. Trump ran on an unapologetically nationalistic platform that enthusiastically attacked immigrants and Muslims, while also insulting women, people with disabilities and other groups of Americans along the way.[6] Advancing his campaign under the tag line "America First," Trump claimed the essential purpose of his candidacy and presidency would be to "Make America Great Again."[7]

Now, ironically, in the aftermath of Trump's victory, for many, the former businessman and television personality's election and subsequent, chaotic service in office have signaled a possible end to America's century of global leadership. Only six months into the Trump presidency, record low numbers of Americans expressed confidence in the new executive or the direction of our nation. According to the Gallup Organization, in July 2017 some sixty percent of Americans of all political persuasions already disapproved of Trump's performance in the White House. No post-World War II American president has ever received such low marks in such a short period of time following his election. And according to Rasmussen's Summer 2017 polling data, only one-third of likely American voters believed the nation was on the right track.[8]

Americans' concerns about the nation's most recently elected chief executive were unprecedented in our modern history and disconcerting. Through a combination of bizarre policy advancements and retreats, public remarks and tweets, Trump spent his first two years in office defying established presidential decorum and conventional political rules of the road.[9] While candidate Trump had threatened to do as much during his 2016 campaign, once in office, it quickly became apparent that his views and approach carried real-life and highly troublesome consequences. In August 2017, for example, the Trump presidency sunk to new lows when in the aftermath of several deaths resulting from a violent rally of white supremacists at the University of Virginia in Charlottesville the president asserted that counter-protesters were equally reprehensible and responsible for the violence. Trump's inflammatory remarks on the events in Charlottesville were publicly condemned by Americans of all racial backgrounds, even by members of the president's own Republican Party, as well as by leaders around the world.[10]

At a well-attended rally in Alabama in September 2017, Trump mocked the Black Lives Matter (BLM) Movement's legitimate concerns about increasing incidents of African American deaths at the hands of police and allied authorities during recent years. Challenging the decision taken by many African American professional football players to peacefully protest in solidarity with BLM by kneeling in silence during the national anthem at National Football League (NFL) games, Trump brashly asserted that he would like to encourage NFL franchise owners to disallow such conduct, saying, "Wouldn't you love to see one of these NFL owners, when somebody disrespects our flag, to say, 'Get that son of a bitch off the field right now. Out! He's fired. He's fired!'"[11]

Also in September 2017, the president moved to rescind former President Obama's executive order allowing nearly 800,000 mainly non-citizen Latino immigrants brought to the United States without documentation as minors to remain in the country to work and study under the Deferred Action for Childhood Arrivals (DACA) Program. By all reasonable accounts, DACA status holders have been overwhelming contributors to American society and the economy over recent years.[12] The decision to end DACA thus has posed serious deportation threats to upstanding individuals who have effectively known life in no other country than ours—threats that would materially and detrimentally impact not only the affected individuals, but also their families (many of which include both mixed, citizen and non-citizen members) and the numerous communities in which they reside. Trump later doubled down on his anti-immigrant proclamations, introducing in Spring 2018 the most heinous US policy since the Japanese American internment of WWII, separating Central American refugees from their children at the US-Mexico border, by isolating the children, toddlers and even infants in prison-like facilities across South Texas in defiance of US obligations under established international law.

In December 2017 through early 2018, credible reporting (covered only briefly during the 2016 election cycle) surfaced regarding numerous women who, over the years, have accused the president of sexual misconduct. Such coverage closely followed revelations of major sexual impropriety against women by numerous well known male media and political figures, including Trump's White House Secretary Rob Porter.[13] Amid growing calls for the president to address the allegations and the general phenomenon of sexual impropriety in society and at the workplace, a tone-deaf Trump tweeted statements that reflected his concern for the men accused of sexual misdeeds, rather than the women subjected to unacceptable encroachments on their physical integrity and feelings.[14] This response, coupled with earlier incidents suggesting related sexual abuse and misconduct involving Trump and/or close allies of the president, fueled a wave of righteous public outrage.[15]

In February 2018, following several mass shootings, including the one at Marjory Stoneman Douglas High School in Parkland, Florida, affected youth and community members initiated one of the most forceful calls ever for new restrictions on the sale and possession of semi-automatic firearms. Key retail vendors responded with surprising swiftness to the resulting #NeverAgain Campaign, changing their sales policies in hopes of preventing future massacres.[16] Walmart and Kroger made significant changes, raising their minimum age for firearms sales from 18 to 21. Dick's Sporting Goods went further, discontinuing its sale of assault weapons and ceasing to do business with companies represented in its non-firearms-related product lines that also manufacture such products. President Trump and Congress, on the other hand, proposed a range of minimum-level policy responses, including almost everything except the obvious: banning assault weapons altogether for civilian use. Indeed, rather than focusing on reducing the weapons available to cause more school shootings, Trump's main proposal after Parkland was to more fully arm school personnel with hand guns.

The Future of America in the Balance

Trump's actions have set the stage for a dangerous new era of racially and culturally charged conflicts across the nation by reopening old wounds and sensitivities flowing from the US's deep history of racial inequality, violence and injustice. Indeed, one of the central issues the Trump presidency has brought to the surface is the nation's growing multicultural diversity and how white Americans are challenged by its implications for future policy and power-sharing in national governance. It has been well-documented that Trump's core base of supporters include a broad swath of disaffected white Americans, many of them non-college educated and predisposed to notions of white supremacy.[17] Among non-college educated whites, Trump's 2016 election margin of victory over his Democratic opponent Hillary Clinton was especially significant. According to the Pew Research Center, " . . . Trump's margin among whites without a college degree [was] the largest among any candidate in exit polls since 1980. Two-thirds (67%) of non-college whites backed Trump, compared with just 28% who supported Clinton, resulting in a 39-point advantage for Trump among this group."[18]

In effect, the Trump Presidency has raised the fundamental question: What kind of nation will America be in the future? Will it continue to strive towards being an open and inclusive society that builds constructively on its growing multiculturalism and a robust middle class? Or rather will the United States become an exclusive and closed society that disproportionately benefits a shrinking uber-class of already wealthy and privileged white Americans? As America approached the mid-term elections of 2018, these issues hung in the balance and were increasingly bubbling over into additional public discord and violence.

To be sure, our nation's democracy and economy have faced other major crises and moral challenges that we have successfully overcome or otherwise reconciled in the past. We can think back to the Civil War, the widespread labor strife of the late nineteenth and early twentieth centuries, the Japanese American internment of the World War II era, the McCarthy era witch hunts for communists in the 1950s and the Civil Rights movements, the movement to end the war with Vietnam and the Watergate scandal in the 1960s and 1970s; these were comparably violent and transitional chapters in our history that presented similarly daunting challenges to our national political integrity and domestic tranquility. And we can also think back on other hard economic times in our past, such as the Great Depression of the 1930s and the economic challenges of the late 1970s, the early 1980s and the early 1990s to be reminded that we are not entirely on untraveled terrain.

We made it through those traumas, with a more broadly shared sense of collective purpose, goodwill and optimism. Sadly today, however, something new and different is happening. Americans seem to be increasingly dividing irreconcilably along racial, religious, ideological, economic and regional lines. Indeed the United States is entering its next decade as an angry nation at odds with itself and the world, a nation that is in danger of losing its center.

The evidence suggests that the United States has entered largely unchartered territory—a space in which its inhabitants are effectively lost in the wilderness, unable to acknowledge or accept the depth of their wants. How else would a nation of our many epic past accomplishments and continuing possibilities elect to be led by the likes of Donald Trump and a national administration that appears intent on undermining America's most progressive domestic achievements and global advances? Manifestly, many in America are suffering from collective denial about these realities. However, a new and better course is available and achievable over the coming years if the sane and rational majority of Americans are prepared to organize and join forces to fight for it.

Constructive Protest and Resistance Is Needed

A new and different course, informed by active organizing and innovation, is necessary if our country and the world are to avoid an even more perilous future. Recent years have provided important new examples of constructive protest and resistance, ranging from the valiant efforts of the Marriage Equality, Black Lives Matter and Dreamer movements to the increasingly successful organizing efforts of workers seeking living wages and improvements in labor conditions across our economy. Comparable efforts have been waged by Native American spiritual and environmental leaders at Standing Rock, North Dakota, as well as by #MeToo gender equality activists during the 2017 and 2018 Women's Marches in cities and towns around our nation. Likewise, people and communities affected by mass gun violence have rallied to say #NeverAgain.[19]

In writing this book I hope to inspire more reasoned, purposeful and nonviolent efforts along these lines with an eye to resuscitating the vibrancy of our political democracy and the sustainability, robustness and fairness of our national economy. In doing so, I hope to make the case for fundamentally new ways of thinking about and organizing our national governance and economy. Along the way, I will highlight models of democratic engagement and economic development that are helping to move us in these directions. One of the premises of this work is that there is presently too much public and private discussion about our failing democracy and economy, but not nearly enough corresponding remedial action. We must address the worst manifestations and impacts of recent American decline, such as growing intergroup tension, public violence and international conflict. But so much of our current leadership and public discourse seems to be taking us in the opposite direction. Part of the problem is the proliferation of social media and its tendency to calcify, if not intensify, social and ideological divides.[20]

More profoundly, there is presently very little leadership addressing the underlying causes of our aforementioned national challenges: systemic poverty and inequality, excessive commodification and resource depletion. Equally, there is too little attention being paid to the many emerging solutions that progressive community-based leaders and residents all across America are advancing in their respective local domains of influence to address our growing societal challenges. Properly supported by enabling public policy and resourcing innovations along these lines could help put our nation on a path that is more consistent with the best of its values and commitments.

These are not new ideas by any stretch of the imagination. Progressive community leaders, such as Angela Glover Blackwell, founder of California-based PolicyLink, and important social investment organizations, such as the New York-based Nonprofit Finance Fund, have increasingly focused on investing in the proven successes of community- and place-based innovators in fields ranging from regional economic development and transportation to human services delivery, education and the arts.[21] But much more needs to be done by public institutions and leading private actors to normalize this approach to problem solving across various communities, fields and geographies. Even beyond that, what has not been sufficiently seized to date is the opportunity to harmonize efforts along these lines across the increasingly diverse communities that are still largely unaligned. Thus, in the pages of this book, I will emphasize opportunities for coordinating efforts by progressive leaders and institutions in support of new and better courses of action based on the strategic and collective advancement of our most promising policy priorities and models.

To bring to the surface the best of these priorities and models, I enlisted the input of more than sixty leading progressive voices from across the nation via a dynamic group of advisors and experts on the issues (See the Appendix). I interviewed these progressive thought leaders and practitioners across the nation specifically to learn about how their recent work and advocacy might help to lay a better foundation for American democratic action and economic justice. Most of their innovative approaches are featured or referenced throughout the pages that follow.

Marginal and Incremental Change Is Not Enough

One final assertion underlies much of what I have advanced in these pages: the change America needs to right its course is not simply to make existing policies, practices and conventions more tenable or inclusive for people and communities that have been increasingly disconnected from America's centers of power over the past several decades. Instead, I call for fundamentally new approaches to demo-

cratic governance and wealth creation based on a more open and
accessible democracy and a far more socially and environmentally
responsible economy—that is, an economy focused on the well-being
and sustainability of the majority of Americans (especially society's
most vulnerable members) and the natural world upon which our collective survival ultimately depends.

At the end of the day, our core purpose as a society—and all the
associated elements of our public policy—cannot just be about making more money and things for a shrinking population of beneficiaries without attention to the larger human, societal and environmental
costs. When average people are often forced to work at two or three
jobs just to get by, while wealthy elites (many of whom merely inher-
ited, rather than produced, their wealth) get all the breaks and privileges in society, something has gone awry with our national political
economy and civic culture. The situation is exacerbated when,
increasingly, working and middle-class Americans are pushed to
shoulder lower and lower pay, ever more contingent and dangerous
working conditions, and greater and greater shares of their health and
retirement costs.[22]

We Need to Forge a New Social Contract

What is badly needed is a sustainable new social contract for the
emerging realities of the twenty-first century, one that helps our working and middle class populations through expanded public investments intended to build their skill sets, household assets and collective bargaining power vis-à-vis the nation's most privileged interests,
while improving their quality of life more broadly. In that context, we
need to learn from the work of progressive labor and community
organizers, social and environmental justice advocates, social investment and social enterprise leaders and leading progressive scholars
and thinkers. All of these actors are advancing important pilot efforts
and ideas that encourage the broader inclusion of talent and leadership
from historically excluded—or otherwise disconnected—communities in ways that help to responsibly advance our nation's progress and
global economic competitiveness.

Contrary to the claims and suggestions of many conservative leaders, all Americans, even the most left leaning, progressive thinkers and activists among us, want expanded economic opportunity and prosperity, and we are willing to work mightily for those things. But we want vast improvements in the levels of fairness, inclusiveness and sustainability of our economy. In short, we want to work to achieve a newfound balance in our political economy where prosperity meets justice for the average American.

Economic justice is a huge part of what is still woefully lacking in America and will accordingly be a central topic here. But our recent history makes crystal clear that the most glaring injustices across our nation still relate to racial disparities in criminal justice and law enforcement. Justice in this context has been a growing casualty of recent American demographic diversification, with increasingly disturbing implications for the future of our democratic culture and institutions. The data on Americans of color being subject to double standards under US law–especially American criminal and immigration law–are rampant and disturbing.[23] Indeed, today in America it is clear: People of color, especially young men of color, are disproportionately surveilled, arrested and sentenced to long jail and prison terms (and, in the case of immigrants, eventual deportation).

Looking ahead, it is vital for our nation to address the growing costs of the past generation's systematic crackdown on communities of color through over policing, unequal application of the law, the excessive use of force and prison privatization policies. Beyond the worst of these racial disparities in criminal justice, people and communities of color in America remain disproportionately disserved across the nation's various systems of economic and employment opportunity, education, housing, healthcare and political representation.[24] Other diverse populations of American women, LGBTQ community members, and Americans with disabilities face comparable injustices and inequalities that have only recently begun to be addressed through the authority of American law and policy.[25]

In addition, there is a growing contingent of white working-class Americans who face their own challenges as a result of America's increasingly unequal society and economy. Many of these Americans

now suffer from levels of economic dislocation and oppression that
have previously been known mostly to Americans of color. Many of
them are impacted by growing rates of opioid addiction, alcoholism
and suicide.[26] While these Americans (and white voters generally)
voted overwhelmingly for Donald Trump in our last national election,
it is also clear that they need and want help too. Indeed, their growing
desperation may account for much of Trump's success in gaining the
presidency. But this new president's clear ineffectiveness in office so
far presents many opportunities over time for his white voters to seek
new and different alternatives to the status quo in coming cycles—not
all of which reside on the far right. In fact, like most Americans, many
white American voters who supported the Trump presidency are not
deeply ideological nor doctrinaire.[27] Rather, many of them are badly
hurting, confused about the implications of America's changing culture and economy, and desperate for relief. Like socially and economically distressed Americans of color, working class and struggling
white Americans would benefit greatly from a wider democratization
of the ways in which our nation informs its decision-making and dis-
tributes its wealth. Ultimately, this implicates a stronger role for government and public policy, and more progressive approaches.

Government Must Lead the Way Forward

To be sure, only the state, and for that matter only a state that is
truly committed to promoting the common good, can facilitate the
kind of change needed in America today for all who find themselves
increasingly disadvantaged by recent developments in our political
economy. We have a long national history of structural inequality facing diverse groups and their communities, and following forty years
of policy favoring capital accumulation for the few at the expense of
the many, now, only the power of government, especially the federal
government, can serve to reorganize our society in a more equitable
and just way.

There is nothing new about this. As we saw in prior eras when
evolutionary change was achieved (such as during the progressive era
of the early twentieth century, the labor organizing and WPA years of
the 1930s and the Great Society years of the 1960s), American polit-

ical leaders took bold and affirmative steps that improved the lot of the many. It took active and intentional central government leadership to make these advancements possible, because no other single actor in our society was positioned to create the changes needed at a sufficient level of scale to finally matter. The lessons of this history and our recent experiences are clear; in order for America to prosper and succeed as a multicultural nation, it is vital for the federal government to play an expansive, facilitating and supporting role.

We Are Going in the Wrong Direction and Must Change Course

As a nation, we are headed in the wrong direction. Recent decades have witnessed the reversal of the basic operating principles of American governance, with conservative and neoliberal politicians and thought leaders advocating the disengagement of government in order to benefit the overwhelmingly white, wealthy and privileged classes, with little regard for the social, economic or environmental consequences. This is in stark contrast to the longstanding fundamental role of government, namely, to level the playing field in order to create opportunities on behalf of the poor, working and middle classes; and to ensure responsible stewardship of America's vast natural resources—a worldview shared by both conservative and liberal icons of the early twentieth century, such as Republican President Theodore Roosevelt and his younger liberal cousin, President Franklin D. Roosevelt.

We need to get back to a government that first and foremost puts the longer term interests of people and nature first, rather than the shorter term interests of capital and privilege. And we need to do this in the new and different ways recommended in the following pages. Today's new challenges require fresh approaches that go beyond merely trying to recreate past efforts and even successes. As previously asserted here, we are increasingly in unchartered territory; finding our way through the new realities we are facing requires innovative ideas to be implemented by people and organizations interested in creating new standards and successful frameworks for needed reform and action.

The thinking and leadership of the commentators and stakeholders I consulted for this work were vital to my analysis and assertions here;

they are on the front lines. I thank each of them profoundly for both their inspirational work and insights. But, if any issues and ideas presented here inspire rancor or negative reaction, I take full responsibility for the content and configuration of this book and for the recommendations that flow from them. Indeed, I hope that some of the ideas and content of this work will inspire dynamic public debate and refinement in thought and practice for the common good. It is a vitally important time for expanded public discourse about the best path forward to right our nation's troubled course.

The Road Ahead Is Ours to Pave

Nostalgia will not make America great again. It is not enough for the conservative leaders of the moment to seek a backward path to some past time that makes many Americans feel safer and stronger; but neither is it a time for more liberal- and progressive-leaning Americans to rely on our own past ideas and inclinations to fix what has unraveled in recent years. Rather, it is a new day in America, representing a pivotal moment in our history that requires some new thinking and unprecedented action, if we are to survive and thrive in a way that is consistent with our nation's best ideals and traditions.

Just as global communism met an unceremonious and unexpected death in the late 1980s with the fall of the Berlin Wall and the former Soviet Union, we are now on the historical front line of hypercapitalism's inevitable decline. What will replace this dying system of relentless wealth concentration, human and environmental degradation, and expanding militarism is up to us. Past moments in history have seen revolutionary and theretofore unimaginable change occur with relatively astonishing speed as the dictates of nature and human will have ultimately required, even against all conventional odds. Our own American Revolution was such a moment, a moment that saw a small upstart nation of rebelling colonists defeat the world's strongest military power, Great Britain, in order to gain its independence and right to self-rule.

We have seen similar leaps forward in other chapters of our history as a nation, including the extension of voting and other fundamental rights to women and people of color, the elimination of child labor, and the widespread recognition of LGBTQ and disability community rights, among other important breakthroughs that could be considered. But none of these gains came just because. They came because dedicated agents of change united in large numbers to take a principled stand by pursuing collective action, by challenging naysayers and various powers-that-be with evidence and compelling lines of argument, by forcing public leaders to impose corrective policy, and by engaging the larger public in inspiring and galvanizing ways that led to needed changes in laws and public mores.

It took extraordinary commitment, initiative, planning and coordination to achieve those successes over the decades. With America being so exhausted and angry these days, it will take special care and effort to successfully bring about a higher level of community and political organizing that in turn can inspire the constructive change forward-looking Americans seek. Such change will require extensive strategic consensus-building, mass peaceful protest, a significant reshaping of partisan politics and a fundamental re-envisioning of our essential means of building wealth to rise to our generation's particular calling in service to democracy and a new and better American economy. It will require us to rise as well to advance compelling new proposals and models that actively promote expanded political and economic justice. And it will require those of us on the American left to rise to significantly new levels of trust and investment in one another as we strive to see this work through. But rise we must and, with the benefit of good works and good ideas such as those featured in the pages that follow, rise we will!

Endnotes

[1]Wheatley, Margaret J., *So Far From Home: Lost and Found in Our Brave New World*, Berrett-Koehler Publishers, Inc., San Francisco, 2012, p. 67.
[2]While I underscore the United States' history of liberal democracy and progressive achievements over its now two and a half centuries of national evolution, it is important to recognize here as well the darker realities of the American journey that remain to be fully accounted for. These include, among other things, the nation's shameful history of African slavery, state-supported genocide against the indigenous nations of North America, the unjustified annexation of extensive Mexican ter-

ritories following the US-Mexico War of 1846–48 and the extensive racial exclusion and injustice perpetrated against Chinese American and Japanese American immigrants and citizens alike throughout the nineteenth and twentieth centuries.

[3]See, e.g., Ingraham, C., "How the Unrest of the 1960s Compares to Today According to the People Who Lived Through It," July 12, 2016, Washington Post at: https://www.washingtonpost.com/news/wonk/wp/2016/07/12/reddit-remembers-the-1960s-we-probably-dont-have-to-kill-all-of-them-just-the-agitators/?utm_term=.4ffb2b15c60e.

[4]See, e.g., Mellman, M.S., "Mellman: Tea Party vs. Occupy Wall Street," February 11, 2014, The Hill at: http://thehill.com/opinion/mark-mellman/198157-mark-s-mellman-tea-party-vs-occupy-wall-street.

[5]See, e.g., Gallup Organization polling dating back to the 1970s at: http://www.gallup.com/poll/1597/confidence-institutions.aspx.

[6]See, e.g., Kopan, T., "10 Groups Donald Trump Offended since Launching His Campaign," November 29, 2015, CNN.com at: http://www.cnn.com/2015/11/27/politics/donald-trump-insults-groups-list/index.html.

[7]See, e.g., Goldberg, J., "What Trump Means When He Says, 'America First'," January 25, 2017, National Review, Washington, DC at: http://www.nationalreview.com/article/444211/donald-trump-america-first-slogan-stands- nationalist-identity and Trump, Donald J., Great Again: How to Fix Our Crippled America. NY: Simon & Schuster, 2015.

[8]See the following Rasmussen tracking report from July 2017: http://www.rasmussenreports.com/public_content/politics/mood_of_america/right_direction_wrong_track_jul24 An October 2017 national poll found an even more dismal data point: only 24 percent of Americans surveyed felt the nation was on the right path under Trump's leadership. See, Pace, J & Watson, E., "NORC-AP Poll: Just 24 Percent Say US Heading in Right Direction," October 7, 2017, Associated Press, Washington, DC at: https://apnews.com/f7d770542f334a218398b2f9b2ae1102/ AP-Poll:-Just-24-percent-say-US-heading-in-right-direction?utm_campaign=SocialFlow&utm_source=Twitter&utm_medium=AP_Politics.

[9]See Baker, P., "For Trump, a Year of Reinventing the Presidency," December 31, 2017, The New York Times at: https://www.nytimes.com/2017/12/31/us/politics/trump-reinventing-presidency.html. It is important to note here the Baker article's headnote, which reads as follows: "In ways that were once unimaginable, President Trump has discarded the conventions and norms established by his predecessors. Will that change the institution permanently?"

[10]See, e.g., Phillip, A., "Trump's Isolation Grows in the Wake of Charlottesville, August 17, 2017, Washington Post at: https://www.washingtonpost.com/politics/trumps-isolation-grows-in-the-wake-of-char-

lottesville/2017/08/17/5bf83952-81ec-11e7-82a4-920da1aeb507_story.
html?utm_term=.644578287259. Notably, Trump's clumsy and inappropriate reaction to Charlottesville led directly the following week to the
members of his major corporate advisory boards resigning and those advisory bodies being effectively disbanded. It also led to the dismissal of
Trump's most celebrated far right advisor, Steve Bannon, from his position as the president's chief strategist. See Haberman, M., "Stephen Bannon Out at the White House after Turbulent Run," August 18, 2017, *New
York Times* at: https://www.nytimes.com/2017/08/18/ us/politics/steve-
bannon trump white house.html.

[11]See "Donald Trump Blasts NFL Anthem Protesters: 'Get the Son of a
Bitch Off the Field,'" *The Guardian* 23 September 2017:www.the
guardian.com/sports;trump-nfl-national-anthem-protests.

[12]According to recent analysis by the Center for American Progress,
deportation of the nation's current DACA status holders would cost the
US economy more than $400 billion in lost GDP over the coming
decade. See Prchal Svajlenka, N., et al, "A New Threat to DACA Could
Cost States Billions of Dollars," July 21, 2017, Center for American
Progress, Washington, DC at: https://www.americanprogress.org/issues/
immigration/news/2017/07/21/436419/new-threat-daca-cost-states-bil-
lions-dollars/.

[13]See Hartmann, M., "What Happened to the 19 Women Who Accused
Trump of Sexual Misconduct," December 12, 2017, New York Magazine at: http://nymag.com/daily/intelligencer/2017/12/what-happened-
to-trumps-16-sexual-misconduct-accusers.html. In late 2017.

[14]See Ducharme, J., "Trump Just Went After the #MeToo Movement:
'Lives Are Being Shattered'," February 10, 2018, *Time*: http://time.com/
5143101/donald-trump-tweet-allegations/. On February 10, 2018,
Trump tweeted a telling commentary expressing concern for the men
accused by a growing number of women reporting systemic sexual
abuse under what has come to be known as the #MeToo Movement. In
that tweet, Trump texted the following statement of concern about the
alleged male transgressors: "Peoples lives are being shattered and
destroyed by a mere allegation. Some are true and some are false. Some
are old and some are new. There is no recovery for someone falsely
accused—life and career are gone. Is there no such thing any longer as
Due Process?"

[15]See Cillizza, C., "What Makes No Sense About Donald Trump's Rob
Porter Response," February 12, 2018, CNN.com/Politics at: https://www.
cnn.com/2018/02/12/politics/rob-porter-trump/index.html and Levine, J.,
"Internet Mocks Trump for Chris Brown Tweet After President Defends
Rob Porter," February 9, 2018, , Los Angeles at: https://www.thewrap.

com/donald-trump-mocked-for-chris-brown-tweet-after-defending-rob-porter/. In addition to Trump and his White House disrespectfully responding to female accusers of the president on the issues, and Trump's clumsy statements in support of his disgraced former White House Secretary Rob Porter, the president had forcefully defended former Alabama US Senate candidate Roy Moore in late 2017, despite credible allegations from multiple women that he had sexually abused them as minors, when he had been a county prosecutor in the 1970s and 1980s.

[16]See Bomey, N., "NRA fallout: See the List of Companies That Cut Discounts for NRA Members after Parkland, Florida School Shooting," *USA Today* 26 February 2018: https://www.usatoday.com/story/money/2018/02/26/nra-companies-parkland-school-shooting/372271002/.

[17]See Millbank, D., "Yes, Half of All Trump Supporters are Racist," *Washington Post* 22 September 2016: https://www.washingtonpost.com/ opinions/clinton-wasnt-wrong-about-the-deplorables-among-trumps-supporters/2016/09/12/93720264-7932-11e6-beac-57a4a412e93a_story.html?utm_term=.0cb4785f98a9 and also López, G., "Study: Racism and Sexism Predict Support for Trump Much More Than Economic Dissatisfaction," January 4, 2017, from Vox.com at: https://www.vox.com/identities/2017/1/4/14160956/ trump-racism-sexism- economy-study.

[18]See, Tyson A. & Maniam, S., "Behind Trump's Victory: Divisions by Race, Gender, Education," November 9, 2016, Pew Research Center, Washington, DC at: http://www.pewresearch.org/fact-tank/2016/ 11/09/behind- trumps-victory-divisions-by-race-gender-education/.

[19]See Equal Voice Action national podcast, "Resistance: Action for Equity in a New Political Era," of January 19, 2017 at: https://www.equalvoiceaction.com/podcast-resistance-action-for-equity-in-a-new-political-era/, as well as it's subsequent national webinars on immigrant and refugee rights on the Trump era from February 14, 2017 at: https://www.equalvoiceaction.com/podcast-immigrant-refugee-rights-in-the-trump-era-next-stage-advocacy-strategies/, and its March 7, 2017 national broadcast on civil and human rights under the Trump administration at: https://www.equalvoiceaction.com/podcast-civil-human-rights-under-the-trump-administration/. See also, Witt, E., "Urgency and Frustration: The Never Again Movement Gathers Momentum," *The New Yorker* 23 February 2018: https:// www.newyorker.com/news/news-desk/ urgency-and-frustration-the-never-again-movement- gathers-momentum.

[20]See, e.g., Rabasca-Roepe, L., "America's Obsession with Social Media is Undermining the Democratic Process," *Quartz*, 24 March 2016: https://qz.com/647064/americas-obsession-with-social-media-is-undermining-the-democratic-process/.

[21]See, e.g., Oakland, CA-based PolicyLink's website at: http://www. whatworksforamerica.org/angela-glover-blackwell-policylink/ and *What Matters: Investing in Results to Build Strong, Vibrant Communities*, Federal Reserve Bank of San Francisco and Nonprofit Finance Fund, Erickson, D., Bugg-Levine, A., et al, editors, 2017: http://www. investinresults.org/.

[22]Another manifestation of the problem is the growing incidence of forced arbitration clauses in worker employment and purchasing contracts, which preclude growing numbers of workers and consumers from challenging health, safety and fairness breaches at the workplace through court-based litigation. See the report from the Economic Policy Institute by Stone, K.V.W. & Colvin, A.J.S., "The Arbitration Epidemic: Mandatory Arbitration Deprives Workers and Consumers of Their Rights," December 7, 2015: http://www.epi.org/publication/the-arbitration-epidemic/.

[23]See Kirby, S., "The Top 10 Most Startling Facts About People of Color and Criminal Justice in the United States," March 13, 2012, Center for American Progress, Washington, DC: https://www.americanprogress.org/ issues/race/news/2012/03/13/11351/the-top-10-most-startling-facts-about-people-of-color-and-criminal-justice-in-the-united-states/.

[24]See, e.g., the following important ACLU reports, respectively on racial disparities in sentencing (2014) at: https://www.aclu.org/sites/default/ files/assets/141027_iachr_racial_disparities_aclu_submission_0.pdf; racial inequality in American public schools (2014) at: https://www. thenation.com/article/14-disturbing-stats-about-racial-inequality-american-public-schools/; and racial disparities in health (2015) at: https://hbr.org/2015/10/the-costs-of-racial-disparities-in-health-care; as well as this *New Republic* report by Danny Vinik on continuing gender and racial inequality in American governance (2014) at: https://newrepublic.com/article/119737/report-women-minorities-underrepresented-all-levels-government.

[25]See Wolfers, J., "Evidence of a Toxic Environment for Women in Economics," *New York Times* 18 August 2017: https://www.nytimes.com/ 2017/08/18/upshot/evidence-of-a-toxic-environment-for-women-in- economics.html?rref=collection%2Ftimestopic%2FDiscrimination&action=clic k&contentCollection=timestopics&region=stream&module=stream_unit& version=latest&contentPlacement=2&pgtype=collection; as well as Shear, M.D. & Savage, C., "In One Day, Trump Administration Lands 3 Punches Against Gay Rights," *New York Times* 27 July 2017,: https://www. nytimes.com/2017/07/27/us/politics/white-house-lgbt-rights-military-civil-rightsact.html?rref=collection%2Ftimestopic%2FDiscrimination&action=cl ick&contentCollection=timestopics&region=stream&module=

stream_unit&version=latest&contentPlacement=26&pgtype=collection; Black, E. R., "Why Is Our Existence as Humans Still Being Denied?" *New York Times* 26 July 2017: https://www.nytimes.com/2017/07/26/opinion/why-is-our-existence-as-humans-still-being-denied.html; and "Discrimination, Inequality & Poverty: A Human Rights Perspective," January 11, 2013, Human Rights Watch, New York, NY at: https://www. hrw.org/ news/ 2013/01/11/discrimination-inequality-and-poverty-human-rights-perspective.

[26]See "How the Feeling of Falling Behind Fuels Deadly Distress for White Americans," PBS NewsHour, February 23, 2017 at: http://www. pbs.org/newshour/bb/feeling-falling-behind-fuels-deadly-distress-white-americans/ and *Do No Harm: The Opioid Epidemic*, 2017, a documentary film on the issues produced by Media Policy Center, Los Angeles at: http://mediapolicycenter.org/mpc_initiative/opioid-crisis/.

[27]See Cheadle, H., "Turns Out Trump Voters Aren't the Same as 'Republicans'," June 19, 2017, Vice.com at: https://www.vice.com/en_us/article/bj8aqz/turns-out-trump-voters-arent-the-same-as-conservatives. The findings were based on extensive public polling analysis by the Democracy Fund's Voter Study Group. See: https://www.voterstudygroup.org/publications/2016-elections/executive-summary.

DEMOCRACY
WHERE
AND THE
PROSPERITY
NEXT AMERICAN
MEETS JUSTICE
ECONOMY

CHAPTER 1
It Doesn't Have to Be This Way!

So many of the crises we are facing are symptoms of the same
underlying sickness: a dominance-based logic that treats so
many people, and the earth itself, as disposable.

—Naomi Klein
No Is Not Enough[1]

One of the saddest aspects of contemporary life in America is the
growing sense among many that our democratic institutions and economy are increasingly unresponsive to people's basic realities and circumstances. Some would go even further, asserting that our increasingly complex and exclusive systems of governance and wealth
creation are actively hostile to the essential needs of average people
for physical, emotional and economic security.[2] Among the greatest
manifestations underlying these instincts is the sheer disregard for
people and the planet that we see all around us in so much of our political and economic life. The daily news is rampant with stories of
human waste and environmental dislocation owing to decisions and
actions taken by business leaders, political actors of various persuasions and systems that bear down on an increasingly disempowered
population of poor, working-class and middle-class communities. It is
not that any of this is new; indeed, systemic exploitation of people and
nature is sadly an age-old problem. But what is new and concerning
is the unprecedented scale of our national and global challenges and
the emerging view among experts that in the absence of a radical

1

change in production, population and systems management, as well as wealth distribution, the planet may be doomed.

Rage Against the Machine

The drumbeat of relentless production and growth; the rationalization of increasing inequality and structural poverty; the churn of labor and consumer markets that increasingly leave people behind; the decimation of longstanding small businesses, communities, and neighborhoods; the numbing violence that now regularly meets our daily lives; the environmental degradation of our cities, forests and waters—all of these ever-intensifying phenomena reveal that something fundamental has gone awry. It is all, as environmental and human rights activist Naomi Klein observes in her book *No is Not Enough: Resisting Trump's Shock Politics and Winning the World We Need*, the product of an underlying sickness in our culture and world that treats humanity and natural resources as merely disposable commodities that are to be dominated, divided and deployed by the powerful and wealthy to maximize their gains.

The Hidden Costs of Modern Production

A central, if increasingly disturbing reality is the modern economy's hidden dependence on production externalities to fuel profitability and growth—that is, systematically hiding and passing on to the public the real environmental and societal costs of production. Masking the true costs of production, while facilitating market competitiveness and lower consumer costs, discourages more responsible and sustainable practices. Looking at just the environmental aspects of this for a moment, the scope of the problem is epic. According to a 2013 Trucost report commissioned by the United Nations-supported Economics of Ecosystems and Biodiversity Program, the unpriced natural capital costs of industrial production among the world's twenty leading economic regions came to about $7 trillion in 2009 alone— or 13 percent of all global GDP.[3] The extent of this hidden production subsidy is so great that, according to Trucost, of the regional production centers studied for environmental impacts, none would have been profitable if the full costs of producing their goods and services had been factored into their pricing.

If we consider as well the additional hidden social costs of production flowing from the outputs of these industrial centers in the form of worker discrimination, abuse and injury, as well as associated stress, long term negative health impacts and family and community disruption, the extent of the problem comes into relief in an even more profound way. According to a 2012 report by the Center for American Progress, the annual estimated cost of workplace discrimination in America is now more than $60 billion—that is, the annual aggregate expense of losing and replacing more than two million American workers who leave their jobs each year due to unfairness and discrimination.[4] During 2016 alone, the US Equal Employment Opportunity Commission (EEOC) treated nearly 100,000 cases of race-, gender-, disability- and related workplace discrimination claims and ordered employers found guilty of actionable violations to pay nearly $500 million in penalties and fines.[5] However, by the federal government's own admission, workplace abuses are rarely successfully reported.[6] In fact, a recent article by the business weekly *Fast-Company* reported that, while many suits brought by employees end up being settled or dismissed, when worker claims do make it to litigation in our courts, employees prevail in only about one percent of the actions brought.[7] A large part of the equation is an increasingly employer-friendly legal environment that imposes unduly large legal and financial burdens on aggrieved employees or requires them to address their claims through mandatory binding arbitration.[8] As a result, the total real costs of workplace discrimination are never fully accounted for in marketplace transactions, despite the fact that the costs to victims are very real indeed.

Moreover, the larger societal costs of our economy's increasingly disruptive nature has imposed growing human costs across our society that are never fully factored into the prices of the goods and services we all purchase. As recently reported by ScienceDaily.com, just considering the current opioid epidemic afflicting so many US households and communities under growing duress across our nation today, experts estimate that the economic burden on our hospitals, business-

es, schools, prisons and communities responding to that single important problem now totals nearly $80 billion, with only about one-quar-
ter of that total being covered by public funding sources.[9] The upshot
is that systemic disparities between the real and the charged prices of
goods and services across our economy fundamentally camouflage
the growing, unsustainable costs of our current production system and
its worsening impacts on the natural world and humanity.[10]

Complexity and Civic Disempowerment

Faced with these complex, systemic and monumental challenges,
many people feel a growing desire and need to bring about meaningful change. At the same time, all but the most well-endowed and
resilient among us are finally left feeling that things simply cannot be
changed. This truly is not so. According to the New Economic Theory Group, co-sponsored by the World Academy of Art & Science and
the Club of Rome, for example:

> Efforts to reform current economic policy and institutions are
> invariably opposed by both an intellectual orthodoxy and
> vested economic interests. They draw on the conventional
> wisdom of prevailing economic theory to support prevailing
> policies. They argue that given the laws of economy and cur-
> rent circumstances, we are living in the best possible world.
> This simply is not true. The multidimensional challenges con-
> fronting humanity today are human-made and can be changed
> by a change in thought and action. Theoretical limitations and
> misconceptions are a primary root cause of persistent pover-
> ty, rapid and rising levels of unemployment, inequality, and
> calamitous environmental threats. Contemporary economic
> thought is built on a mind-frame that originated prior to the
> Industrial Revolution when scarcity of goods was the primary
> concern, economic growth was considered synonymous with
> human welfare, and impact of humanity on the environment
> was completely ignored . . . Conditions have radically
> changed since then.[11]

At the end of the day, societies, systems, and their supporting institutions and rules are human constructs. People make choices every day, both individually and en masse, that ultimately bear on all of our possibilities going forward. Even in instances where we collectively take no action or invoke no change, in effect we are still making choices. In times like these, it is vitally important to remind ourselves that people have power. Indeed, historical evidence to that effect is all around us, notwithstanding our frequent tendency to forget how much has changed for both better and worse over even the relatively short course of our respective lifetimes as a result of the choices we have made.

In the last century alone, in spite of resistance from many reactionary interests, our nation has seen previously denied voting and civil rights extended to women and communities of color that had been historically excluded from full citizenship under the law. It also has seen significant, long overdue, legal and social gains for LGBTQ Americans and people with disabilities, the formal establishment of minimum federal protective standards in areas ranging from automobile safety to environmental protection, and the mandated expansion of private health insurance coverage and benefits for American consumers following decades of prior failed efforts to make basic healthcare more accessible and affordable across our nation. All of these advances have been the byproduct of popular support and organizing that enabled justice and the will of the people to finally prevail after decades-long struggles leading to each respective breakthrough.

On the other hand, in recent years choices have prevailed that have not been so supportive of people's rights and well-being in America. Over the past decades, for example, as a direct result of public choices or inaction, we have seen sharp systemic increases in wealth and income disparities (especially between white Americans and various minority groups), expanding incarceration rates and police violence against people and communities of color, the widespread abridgement or denial of hard-earned worker rights, accelerating disinvestment in the nation's public education system, the proliferation of modern servitude in the form of growing undocumented immigrant exploitation, and a dramatic reduction in poor people's access to jobs, housing and legal and other social services. All of this has resulted from choices we the people have made or otherwise enabled.

Sadly, and somewhat mysteriously, over the past four decades, American voters have tended to err on the side of choosing the strong over the weak, the haves over the have-nots, and the materialistic over the socially and environmentally responsible. That is to say that through decidedly deregulatory and neoliberal policies advanced under both Republican and Democratic leadership, America has chosen to pursue policies that are largely at odds with its foundational commitments to democracy and the common good. By advancing tax and regulatory policies that cater principally to the interests of the already wealthy and powerful, by undercutting basic worker and human rights, and by privileging older, dying industries such as oil and coal over sustainable new energy sources and industries, American policy has privileged the few at the expense of the many and retarded the nation's prospects for true economic, social and environmental progress in the years to come.

America at a Crossroads: Signs of Decline Are on the Rise

There are unprecedented and growing challenges for the coming generations of Americans, who will be the most significant losers if the processes of the present continue. Our systems of politics, economy, education, health, housing and upward mobility have been hijacked, stymied by growing dysfunction and ineffectiveness. Evidence of these assertions is ample and painful for a nation that for the past century has fancied itself as the world's leader in all manner of political, social and economic performance. The data shows that our nation has been experiencing a rapid decline in key areas of its civic and economic life over the past several decades. While many Americans remain in denial about these realities, many more have expressed growing concern and anger over our present course. Indeed, evidence strongly suggests that most Americans are now seriously rethinking the path we have been on. In so many areas of our public life, people all across the nation want to pursue substantially different policies to address the problems enumerated above. Yet resistance or inaction from increasingly conservative

Republican politicians and tepid Democrats seems to preclude the opportunity to pursue improvements in course at every turn. The list of examples supporting this last point is long.

Growing Public Debt

According to recent data from the Organization for Economic Cooperation and Development (OECD), for example, US public debt has skyrocketed in recent decades, totaling now more than 125 percent of the nation's Gross Domestic Product (GDP).[12] In 2013, an International Monetary Fund study showed that America's national debt was second only to Japan's and nearly twice that of the next ranking nations in country indebtedness; included on the list were Brazil, India and Pakistan, respectively.[13] All of this is largely the result of America's ever-bulging defense spending,[14] its substantially unregulated, pay-to-play campaign finance system (which inherently privileges the policy and expenditure preferences of corporations and the already wealthy)[15] and, by extension, its support of now more than a generation of ideologically driven, anti-government tax- and budget-cutting policies that have made deficit spending and ever-growing debt permanent fixtures of our national governance.

The recent passage of the Trump tax bill of 2017 and the early 2018 budget deal have combined to ensure a doubling down in this direction. According to *Business Insider*, "the deficit would grow by about $1.5 trillion in the decade after the bill is implemented."[16] Republican leaders insisted that by expanding profits and tax receipts, the tax cuts built into the legislation would ultimately close the gap, but no less than the conservative Tax Foundation's best-case scenario shows that, even with new growth, the bill would increase the federal deficit by $448 billion over 10 years. Such leading authorities as the Joint Committee on Taxation and the Tax Policy Institute have been less optimistic, estimating that the bill would add as much as $1 trillion or more to the deficit. To make matters even worse, in February 2018, Senate Republicans and Democrats reached a budget compromise calling for an additional $300 billion in deficit spending and an extension of the debt ceiling limiting federal spending through March 2019.

Diminishing Investment in Public Education and Social Well-being

An unhappy byproduct of America's growing debt and declining support for government initiatives has been the steady diminution of public investment in essential centers of human development and well-being. One of the most significant of these has been public education. During the mid-1970s, total national spending on public education totaled 5.7 percent of the nation's GDP. But by 2014, when educational preparation had become even more linked to economic security,[17] it constituted only 5.5 percent.[18] Local public school investment, the real center of gravity for education spending in America, saw an even greater reduction over recent decades, from around 4 percent of GDP in 2002 to only 3.4 percent of GDP by 2015.[19]

The United States led the world during prior decades in public school quality and higher education attainment,[20] but largely as a result of this decline in funding, our country now ranks only eighteenth among all nations in student reading performance,[21] twenty-third in science test scoring[22] and thirty-sixth in international math rankings.[23] Because of our slipping education standing, adult skill levels and labor force competencies in the United States now rank only twelfth among advanced nations.[24] Similarly, key areas related to US quality of life have also experienced recent significant decline: health status,[25] rates of incarceration[26] and violence[27] and home ownership.[28] Correspondingly, the percentage of wages directed to low paid workers has risen.[29]

The Continuing Healthcare Conundrum

Recent surveys by such credible sources as the Kaiser Family Foundation show that Americans overwhelmingly support government initiatives to expand affordable, quality healthcare for people and families in need through Obamacare[30] or even more aggressive efforts to build out Medicare, Medicaid or some other single-payer system of universal healthcare coverage.[31] Yet, despite prevailing public opinion and manifold defeats over recent years on the issues, Republicans in Congress and the Senate continue to seek a "Repeal and Replace" strategy for Obamacare, substantial reductions in

Medicare and Medicaid spending, and allied efforts to accelerate healthcare privatization.[32] Indeed, as of this writing, during the past eight years, the Republican-controlled House of Representatives has voted more than fifty times to repeal Obamacare, without any viable alternative to offer the American people.

The Ever-Elusive Fight for Fair Wages

On matters of the economy, reliable survey data reveal that an overwhelming majority of Americans favor substantially increasing the national minimum wage, which has not been augmented since 2009; presently, a family of three living on minimum wage pay does not even meet federal poverty level earnings.[33] Over the past several years, a super-majority of nearly three-quarters of Americans (including business leaders) has expressed significant support for an increase in the federal minimum wage from $7.25 to at least $9.00 per hour.[34] (Leading activists in the labor space contend that a true "living wage" would be $15 per hour.[35]) Twenty-nine states have passed their own legislation to pay their workers more than the federal minimum; but fully twenty-one still maintain the current low federal pay requirement. If no change is made in the coming years, experts estimate that workers in states stuck at the current federally mandated minimum level will make more than 30 percent less than their counterparts in states that have increased their minimum hourly pay rates.[36]

The ultimate effect of the aforementioned approach to wage and economic policy is bad for the economy and most of the nation. At the end of the day, maintaining low wage levels reduces the rate of consumption necessary to fuel our economy.[37] The decided unfairness of current worker pay in America is amplified by the fact that, unbeknownst to most Americans, millions of workers in key sectors, such as agriculture and food service are intentionally excluded from minimum wage protections that govern other workers' hourly wages.[38] If more Americans understood these policies, it is unlikely they would support their continuation. Perhaps owing precisely to that prospect, political leaders who control the federal power structure have refused even to hold hearings on these issues in recent years.

Redoubled Military Spending at the Expense of Addressing Domestic Priorities

Recent public polling has established that a growing majority of Americans favor expanded public investment in support of education, veterans' services and national infrastructure. According to an April 24, 2017 national polling report from the Pew Research Center, nearly 50 percent of American adults surveyed said they prefer more rather than less national investment in these cost centers, as opposed to 45 percent who reported otherwise. According to the Pew Center's research, the comparative survey of voter views showed public endorsement of expanded spending in eleven of fourteen budget categories highlighted, representing a substantial increase in respondent support for more affirmative government action in these areas.[39] Yet the Trump budget proposal submitted to Congress in Spring 2017 requested large cuts in most categories of public spending, including for education and veterans' programs, as well as significantly less infrastructure investment than the president suggested he would make during his campaign. At the same time, Trump's proposed military spending for 2018 would increase markedly, by roughly 10 percent over Barack Obama's last approved military budget.

Growing Racial Bias in Law Enforcement

Over recent years, the killing of unarmed civilians, and especially African American men and boys, has led to deteriorating police-community relations in the United States. According to census data extrapolated by the *Washington Post* (11 July 2016), African Americans are 2.5 times as likely as white Americans to be shot and killed by police officers.[40] The *Post*'s analysis showed, furthermore, that unarmed black people are five times as likely as unarmed whites to be shot by police.

While police brutality and the unjust killing of people of color is sadly not a new phenomenon in America, recent years have seen a notable increase in the number of highly-publicized police shootings of unarmed African American men and boys, including among others those of Tamir Rice in Cleveland, LaQuan McDonald in Chicago, Eric Garner in New York, and Michael Brown in Missouri in 2014;

Walter Scott in South Carolina in 2015; Philando Castile in Minnesota and Alton Sterling in Baton Rouge in 2016; and, most recently, Stephon Clark in Sacramento and Antwon Rose in East Pittsburgh in 2018. In each instance, subsequently-released video footage revealed the absence of any real impending threat to the police officers responsible for these heinous incidents. Yet, in the vast majority of these cases, the offending police officers were not held accountable under the law, owing to legal rules that give law enforcement officials almost carte blanche to shoot and kill if they claim to have felt themselves to be at risk of death or serious injury at the time of the incident.[41]

According to a Roper Center for Public Opinion Research poll conducted in 2014 and 2015, Americans of all races are increasingly and substantially unified around the need to reduce incidents of racially-implicated police shootings and civilian deaths through the use of police body cameras (over 90 percent approval by Americans of all races) and independent public prosecutors (over 85 percent approval by Americans of all races).[42] But only about half of the nation's police departments have deployed police body cams as part of their official practice[43] and only about 200 of some 18,000 law enforcement agencies have empaneled independent reviewers to examine purported police misconduct in cases of officer shootings.[44] Recent data reveals that, presently, even in the most egregious cases of excessive force and racial profiling, police officers rarely face criminal consequences.[45]

If the summary killing of unarmed Americans of color by law enforcement professionals is not an indicator of bias in the US system of justice, then the gross over-incarceration of black and brown people surely is.[46] Indeed, Americans of color are overwhelmingly more likely than whites to be apprehended and arrested; and increasingly they are being jailed in private facilities whose owners have a profit motive to keep them there.[47] Today in America, it is estimated that nearly 1.5 million individuals are incarcerated in state prisons, with African Americans and Latinos being substantially overrepresented in the inmate population relative to their share of the domestic population.[48] According to the Sentencing Project's analysis of US Bureau of Justice statistics, owing largely to racial and ethnic disparities in the law and its administration, whites comprised only 35 percent of state prison inmates in 2015, despite constituting more than 60 percent of the total US population. By contrast, African Americans made up nearly 40 percent of the state prison population, despite constituting only 12 percent of the US population; and Latinos made up 21 percent of state prison inmates, despite constituting only 18 percent of the national population.[49] Highly informed organizations and networks, including the Movement for Black Lives, the Alliance for Boys and Men of Color, and the ACLU have proposed policy reforms and guidelines for change; and opinion polls by such credible organizations as the Pew Charitable Trusts show growing public support for less draconian and racially disparate approaches to criminal justice policy.[50] As the problems have mounted, federal officials have begun to seriously consider major sentencing reforms, but paid little attention to continuing police brutality and overreach in communities of color.

Continuing Challenges to Women's Reproductive Rights

American women and their families are supposedly invested with full legal agency to purchase basic health services, including constitutionally protected reproductive health services and abortions. According to the Pew Research Center for Religion and Public Life, nearly 60 percent of all American adults believe that abortion services should be available in most cases to women.[51] Responsible organizations like Planned Parenthood provide such services safely and affordably to women of all social and economic backgrounds, along with allied basic health services that low and moderate income women too often lack access to. Yet, in state after state, and at the federal level as well, conservative lawmakers have made it virtually impossible for many women to access Planned Parenthood's services.[52]

Legislative actions have placed burdensome financing, reporting, technical and facilities restrictions that are not justified by medical science or necessity. Lawmakers have hyper-complicated the already difficult decisions women and their families often have to make to terminate pregnancies owing to a wide variety of health, economic and other private considerations.[53] Over the past several decades, moreover, the heightened rhetoric of anti-abortion activists and their conservative sponsors in Congress and legislatures across America has increasingly emboldened extremists to use violence against abortion providers as a means of advancing their cause. According to NBC News, based on survey data from the Feminist Majority, an all-time high of "34.2 percent of US abortion providers reported 'severe violence or threats of violence' in the first half of 2016 . . . up from 19.7 percent in 2014."[54] The prior high mark of 24 percent was recorded in 1995.

"Too Big To Fail" and Unregulated Corporate Greed

During recent years, American consumers have experienced increasing corporate greed and malfeasance with little or no resulting institutional or executive accountability. In advance of the 2008 Great Recession, banking, finance and insurance companies, such as Lehman Brothers, AIG and Moody's wreaked havoc on the nation's and the world's economies through over speculation and manipulative practices. According to NBC News, the Great Recession that was mainly triggered by the subprime mortgage industry meltdown of 2007 resulted in at least 8.4 million jobs lost and nearly three million homes foreclosed.[55] The highly reported shenanigans of corporate leaders and the impact of their misconduct on consumers between 2007 and 2009 helped to fuel a significant national outcry from both the left and the right, emerging first in 2011 with the progressive-leaning Occupy Wall Street Movement and, then, subsequently in 2013 with the conservative Tea Party Movement. Yet, despite considerable public discontent on all sides, not a single US corporate leader in the financial sector was ever prosecuted for committing the crimes that led to one of the American housing market's largest declines ever and the bankruptcy of millions of businesses and households as a result.[56] On the contrary, many of the leading banking, finance and insurance leaders implicated in these scandalous activities were rewarded by the federal government with massive working capital loans that enabled their firms to weather the worst of the storm because, in the eyes of our national leaders, they were considered "Too Big to Fail." More recent examples of amply documented corporate overreach and greed at large leading companies, such as Wells Fargo, Volkswagen, and

Equifax underscore how vulnerable people remain even now a decade later, as a result of continuing lax public oversight and insufficient firewalls to prevent ongoing corrupt corporate practices.

Diminishing Public Confidence and Satisfaction

There can be no doubt that all of these examples of our national leadership's unwillingness to respect the public will for real change have increasingly undercut national confidence in political and democratic processes. In recent national elections, more than 90 million eligible voters (fully 40 percent of the nation's voting populace) have opted to stay home and not vote. Even among those Americans who do turn out to vote, many express extreme and growing unhappiness with their limited choices.[57] During the 2016 election cycle, for example, nearly 2.5 million citizens who voted opted not to cast a ballot for any of the presidential contenders. Such is the level of voter disaffection with the state of American politics and political leadership in the early years of the 21st century.

All of these data have ominous implications for America's future as a beacon of democracy and economic opportunity. Yet the nation's current political leaders on the conservative right, rather than seeking common ground to address America's increasingly problematic realities after the close and contentious election of 2016, seem each day instead to double down with ever more reckless actions and misguided proposals designed to advance their most extreme aims and already-proven failures in policy application. In each instance, their extremism defies the preferences of a majority of the American people. This includes decisions such as pulling out of the Paris Global Climate Accord designed to reduce greenhouse gas emissions and ending the Deferred Action for Childhood Arrivals (DACA) program that over recent years has enabled non-citizen youth brought into the country without proper documentation during their childhood to remain in the United States with temporary work and study privileges. It also includes allied proposals, such as building an expensive and impractical wall to stem the significantly declining illegal immigration along our southern border, defunding family planning and basic health services for poor and moderate income women and their families, advancing international oil pipeline development in the Dakotas on disputed sacred Native lands, and pursuing yet another large Republican tax cut for our nation's already wealthiest citizens and corporations.

Recent trends in the political economy are increasingly antithetical to America's best experiences and traditions. And only the most uninformed or intellectually dishonest observers would deny that it does not have to be this way. In fact, public policy choices and preferences since the early 1980s have created the conditions for the downward trend lines that American society has experienced in recent years. According to University of Michigan researcher Charles Ballard:

> Income inequality decreased dramatically in the middle decades of the 20th century, largely as a result of policies that were designed to help the bottom 99 percent of the population more than the top one percent. These policies included strong support for [public] education, a highly progressive tax system, strong financial regulations, protections for labor, and [a living] wage.
>
> Income inequality has increased in the last 40 years, largely because earlier policies were diluted or reversed. So far, the main thrust of policy proposals from President Trump is to maintain, and even accelerate, the anti-egalitarian policies of recent decades.[58]

Reaganomics: Where It All Began

Most of the worst outcomes of recent American economic policy have been the predictable consequence of our nation's decidedly conservative and neoliberal policy choices since the Reagan era. Now, after nearly forty years of American policy flowing from the Republican Revolution that Ronald Reagan began in California in the mid-to-late 1970s, all objective evidence reveals that the basic premises and promises of Reagan's so-called "Morning in America"[59] campaign and undergirding supply side economics[60] have proven to be entirely unfounded.

Reagan and his conservative movement promised to renew American democracy and the vitality of our working and middle classes based on cutting government spending and enabling more unfettered corporate largesse and investor freedom. Reagan and his followers argued that if only federal policy could substantially reduce government impediments to productivity and profitability, average workers would benefit from a "trickle down" effect that would put more money in their pockets. In fact, the trickle down benefits that Reaganomics asserted would flow to average Americans as a result of major tax breaks for the already wealthy and massive cuts in public spending and regulation never materialized.[61] To the contrary, what has resulted is just the opposite: an economy that has more wealth concentrated at the top than ever before in our national history, and that has produced at the same time an increasingly robust "gig economy" of part-time worker-entrepreneurs who are otherwise unable to make a living through full-time employment.[62] In effect, the essential properties of the conservative policy platform Ronald Reagan sold to America in order to get elected in 1980 have produced a radical "trickle up" phenomenon; namely, a massive wealth transfer from America's working and middle classes to the nation's most well-endowed individuals, families and businesses.

The Changing Nature of Jobs and The Economy

To be sure, one of the biggest reflections of this shift has been the changing nature of work and jobs in the evolving American economy, a trajectory fundamentally characterized by expanded low-wage and contingent employment, and a related decline in the economic security of most Americans. According to journalist Patrice Hill:

> The increase in low-wage employment accelerated during the Great Recession of 2007 to 2009 when millions of higher-paying jobs in construction, manufacturing and finance were lost. Of the 7.2 million jobs that have opened since the recession, more than half have been in low-wage professions such as retail and restaurants, where workers with dependents

often must supplement their wages with federal benefits to make ends meet.[63]

Given the economy's remarkable production of wealth over the past decades, the real-life impact of these trends is profound. Economist Charles Ballard puts it this way:

> On a per capita basis, the US economy is more than twice as large as it was in 1973. But the average man, who works full time, year round, earns less now than in 1973, after adjusting for inflation.
>
> Meanwhile the share of income going to the most affluent one percent of American households has skyrocketed from about nine percent in the 1970s to more than 20 percent in recent years. That's a redistribution of more than one trillion dollars per year.[64]

American working and middle class families have borne the brunt of this shifting job market and redistribution of wealth to the point now where in many households, just to stay even, it has become necessary for heads of household, their spouses and even their children to take on supplemental and contingent employment. Such employment, however, typically does not offer meaningful benefits or upward growth opportunities. As of mid-2015, the incidence of contingent and alternative employment had begun to outpace traditional job opportunities for American workers. According to a March 31, 2016 report by *New York Times* senior economics correspondent, Neal Irwin:

> [T]he proportion of American workers who don't have traditional jobs—who instead work as independent contractors, through temporary services or on-call—has soared in the last decade . . . the number of Americans using these alternate work arrangements rose 9.4 million from 2005 to 2015. That was greater than the rise in overall employment, meaning

there was a small net decline in the number of workers with conventional jobs.[65]

In addition to the significant lower pay and benefits the kinds of jobs that are increasingly available in today's economy offer, encroaching structural adjustments in the labor market portend the disappearance of millions of "good jobs" with decent pay and benefits in the future, resulting in part from automation and artificial intelligence (AI).[66] The political and economic implications of this sea change are profound.

Compounding Effects of the Great Recession

The problems of diminishing job and income-earning opportunities for society's already vulnerable working and middle classes are further exacerbated by the lingering fallout of the national mortgage meltdown that fueled the Great Recession from 2007 to 2009. That catastrophic event caused the American economy to lose some $20 trillion and had an especially negative effect on property owners of color, who were disproportionately impacted by the resulting foreclosure crisis. As reported by the Alliance for a Just Society in May 2013,

Communities of color received a disproportionate share of subprime mortgages in the years before the housing crash and were therefore at a higher risk of facing foreclosure. Prior to the Great Recession, 35% of subprime loans were issued to borrowers who qualified for prime loans, and blacks and Latinos were 80% and 70% respectively more likely to receive subprime loans than white borrowers, after controlling for income, credit scores, and other factors.

Furthermore, when facing foreclosure, black and Latino mortgage holders were 76% and 71% more likely to have lost their homes than white borrowers. The authors also found that in ZIP codes where more than half of the population includes people of color, there were 17 foreclosures per 1,000 households. In comparison, there were just 10 foreclosures per 1,000 households in ZIP codes with predominately white households.

The average wealth lost per household in majority people of color ZIP codes was $2,200, compared to just $1,300 in majority white ZIP codes. This loss of wealth in the form of home equity is especially devastating in communities of color because black and Latino communities hold 49% and 52% of total assets in home equity, compared with just 28% for white families.[67]

The impact on net wealth for households of color was devastating. According to Rakesh Kochhar and Richard Fry in a late 2014 report by the Pew Research Center, racial wealth inequality widened substantially in the wake of these developments:

The wealth of white households was 13 times the median wealth of black households in 2013, compared with eight times the wealth in 2010, according to . . . the Federal Reserve's Survey of Consumer Finances. Likewise, the wealth of white households is now more than 10 times the wealth of Hispanic households, compared with nine times the wealth in 2010.[68]

The growing stresses these factors are creating across the American landscape in household after household have great implications for the quality of our lives. We have diminished the capacity of the American working and middle classes—and especially America's rapidly growing populations of color—to save and invest in ways that ensure a secure retirement and the prospect of leaving something meaningful behind for the next generation. Family leisure time and community volunteering have diminished, and economic stress has heightened racial and regional tensions, perhaps even increasing the incidence of violence across America. By almost any meaningful measure, American well-being has been substantially diminished as a result of these multiple, related factors.

The massive shift in public policy logic and practice that the Reagan presidency initially brought forward in the early 1980s set all of this in motion and is a central culprit in the evolving decline of American civic culture. That shift informed a significant and sadly still-enduring myth that a less regulated market, rather than a more activist government, is the best prescription for both reinvigorating American democratic vitality and shared prosperity. The nation's decided move to the political and economic right in recent decades has led to analogous, though perhaps not as extreme inclinations towards the market and the state among Democrats over the years (even despite growing evidence that Reaganomics and the modern conservative agenda offered counterproductive responses to the nation's lingering woes).

Democrats Have Also Contributed to This Crisis

Included in President Bill Clinton's acknowledged achievements were highly conservative policy "wins." These include the North American Free Trade Agreement, which has cost American workers considerable employment and income generating opportunities over the years; Welfare Reform, which tossed millions off of public assistance and further incentivized low-wage employment across the national economy; the highly punitive Federal Crime Bill of 1994, which established mandatory minimum sentences for certain crimes with a heavy underlying bias against people and communities of color; and the 1999 repeal of the Glass-Steagall Act, which for nearly seven decades predating the 2008 global economic crisis separated commercial and investment banking in order to protect investment consumers from the kinds of conflicts of interest and overreach that produced the Great Recession.[69]

New Democrats and the Democratic Leadership Council

Bill Clinton's essential distinction when he sought the Democratic presidential nomination in 1992 was his aim to move the party to the center.[70] As Governor of Arkansas, Clinton had been a leading member of the Democratic Leadership Council (DLC), an emerging national group of moderates in the party, consisting of so-called New Democrats. The DLC's New Democrats proposed to inoculate the party from defeat in the context of America's increasingly conservative bent in the post Reagan-era by promoting more business-friendly policies and more moderate views on government social spending. In fact, since the Clinton presidency, Democrats have tended consistently to moderate their policy positions towards the center-right in order more closely to align with the national political landscape. But even when the Democratic Party regained the White House with Barack Obama's 2008 landslide presidential victory, which for the first time in a generation gave Democrats simultaneous control of the Senate and the House of Representatives, with the exception of the Affordable Care Act, its leadership was only able to move legislation intended to address the worst of the Great Recession in advance of the 2010 mid-term elections, when they lost control of the House.

The Complicated Legacy of the Obama White House

Clearly, from its beginnings, the Obama White House was disadvantaged in unique ways that account for much of its inability and, in many cases, its unpreparedness to advance more progressive public policy. The young new president ascended to office as the nation's first-ever African American chief executive at a time of severe economic distress and growing associated political turmoil, and even prospective violence in reaction to his presidency.[71] Moreover, without Obama even having begun his new job, literally on his first day in the White House, Republicans in Congress vowed to unite against every measure the incoming president might advance, in order to ensure that he would be only a one-term president. Under these circumstances, Obama's and his Democratic Party's options were severely limited. Nevertheless, to many observers on the left, Obama and the Democrats generally failed to push back in areas where it ultimately proved to be unnecessary and even unproductive to appease the political right.[72] For eight years, Obama and the Democratic Party—like the Clinton White House in the 1990s—supported numerous policy positions that unnerved and unsettled important elements of the party's progressive base. Particularly significant in these respects were President Obama's continuation of the military actions his predecessor George W. Bush had initiated in Afghanistan and Iraq, his aggressive deportation of nearly three million undocumented individuals (many of whom were law abiding longstanding residents with deep community roots and US-based families), and his decision to support banking and financial institutions, rather than aggrieved consumers during the immediate aftermath of the Great Recession.

Democrats and the Political Money Game

A large part of the problem contributing to the Democratic Party's now generation-long move to the political middle has been the expanding role of money in our politics over the past two decades and the party leadership's adeptness and intentionality under Bill Clinton, Barack Obama and Hillary Clinton in securing more and more of it over recent election cycles. With the ever-increasing premium on big money in our contemporary politics and the Democratic Party leadership's growing fundraising appeals to the wealthy and privileged, the party has increasingly lost touch with its traditional base of working- and middle-class Americans. For all intents and purposes, the Democratic Party and its leaders have increasingly positioned themselves as a moderate version of the nation's traditional Republican Party, rather than as a real alternative to the increasingly extreme conservative elements that now largely control the White House and much of Congress. As a result, Democratic Party efforts to advance more aggressive and progressive policy alternatives on behalf of average Americans, who continue to struggle, have been relatively weak.

The Tyranny of Hyper-Capitalism and Neoliberalism

Over the better part of the past four decades, conservative and neoliberal politics have clearly ruled American policy. Conservative politicians have controlled our national and state political apparatus, and been hostile toward government in general. They have cuts taxes and deregulated much economic activity across the land. They have championed the rights and privileges of capital and wealth over humanity and nature at large; and they have imposed increasingly dehumanizing policies on groups ranging from women and workers to immigrants and the incarcerated. Moderate and conservative Democrats have advanced their own version of these policies out their own financial self-interests and class privilege. Yet, despite all the power and prerogative that conservative and neoliberal leaders have wielded, and all of their promises of eventual "trickle down" benefits to people, America has continued to decline into economic disrepair and expanding intergroup discord. So many Americans today are fed up with the disfunction in both our politics and our economy. They clamor for change.

Structural Barriers to Change

One of the greatest barriers to a change in course is the 2010 US Supreme Court decision in *Citizens United v. FEC,* which among other things eliminated campaign spending limits for corporations and the wealthy to finance candidates up for election.[73] Another accelerated political practice that impedes change is partisan gerrymandering throughout the nation. Both of these developments have imposed monumental impediments to meaningfully addressing the will of the American people in our political and economic life as a nation.[74] *Citizens United* has made elections more fully than ever before a pay-to-play proposition, leaving average citizens and smaller donors largely on the sidelines as a result of the massive scale of unfettered campaign giving by billionaires and millionaires, some of whose individual contributions exceeded $20,000,000 during the 2016 election cycle.[75] Hyper-partisan conservative gerrymandering, moreover, has made it virtually impossible to advance even the most basic legislative or regulatory reforms that American voters of all persuasions largely support, as noted earlier in this chapter.

The present and long-term effects of allowing increasingly unfettered campaign spending by a select club of corporations and independently wealthy donors should be troublesome to all Americans. The growing role of Super PACs—a direct result of the *Citizens United* decision—reveals the nature and extent of the problem. Super PACs are political committees that can solicit and spend unlimited sums of money with only minimal transparency and accountability to the public. Super PACs cannot contribute directly to a politician or political party, but they can spend independently to campaign for or against particular political figures our causes. Not surprisingly, Super PACs have tended to benefit more conservative interests that have disproportionately substantial resources and a vested stake in the status quo. According to a September 2016 report to the Congressional Research Service:

[A]lthough all super PACs combined spent less than $100 million in 2010, two Republican super PACs alone—Restore Our Future and American Crossroads—each spent more than $100 million in 2012. These two groups were the only super PACs that raised or spent more than $100 million in 2012.[76]

A recent report by the Center for Responsive Politics further reflects the dramatic growth of Super PACs during recent American elections. According to the report findings:

Super PAC spending in the 2016 cycle was almost double its level in the last presidential election, $1.1 billion compared to $609 million in 2012. The number of super PACs likewise nearly doubled, going from 1,300 to more than 2,400 in just four years.[77]

With so much concentrated wealth and spending increasingly driving our election system, who can honestly say that our modern day democracy works in service to the common people? In these circumstances, who can honestly say that our democracy is not for sale?

The related, negative impact of recent Republican Party gerrymandering has resulted in a marked skewing of the congressional balance of power that presently protects conservative policy preferences over more progressive legislative and regulatory aims. According to a June 2017 Associated Press in-depth analysis of the 2016 elections, for example, as a result of gerrymandering,

. . . Republicans won as many as 22 additional US House seats over what would have been expected based on the average vote share in congressional districts across the country. That helped provide the GOP with a comfortable majority over Democrats instead of a narrow one.[78]

Similar skewing because of gerrymandering at the state level afflicts our lower-level politics as well, owing to the lack of national standards for the governance of states.[79] Given these realities, who can honestly say that our elected officials are working to represent the authentic interests and will of the people? Who can honestly say that this is true democracy?

The Commodification of American Political and Civic Life

The primacy of priviledged money and exclusive rules that serve to retard democratic engagement and the will of the American people reflects a value system that makes everything a commodity and a transaction. It speaks to a world view in which people and nature are up for sale or the rubbish bin, depending upon the carrying capacities, needs and whims of big corporate and monied interests. Advancing our politics in this vein may have defined past eras of our national journey, dating back to Tammany Hall and the Victorian era of the nineteenth century, but it is hardly the best we can do in our day and age. With all of our modern knowledge and technology, and all of the emerging consciousness that humanity has recently achieved about the dangers of political corruption, poverty, social unrest, global climate change and species elimination, we certainly can and should be doing much better.

We Need to Find a New and Better Way Forward

Let's be frank. Our nation has lost its way in recent years. The best elements of what defined us (however imperfectly) in the past—our expanding national commitments to intergroup tolerance, equal opportunity, human rights, responsible environmental stewardship and meaningful bipartisan policy making–are at risk of being lost. What we have in America today is a political economy and society that manifest the tired mentality and ways of now forty years of misguided policy defined by conservative extremism, selfish short-sightedness, exclusivity, exploitation, greed and waste. What we have in America today is an unsustainable system that fundamentally over-relies for its "success" on the vagaries of barely regulated private markets and growing militarization—a reliance that is increasingly at odds with our society's democratic claims and long-term interests. What we have, in short, is a dramatic disconnect between what our current systems allow and what humanity and the planet now demand.

If our present approach to governance and policy ever worked in our waning industrial past (a dubious proposition on many levels), it surely is out of step with the emerging culture, values and needs of the post-industrial era in which we now live. Yet we remain mired in the proven political and economic failures of the past several decades; and therefore we find ourselves increasingly living in circumstances that a vast majority of our people find unacceptable. Gratefully, it doesn't have to be this way. As this book seeks to make clear, there are many promising new ideas, visions, models and templates emerging from progressive leaders and grassroots communities all across the country, that properly adapted and scaled could provide a working roadmap to a more inclusive, successful and sustainable reality for our nation and its people. It is high time we pursue this course to ensure a more productive, purposeful, and peaceful future for the decades to come.

Stronger Together

The fact is that by coming together and organizing around the normalization and scaling of various policy and practice alternatives that are already showing their real value and potential transformative powers across our nation and world, progressive Americans can change the course of our current trajectory in vitally important and essential ways. In the main, the chapters that follow seek to make clearer to interested parties who are committed to progressive transformation specific examples of how we can best advance change of the most timely and important kind. If progressive American leaders and communities can align around the best and most strategic of these possibilities in the years to come, there can be greatly expanded hope and benefits for all of us to share in ways that would make our country and planet saner, safer and ultimately more democratic and prosperous.

Putting People and the Planet over Privilege and Profits

When all is said and done, people, communities, and the natural world that sustains them are either bound together or torn asunder by the values and policies we support in our national decision-making processes. For nearly two generations, our national and global political economies have chipped away at the common good and our collective well-being to advance the interests of a select few. The case made throughout this book is that, moving forward, we stand to gain far more by putting common people and the environment first before hyper-profits and privilege. This is owing to the intrinsic value of all living things and the mutuality that is required to advance any successful enterprise or sustainable community over time.

In effect, what this book asserts at its core is that people and the planet must be re-centered in our systems of governance and economy to make life as we know it more sustainable and worthy. They cannot continue to be considered as expendable or otherwise disposable objects that merely serve at the pleasure of the wealthy and the powerful. Rather, humanity and nature must be the central focal points of all of our forward-going politics and economic investment priorities.

Attacking Age-Old Problems in New and Different Ways

Our evolving and increasingly complex modern culture and economy require new modalities, strategies and constructs to achieve change and, along with it, the different and better outcomes we all seek. Hence, the emphasis here rests on innovation. Without new approaches and applications of emerging thinking and technologies to the increasingly thorny problems we face, it is practically unlikely that we can achieve real and profound improvements. Our current systems and thinking have manifestly begun to run their course. This is true not only for established conservative practice and thought, but also for more traditional liberal practice and thought, as well.

What we need now, therefore, is the creative advancement of new ideas and models for a new day and time that simultaneously honor and respect the perennial, time-tested values of progressive people and communities. Using innovation and creativity, we need to build a more inclusive democracy that actively engages the best of what people have to offer in order more effectively to face the challenges and opportunities of our post-industrial era. At the same time, we need to lift up new models of wealth creation, employment and prosperity sharing that are fundamentally based in responsible social and environmental practices. It is the nexus of these destination points that defines the main stage for this undertaking. It is where progress and the living world can best come together in common cause, where private interest and public good can most happily converge and constructively co-exist. This is the crossing point where prosperity meets justice.

Lifting Up Our Voices and Vision

At this vitally important convergence point, we can begin to make our voices and will more meaningfully heard than ever before across our entire political and institutional culture. We can promote and support more active civic engagement by common people across the country, and more reliable, favorable and popular election and public policy outcomes. In short, we can realize the best potentialities of participatory democracy in America—a brand of national governance that we have largely auctioned off to the highest bidders in recent decades. At the same time, we can build a more sustainable social economy that serves the vast majority of our people by employing them at living wages, bolstering their prospects for long-term employment and economic security, and enhancing their overall quality of life.

We can do this by incentivizing more socially and environmentally responsible industry and by nurturing communities that are fundamentally more geared to shared prosperity and more inclusive of all. In these ways, we can begin to experience a more unified and joyful society that is decidedly safer and healthier than our current one, especially for our most vulnerable populations. And we can envision a more stable and strong society based on outcomes and circumstances that inspire more common pride and purpose than recent decades have allowed.

Reweaving Our Tattered Social and Economic Fabric

All of these are most worthy and timely destination points in the evolving American journey. They lead inherently to a new and different kind of logic about what correctly lies at the center of the modern US political economy. Going forward, if we are to survive as an icon of democratic practice and thrive as a worthy global economic leader, we will have to reinvigorate our democracy with more egalitarian and active participation by those who have been too often marginalized in our public decision-making. We will also have to replace our nation's failed experiment in supply-side economics with more practical and inclusive approaches to wealth creation and distribution. The chapters that follow provide more concrete and specific examples of the many exciting opportunities and innovations operating at the intersection of American political culture and economy.

These include, among other possibilities, advancing new rules and applications of digital technology in our electoral system that make registering, voting and securing essential public services easier and more accessible for citizens. They include supporting major system reforms intended to democratize our nation's campaign finance laws, redistricting practices and public engagement in policy decision-making. They include promoting systemic policing and criminal justice reforms geared to expanded racial justice and real rehabilitation and sentencing fairness for criminal offenders, as well as comprehensive immigration reform leading to more humane and consistent treatment of noncitizens living and working productively in our nation. And they include dramatically increased public investments in civic education, arts and culture as essential anchors of evolving American democratic identity and community development.

The opportunities and imperatives that await our next generation include as well investing in the development of smart new infrastructure, twenty-first-century worker training programs and good jobs for our emerging economic future. They include increasing the nation's minimum wage to a livable level and aggressively scaling public and private investments in social enterprises that are both sustainable and more responsive to community needs and concerns. They also involve expanding universal healthcare coverage options for American consumers and essential asset-building opportunities for lower income children and their families.

Finally, the changes that are properly in store for us if we unite to see them through include pursuing aggressive new investment incentives for businesses, government agencies and private foundations to help increase employment opportunities for otherwise marginalized workers (especially in public and community service), developing affordable new housing and creating smarter transportation systems and production processes that can sustainably fuel a next generation of economic progress for people all across our nation. Through policy efforts and private initiatives like these, the future of America can be made far more harmonious and prosperous. New strides can be made toward reweaving our fraying social and economic fabric. New opportunities for a next generation of national achievement and reunification can be realized. And new anchors for continuing American global inspiration and leadership can be established. These are the promises and potentialities of advancing a new American social contract that better meets the emerging needs of both our people and our planet. These are the ultimate benefits of intentional efforts today to ensure that we evolve as both a prosperous and a just society in the decades ahead.

For enhanced confidence that initiatives and outcomes along these lines are achievable if we aggressively and collectively pursue them, one need only look to the State of California, whose often controversial and contrarian views serve as a perennial harbinger of the change that will take place in the rest of America. As reported in Manuel Pastor's important new book *The State of Resistance: What California's Dizzying Descent and Remarkable Resurgence Mean for America's Future* (2018),[80] the Golden State's trajectory over recent decades, from failed hyper-conservatism to more recent prosperity and social cohesion under liberal and progressive policy leadership, offers inspiring lessons. California, long the nation's leading innovator and bellwether, was the first significant state to embrace the new Republicanism of Reaganomics and the politics of intensified social and economic division. The Reagan era proved a formidable elixir for many across the nation, and indeed many climbed aboard its train with gusto, so much so that nearly half a century after Reagan's presidential election we are still not fully free from the misplaced logic of Reaganomics.

Like the United States today, the California of the late 1970s lost its mind to the myths that government was the enemy of the people and that relentless budget- and tax-cutting, along with heightened cultural animus, could be formulas for long term-societal success. California took that path to its own great detriment from 1978 through the early 2000s, during which time the state saw its once leading public education system implode, its world class economy falter, its burgeoning population of young black and brown men incarcerated at unprecedented levels and its poverty rate balloon. But, as Pastor meticulously documents, over more recent years, by re-investing as a state, by rejecting hyper-divisive politics and by re-establishing California's more long-held commitment to forward- (rather than backward-) looking policies, the Golden State has regained its greatness. Recently, California surpassed the United Kingdom as the fifth largest economy in the world, and is widely considered again to be the nation's leading hub of technological and cultural innovation, and global influence. In its remarkable recovery, based on lessons learned from its darker recent past, the state's voters have essentially rejected the thinking and values of modern conservatism, to the point where it is entirely possible California will never see another Republican statewide official.

There is much historical experience and supporting new evidence to draw on that reveals progressive policy and practices, like those on the rise in California and endorsed throughout this book, are in fact better for society as a whole. That is to say, even despite conventional resistance to new institutional interventions and investments that seek to increase social and environmental equity, both experience and data reveal that the entire society wins when we move in these directions. One example relates to the implementation of protections for Americans with disabilities. Angela Glover Blackwell, writing in the *Stanford Social Innovation Review* examines the broad societal benefits that have accrued since the federal government's mandate in the early 1990s to require new public accommodations for people with disabilities through the Americans with Disabilities Act (ADA).[81] Along with other sections, the ADA requires wheelchair accessibility not only in the construction of places of public accommodation but also in the modification of existing private businesses and local, state and federal facilities. Initially, many Americans resisted this new set of government demands on the basis of cost and inconvenience. However, since the ADA's enactment, many have significantly benefited from the law, extending well beyond the nation's disability population. Most importantly, people with disabilities are now able to enter the workforce and share their robust talents more broadly for the common good, whereas many previously relied solely on government assistance. This is all possible since the passage of the ADA, due to accessible housing, transportation, workplaces and all of the other supportive services one needs to become a contributing member of society. Our country has thus broadly profited, both economically and socially, by having people with disabilities fully integrated into the community as a result of the ADA's passage and implementation.

There are numerous other examples in our contemporary history, where Americans have benefitted from laws and regulations designed to address a targeted portion of the population. Consider the housing and education assistance given to GIs returning from World War II and the building of major public transit systems and bicycle lanes across the nation in more recent years. To be sure, the adjustment to these significant cost outlays and the initial novelty of these new policies and their implementation in contemporary American life was not always easy or immediate for many Americans; however, most today would concur that we are far better off as a nation for their introduction and normalization.

The same will be true one day when the new systems and approaches considered in this book—strange and controversial though they will seem today to all but those closest to their development—have become more standardized and broadly accepted in the future. Making that outcome true will be the mark of our success as progressives during the years and decades to come. By joining together to find new and more fundamentally inclusive ways of making more ethical and durable societal decisions, we can renew and restore democracy to our everyday lives in ways that far better serve humanity and the planet. And by helping to create a wholly new economy that is based fundamentally on helping people to achieve their highest potential and support ecological sustainability, we can improve the duration and quality of life across the planet. In the process, we can create a new meeting point to bind our politics and our economics in more lasting and worthy ways, so that the prosperity we all aspire to meets the justice we all fundamentally need and deserve.

Endnotes

[1]Klein, N., *No is Not Enough: Resisting Trump's Shock Politics and Winning the World We Need*, Haymarket Books, Chicago, 2017, p. 233.

[2]See Brown, Paul, *The Impulse Society* (London: Bloomsbury Publishing, 2014); Meyer, D., *Why We Hate Us: American Discontent in the New Millennium*, Crown, New York, 2008: http://www.npr.org/templates/story/story.php?storyId=93261726; Saleci, R., *On Anxiety*, NY: Routledge, New York (pp.49-66); and Capra, F., *The Web of Life*, Doubleday, New York, 1996 (pp. 3-13, 300). Social discontent in capitalist America, borne precisely out of expanding modernity and complexity, is not a new phenomenon. As far back as the 1970s, writers and scholars such as Eugene Linden (*Affluence and Discontent: The Anatomy of Consumer Societies*, Viking, New York, 1979) and Harvard sociologist Daniel Bell (*The Cultural Contradictions of Capitalism*, Basic Books, New York, 1979) began acknowledging the growing tension between basic human needs and constructed desires as a defining byproduct of America's burgeoning consumer society.

[3]See "Natural Capital At Risk: The Top 100 Externalities of Business," a Commissioned Report by Trucost to the United Nation's Environmental Program-supported Economics of Ecosystems and Biodiversity Program, April 15, 2013: https://www.trucost.com/publication/natural-capital-risk-top-100-externalities-business/. See also Roberts, D., "None of the World's Top Industries Would be Profitable if They Paid for the Natural Capital They Use," Grist.org, April 17, 2013 at: http://grist.org/business-technology/none-of-the-worlds-top-industries-would-be- profitable-if-they-paid-for-the-natural-capital-they-use/.

[4]See Burns, C., "The Costly Business of Discrimination," March 22, 2012, Center for American Progress, Washington, DC at: https://www.americanprogress.org/issues/lgbt/reports/2012/03/22/11234/the-costly-business-of-discrimination/.

[5]See US Equal Employment Opportunity Commission, "EEOC Releases Fiscal Year 2016 Enforcement and Litigation Data," January 18, 2017: https://www.eeoc.gov/eeoc/newsroom/ release/1-18-17a.cfm.

[6]See, Feldblum, C. R. & Lipnic, V.A., *Select Task Force on the Study of Sexual Harassment at the Workplace*, June 2016, Equal Employment Opportunity Commission, Washington, DC: https://www1.eeoc.gov/eeoc/task_force/harassment/report.cfm?renderforprint=1. For allied reporting on the underreporting of gender discrimination issues at the workplace, see also, Noguchi, Y., "Underreporting Makes Sexual Violence at Work Difficult to Address," February 23, 2016, National Public Radio, Washington, DC at: https://www.npr.org/2016/02/23/467826376/underreporting-makes-sexual-violence-at-work-difficult-to-address. According to NPR: "The most recent

data from the Bureau of Justice Statistics estimated there were more than 43,000 workplace rapes and sexual assaults a year. But anti-rape advocates say that vastly underreports the crimes, because many victims are afraid to or discouraged from coming forward." Similar issues pertain to reporting of discrimination issues by other groups of employees on the basis of race, disability and national origin. See Rosenberg, A., "Asian American Employees Underreport Discrimination, Report Finds," January 20, 2009, Government Executive, Washington, DC at: http://www.govexec.com/pay-benefits/2009/ 01/asian-american-employees-underreport-discrimination-report-finds/ 28379/; Nuñez-Smith, M., *Race/Ethnicity and Workplace Discrimination: Results of a National Survey of Physicians*, November 2009, US National Library of Medicine, National Institutes of Health, Washington, DC: https:// www.ncbi.nlm.nih.gov/pmc/articles/PMC2771235/; and Booker, S. J., "Are Scientists With Disabilities the Forgotten Underrepresented Minority?" March 2013, American Society for Biochemistry & Molecular Biology, Rockville, MD: http://www.asbmb.org/asbmbtoday/ 201303/ MinorityAffairs/Booker/.

[7]See Captain, S., "Workers Win Only 1% Of Federal Civil Rights Lawsuits at Trial," July 31, 2017, FastCompany.com at: https://www.fastcompany. com/40440310/employees-win-very-few-civil-rights-lawsuits.

[8]See Stone, K.V.W. & Colvin, A.J.S., "The Arbitration Epidemic: Mandatory Arbitration Deprives Workers and Consumers of Their Rights, December 7, 2015, Briefing Paper 414, Economic Policy Institute, Washington, DC: http://www.epi.org/publication/the-arbitration-epidemic/.

[9]See, e.g., "Costs of US Prescription Opioid Epidemic Estimated at $78. 5 billion," citing recent studies by Wolters Kluwer Health at: https://www. sciencedaily.com/releases/2016/09/160914105756.htm.

[10]Recent, groundbreaking action research by the New York-based Roosevelt Institute on the hidden costs of US political economic policy and structure are most instructive in these connections. See Flynn, A., et al., *The Hidden Rules of Race: Barriers to an Inclusive Economy*, 2017, Cambridge University Press, New York and Stiglitz, J., *Rewriting the Rules of the American Economy: An Agenda for Growth & Shared Prosperity*, 2015, The Roosevelt Institute, New York.

[11]See http://www.neweconomictheory.org/content/need-new-theory.

[12]See OECD Data: United States: https://data.oecd.org/united-states.htm.

[13]See the October 22, 2013 posting by George Mason University Senior Fellow Veronique de Rugy in the Mercatus Center News, building on data from the International Monetary Fund: https://www.mercatus.org/publication/how-does-us-debt-position-compare-other-countries.

[14]During the first decade of the 2000s, the Bush and Obama Administrations combined to expand defense outlays by nearly 120 percent over the preced-

ing decade. Obama's 2016 military budget totaled some $619 billion. See, Shane III, L., "Obama Signs Defense Spending Bill . . ." *Military Times*, December 23, 2016 at: https://www.militarytimes.com/news/your-military/2016/12/23/obama-signs-defense-bill-that-authorizes-pay- raise-more-troops/and Easterbrook, G., "Wasteland," *The New Republic*, November 9, 2010: https://newrepublic.com/article/79066/waste-defense-spending-america-pentagon. The Trump Administration's year one military budget for 2018 totals nearly $670 billion. See Korb, L., "Trumps Proposed Defense Budget . . . " June 8, 2017 Center for American Progress: https://www.americanprogress.org/issues/security/news/2017/06/08/43387 8/trumps-proposed-defense-budget- will-not-support-u-s-national-security/.

[15]Money in politics has always posed challenges to American election integrity and civic participation, but especially so since the 2009 U.S. Supreme Court decision in *Citizens United v. FEC* [558 U. S. 310 (2010)]. In *Citizens United*, the Court found that because corporations and unions have the same legal standing as individuals, their campaign spending (so long as not directed to individual candidates but rather Political Action Committees and Funds) cannot be legally limited "without chilling political speech, speech that is central to the First Amendment's meaning and purpose." The decision also protected the anonymity of political donors to American campaign PACs. While technically the decision placed capital and labor rights on an equal footing, because of the recent relative decline in union membership across the nation and the growing supremacy of for-profit corporations and private wealth, the decision has amplified the recent uptick in casino-style campaign spending, making it more and more difficult for non-wealthy candidates and causes to gain a fair hearing in modern elections at all levels. See, e.g., the following USA Today analysis of the decision's impacts on the five year anniversary of its publication: https://www.usnews.com/news/articles/2015/01/21/5-years-later-citizens-united-has-remade-us-politics.

[16]See Bryan, B., "Here's How the Newly Passed GOP Tax Bill Will Impact the Economy, Businesses, the Deficit, and Your Wallet," December 20, 2017, *Business Insider*: http://www.businessinsider.com/trump-gop-tax-reform-bill-impact-economy-business-debt-income-2017-12.

[17]See "Education Pays: 2013": https://trends.collegeboard.org/sites /default/files/education-pays-2013-full-report.pdf, which reports that, "The difference between median earnings for women ages 25 to 34 working full time year-round with a bachelor's degree or higher and those in the same age range with high school diplomas rose from 43% in 1971 to 56% in 1991 and to 70% in 2011. The earnings premium for men rose from 25% in 1971 to 56% in 1991 and to 69% in 2011."

[18]See Calamaras, D., "Government Spending on Education in the United States: A Historical Perspective": http://www.bidnet.com/bne-cms/content/ bid-resources/business-insights/government-spending-education-in-the-united-states-historical-perspective-en.jsp and also usgovernmentspending.com at: https://www.usgovernmentspending.com/education_ spending.

[19]It should be noted, moreover, that the Trump Administration's initial budget submitted to Congress included cuts of more than $9 billion in federal education outlays for 2018, a nearly 14 percent reduction. See Kamenetz, A., "President Trump's Budget Proposal Calls for Deep Cuts to Education," npr.org, May 22. 2017: http://www.npr.org/sections/ed/2017/05/22/ 529534031/president-trumps-budget-proposal-calls-for-deep-cuts- to-education.

[20]See Kiger, P., "Boomers Once Led the World in Education. What Happened?" June 19, 2013, *AARP: Bulletin Today*: http://blog.aarp.org/2013/ 06/19/u-s-global-education-rankings-slipping-boomers-once-held-strong-lead/?intcmp=AE-WOR-RELBOX1-BL and Ask Mr. History, "Was the U.S. Ever Number 1 in Education?" October 4, 2012, HistoryNet at: http://www.historynet.com/was-the-usa-ever-no-1-in-education.htm.

[21]See https://data.oecd.org/pisa/reading-performance-pisa.htm#indicator-chart.

[22]See https://data.oecd.org/pisa/science-performance-pisa.htm#indicator-chart.

[23]See https://data.oecd.org/pisa/mathematics-performance-pisa.htm#indicator-chart.

[24]See http://www.oecd.org/skills/.

[25]See http://www.keepeek.com/Digital-Asset-Management/oecd/social-issues-migration-health/health-at-a-glance-2015_health_glance-2015-en#.WbCKvLpFydI#page25.

[26]See Lee, M.Y.H., "Yes, U.S. Locks People Up at Higher Rate than Any Other Country," July 7, 2015, Washington Post: https://www.washingtonpost.com/news/fact-checker/wp/2015/07/07/yes-u-s-locks-people-up-at-a-higher- rate-than-any-other-country/?utm_term=.ba613a93f3f7.

[27]See CBS News February 15, 2018: https://www.cbsnews.com/news/ how-u-s-gun-deaths-compare-to-other- countries/, which reports that Americans are currently 10 times more likely than citizens of other developed nations to be killed by guns.

[28]See OECD report http://www.oecd.org/eco/outlook/focusonhouseprices.htm, showing real housing prices in the United States to be higher than all other measured nations except Germany and China, respectively; and http://www.oecd.org/social/affordable-housing-database.htm, underscoring the United States's relative low level of home ownership at just under 23 percent compared to France at nearly 40 percent, Spain at nearly 50 percent, and Italy nearly 60 percent.

[29]See OECD data: https://data.oecd.org/earnwage/wage-levels.htm#indicator-chart, showing that, as a percentage of all wages earned, fully 25 percent of the American workforce is subject to low pay, second only to Colombia at 25.3 percent.

[30]See Kaiser Family Foundation data showing that fully 52 percent of Americans now support Obamacare, with just 39 percent opposing it (down from 44 percent opposition earlier in the year): http://thehill.com/policy/healthcare/346184-poll-majority-of-americans-support-obamacare.

[31]See Catherine Rampell's April 17, 2017 *Washington Post* column, "Sorry, Republicans, but Most People Support Single-Payer Health Care" https://www.washingtonpost.com/opinions/sorry-republicans-but-most- people-support-single-payer-health-care/2017/04/17/f0919bb6-23a6-11e7-bb9d-8cd6118e1409_story.html?utm_term=.9a1b74dce01d, in which she writes, "A recent survey from the Economist/YouGov found that a majority of Americans support 'expanding Medicare to provide health insurance to every American.' Similarly, a poll from Morning Consult/Politico showed that a plurality of voters support 'a single payer health care system, where all Americans would get their health insurance from one government plan.'"

[32]See e.g., the following, October 6, 2017 Politifact report on Congressional plans to reduce Medicare and Medicaid expenditures over the coming decade, http://www.politifact.com/truth-o-meter/statements/2017/oct/06/charles-schumer/are-republicans-paying-tax-cuts-reductions-medicar/.

[33]See the July 24, 2017 letter from Democratic congressional leaders to Virginia Foxx, Chairwoman of the US Congressional Committee on Education and the Workforce: http://democrats-edworkforce.house.gov/imo/media/doc/Committee%20Democrats%20Urge%20GOP%20to%20Hold%20Hearing% 20on%20Raise%20the%20Wage%20Act.pdf. The letter uses federal data to underscore that, for a family of three, the current federal minimum wage still falls $5,000 short of the official federal poverty level for annual earnings.

[34]See the Gallup report from November 11, 2013, http://news. gallup. com/poll/165794/americans-raising-minimum-wage.aspx, showing that more than three-quarters of Americans surveyed favored a federal minimum wage increase to at least $9 from the then prevailing rate of $7.25 per hour. Business leaders have also recently been reported to overwhelmingly favor a national increase in the minimum wage as reported in the *Washington Post* 4 April 2016: https://www.washingtonpost.com/news/ wonk/ wp/2016/04/04/leaked-documents-show- strong-business-support-for-raising-the-minimum-wage/?utm_term=.cc505f6b69f4.

[35]The Fight for 15 Campaign website at: https://fightfor15.org/about-us/.

[36]Economic Policy Institute analysts Janelle Jones and David Cooper, January 9, 2017, "State Minimum Wage Increases Helped 4.3 Million Workers,

but Federal Inaction has Left Many More Behind": http://www.epi.org/publication/state-minimum-wage-increases-helped-4-3-million-workers-but-federal-inaction- has-left-many-more-behind/.

[37]See July 25, 2017 op ed in The Hill by National Employment Law Project Executive Director Christine Owens, "Don't Take Away Our Healthcare, Raise Our Minimum Wage Instead," http://democrats-edworkforce. house.gov/imo/media/doc/Committee%20Democrats%20Urge%20GOP%20to%20Hold%20Hearing%20on%20Raise%20the%20Wage%20Act.pdf.

[38]See Saru Jayaraman's important book *Forked: A New Standard for American Dining*, Oxford University Press, New York, 2016 at pp. 33-37.

[39]See "With Budget Debate Looming, Growing Share of Public Prefers Bigger Government," Pew Research Center, Washington, DC, April 24, 2017: http://www.people-press.org/2017/04/24/with-budget-debate-looming-growing-share-of-public-prefers-bigger-government/.

[40]See Lowery, W., "Aren't More Black People Than White People Killed by Police? Yes, but No," Washington Post, July 11, 2016 at: https://www.washingtonpost.com/news/post-nation/wp/2016/07/11/arent-more-white-people-than-black-people-killed-by-police-yes-but-no/?utm_term=.9cb0719d4407.

[41]See Hirschfield, P., "U.S. Laws Protect Police, While Endangering Civilians," January 18, 2016, The Conversation at: http://theconversation.com/u-s-laws-protect-police-while-endangering-civilians-52737 and, also, "Deadly Force: Police Use of Lethal Force In The United States," June 17, 2015, Amnesty International USA at: https://www.amnestyusa.org/reports/deadly-force-police-use-of-lethal-force-in-the-united-states/. Of the many examples provided here of unarmed African American citizens killed by law enforcement officers, only one victim's death, that of Walter Scott, resulted in the shooting officer being convicted and sentenced to serve prison time.

[42]"Black, White, and Blue: Americans' Attitudes on Race and Police," Roper Center for Public Opinion Research, 2015: https://ropercenter.cornell.edu/black-white-blue-americans-attitudes-race-police/.

[43]McDonald, B. and Bachelder, H., "With Rise of Body Cameras, New Tests of Transparency and Trust," *New York Times,* 6 January 2017: https://www.nytimes.com/2017/01/06/us/police-body-cameras.html.

[44]See the PBS Frontline report by Boghani, P., "Is Civilian Oversight the Answer to Distrust of Police?": http://www.pbs.org/wgbh/frontline/article/is-civilian-oversight-the-answer-to-distrust-of-police/.

[45]See "Police Violence Seems to Result in No Punishment," Bellafante, G., *New York Times*, 4 December 2014: https://www.nytimes.com/2014/12/07/nyregion/police-violence-seems-to-result-in-no-punishment.html.

[46]See, "The Changing Racial Dynamics of Women's Incarceration," The Sentencing Project, New York, February 27, 2013: http://www.sentencing-project.org/publications/the-changing-racial-dynamics-of-womens- incarceration/. According to the report: "Beginning in the early 1970s the United States embarked on an unprecedented escalation of the use of imprisonment. The 2.2 million people behind bars in prisons and jails in 2010 represented more than a 500% increase from the level of 1972. During the highest growth years in the 1980s, state prison populations increased by as much as 12% in a single year."

[47]See "Banking on Bondage: Private Prisons and Mass Incarceration," American Civil Liberties Union, New York, November 2011: http://www.msnbc.com/all-in/private-prisons-and-the-profit-motive. According to the report: "Today, for-profit companies are responsible for approximately 6% of state prisoners, 16% of federal prisoners, and, according to one report, nearly half of all immigrants detained by the federal government."

[48]See A. Nellis, "The Color of Justice: Racial and Ethnic Disparity in State Prisons," June 14, 2016, the Sentencing Project, New York at: http://www.sentencingproject.org/publications/color-of-justice-racial-and-ethnic-disparity-in-state-prisons/.

[49]*Ibid.*

[50]See, "National Survey Key Findings–Federal Sentencing & Prisons," a commissioned report to the Pew Charitable Trusts by the Mellman Group and Public Opinion Strategies: http://www.pewtrusts.org/~/media/assets/2016/02/national_survey_key_findings_federal_sentencing_prisons.pdf. The survey results reveal growing public support for reducing the prison population of nonviolent drug offenders and mandatory minimum sentencing guidelines.

[51]"Public Opinion on Abortion: Views on Abortion 1995-2017," PEW Research Center on Religion & Public Life, http://www.pewforum.org/fact-sheet/public-opinion-on-abortion/.

[52]See the Planned Parenthood Action Fund's website for insight into prevailing restrictions on abortion in America and especially its review of the 1976 Hyde Amendment, which prohibits federal funding for abortions: https://www.plannedparenthoodaction.org/issues/abortion/hyde-amendment.

[53]Benson Gold, R. & Nash, E., "Flouting the Facts: State Abortion Restrictions Flying in the Face of Science," Guttmacher Institute Policy Review, Vol. 20 (May 9, 2017): https://www.guttmacher.org/gpr/2017/05/flouting-facts-state-abortion-restrictions-flying-face-science.

[54]See, e.g., O'Hara M.E., "Abortion Clinics Report Threats of Violence on the Rise," NBC News.com, February 14, 2017 at: https://www.nbcnews.com/news/us-news/abortion-clinics-report-threats-violence-rise-n719426.

[55]See "Study: 1.2 Million Households Lost to Recession," Shoen, J.W., April 8, 2010, NBC News.com: http://www.nbcnews.com/id/36231884/ns/business-eye_on_the_economy/t/study-million-households-lost- recession/#. We5MYLpFwcQ.

[56]See, Cohan, W.D., " How Wall Street's Bankers Stayed Out of Jail," *The Atlantic*, September 2015 at: https://www.theatlantic.com/magazine/archive/2015/09/how-wall-streets-bankers-stayed-out-of-jail/399368/; and also the June 2, 2015 Inman Report by Louis Cammarosano: https://www.inman.com/2015/06/02/bankruptcy-in-america/. Cammarosano's reporting shows that 2007 combined business and individual bankruptcies totaled about 600,000, then increased to about 750,000 in 2008, then to about 1.25 million in 2009, and finally to roughly 1.5 million annually for both 2009 and 2010.

[57]See, Harrington, R. and Gould, S., "Americans Beat One Voter Turnout Record—Here's How 2016 Compares With Past Elections "http://www.businessinsider.com/trump-voter-turnout-records-history-obama-clinton-2016-11.

[58]Ballard, Charles, The Hill, "Many of Trump's Policies Will Further Intensify Income Inequality," February 10, 2017: http://thehill.com/blogs/pundits-blog/economy-budget/318941-many-of-trumps-policies-will-further-intensify-income.

[59]The 1980 Reagan presidential campaign used this language as a marketing moniker to suggest that the Republican candidate's election would vastly improve conditions for average Americans. See, e.g., Beschloss, M., "The Ad That Helped Reagan Sell Good Times to an Uncertain Nation," May 7, 2016, New York Times at: https://www.nytimes.com/2016/05/08/business/the-ad-that-helped-reagan-sell-good-times-to-an-uncertain- nation.html.

[60]Supply-side economics is a theory that says increased production drives economic growth. The factors of production are capital, labor, entrepreneurship and land. Supply-side fiscal policy focuses on businesses. Its tools are tax cuts and deregulation. California economist Arthur Laffer popularized this thinking in the 1970s and gained widespread support from conservative economists and politicians, including Ronald Reagan. See Moore, S., "The Laffer Curve at 40...," December 26, 2014, The Washington Post at: https://www.washingtonpost.com/opinions/the-laffer-curve-at-40-still-looks-good/2014/12/26/4cded164-853d-11e4-a702-fa31ff4ae98e_story.html?utm_term=.c85999ecb588. Evidence over time, however, has strongly undercut the theory's currency and credibility, primarily because of the harsh setbacks those policies imposed on the nation's average and struggling households. For critical analysis on Supply Side Economics, see: http://www.salon.com/2015/06/13/trickle_downs_middle_

class_massacre_failure_of_conservative_economics_should_discredit_
these_ bankrupt_ideas_forever/
[61]During the 1980s, Supply Side Economics came to be equated with purported "trickle down" benefits to working Americans who were supposedly going to benefit as America's wealthy investor classes profited under
more producer-friendly tax and regulatory laws. See the Center for American Progress analysis of Supply side Economics: https://www.american-
progress.org/issues/economy/news/2012/08/01/11998/the-failure-of-sup-
ply-side-economics/.

[62]See Stone, C., et al, "A Guide to Statistics on Historical Trends in Income
Inequality," Center on Budget & Policy Priorities, October 11, 2017, Washington, DC: https://www.cbpp.org/research/poverty-and-inequality/a-
guide-to-statistics-on-historical-trends-in-income-inequality; and Gille-
spie, P., "Intuit: Gig Economy is now 34% of Workforce," May 24, 2017,
CNN: Money at: http://money.cnn.com/2017/05/24/news/economy/gig-
economy-intuit/index.html. According to Intuit and Emergent, the technology finance and research companies cited by CNN as the sources of its
report, there are currently about 4 million quintessential gig—or freelance—
workers in the United States. They expect that number to grow to 7.7 million workers by 2020. A recent KQED-San Francisco Public Television
documentary by Deborah Kaufman and Alan Snitow entitled "Company
Town" reveals the growing negative impacts of gig economy jobs and companies in Northern California, including diminished private housing stock,
rising prices and expanded gentrification pressures, as well as the wholesale undermining of more longstanding formal business players in allied
sectors, such as taxi and limousine services: http://www.snitow-kaufman.
org/company-town/.

[63]See the following article by Hill, entitled: "Welfare-to-Work Law Encourages Low Wages, Raises Dependency on Federal Benefits," *Washington
Times*, 3 November 2013: http://www.washingtontimes.com/news/2013/
nov/3/welfare-to-work-law-encourages-low-wages-increases/.

[64]See, Ballard, Charles, The Hill, "Many of Trump's Policies Will Further
Intensify Income Inequality," February 10, 2017: http://thehill.com/blogs/
pundits-blog/economy-budget/318941-many-of-trumps-policies-will-fur-
ther- intensify-income.

[65]See Irwin, N., "With 'Gigs' Instead of Jobs, Workers Bear New Burdens,"
New York Times, 31 March 2016: https://www.nytimes.com/2016/
03/31/upshot/contractors-and-temps-accounted-for-all-of-the-growth-in-
employment-in-the-last-decade.html.

[66]See *Artificial Intelligence, Automation, and the Economy,* Office of the
President, The White House, Washington, DC, December 2016, p. 2:

https://obamawhitehouse.archives.gov/sites/whitehouse.gov/files/documents/Artificial-Intelligence-Automation- Economy.PDF.

[67]See "Foreclosure Crisis Causes Disproportionate Loss of Wealth among Communities of Color," National Low Income Housing Coalition, Washington, DC, May 31, 2013: http://nlihc.org/article/foreclosure-crisis-causes-disproportionate-loss-wealth-among-communities-color.

[68]Kochhar, R. and Fry, R., "Wealth Inequality has Widened along Racial, Ethnic Lines Since End of Great Recession," *FactTank: News in the Numbers*, Pew Research Center, December 12, 2014: http://www.pewresearch.org/fact-tank/2014/12/12/racial-wealth-gaps-great-recession/.

[69]For an overall critique of President Clinton's many anti-progressive "achievements," see Thomas Frank's in- depth analysis in the March 2016 op ed in Salon: http://www.salon.com/2016/03/14/bill_clintons_odious_presidency_thomas_frank_on_the_real_history_of_the_90s/. Also, on the unintended consequences of Welfare Reform from a labor market and worker mobility standpoint, see Patrice Hill (http://www.washingtontimes.com/news/2013/ nov/3/welfare-to-work-law-encourages-low-wages-increases/), who writes: "The historic welfare reform law of 1996 was widely praised for encouraging Americans to go back to work and not stay on the dole. But after nearly two decades of experience with the law, analysts are finding it created unintended side effects such as a perverse incentive for some employers to pay skimpy wages . . . The provisions were intended to provide incentives for people to go to work and get off welfare, even if they don't have the skills to command wages high enough to fully support their families. The law worked as intended for the most part, and full dependence on welfare programs dropped steeply. But . . . Since the law was enacted, low-wage jobs with no health care or other benefits that barely provide enough for workers to sustain themselves have proliferated."

[70]See, e.g., Robert Pear's June 26, 1992 *New York Times* report, "The 1992 Campaign: Platform; In a Final Draft, Democrats Reject a Part of Their Past."

[71]See Eilperin, J., "The New Dynamics of Protecting a President: Most Threats against Obama Issued Online," *The Washington Post* 4 October 2014: https://www.washingtonpost.com/politics/the-new-dynamics-of- protecting-a-president-most-threats-against-obama-issued-online/2014/10/07/a525ef6c-4b11-11e4-891d-713f052086a0_story.html? utm_ term=.c4673af42afe.

[72]See West, C., "Pity the Sad Legacy of Barack Obama," *The Guardian*, 9 January 2017: https://www.theguardian.com/commentisfree/2017/jan/09/barack-obama-legacy-presidency.

[73]See Dalgo, E., and Balcerzak, A., "Seven Years Later: Blurred Boundaries, More Money," OpenSecrets.org, Center for Responsive Politics, Washing-

ton, DC, January 19, 2017 at: https://www.opensecrets.org/news/2017/01/citizens-united-7-years-later/.

[74]See Potter, T., "Five Myths about Super PACs," *The Washington Post* 13 April 2012: https://www.washingtonpost.com/opinions/five-myths-about-super-pacs/2012/04/13/gIQAGPnEFT_story.html?utm_term=.3858d7e 6378b.

[75]See Garrett, S. R., "Super PACs in Federal Elections: Overview and Issues for Congress," Congressional Research Service, September 26, 2016: https://fas.org/sgp/crs/misc/R42042.pdf.

[76]*Ibid.*

[77]See again Dalgo, E. and Balcerzak, A.

[78]See David A. Leib, *Denver Post* (25 June 2017). The extremity of recent abuses in conservative-led congressional redistricting have met with disapproval even from prominent Republican leaders commenting on the recent case *Gill v. Whitford*, under the U.S. Supreme Court's review as of this writing. The case presents an important opportunity for the nation's highest court to establish new constraints on partisan over-reach in congressional redistricting processes.

[79]See the Ballotpedia overview of state versus federal practices related to redistricting, https://ballotpedia.org/State-by-state_redistricting_procedures, which reports, "The states themselves determine their own redistricting methods. These methods vary from state to state and, sometimes, within a state (for example, different methods may apply to congressional redistricting than to state legislative redistricting)."

[80]See Pastor, *Manuel, The State of Resistance: What California's Dizzying Descent and Remarkable Resurgence Mean for America's Future* (2018), The New Press: New York.

[81]See Blackwell, A. G., "The Curb-Cut Effect," *Stanford Social Innovation Review*, Vol. 15, No. 1 (Winetr 2017).

CHAPTER 2

The Recent Decline of American Democratic Integrity and the Case for Promoting New Models in Civic Engagement

Democracy isn't about paying a little attention once every four years. . . . It's about getting involved and staying involved. And that's the great thing about . . . activism. There isn't a finite supply of it. If anything, becoming engaged actually breeds more engagement.

—Elizabeth Warren[1]

When the American Revolution was successfully waged, average Americans were completely invested. The outcome of the Revolutionary War radically changed human history by normalizing a novel and unprecedented trust in the wisdom of the people to determine the fate of nations—something the world had never seen to that point. The nineteenth-century French observer Alexis de Tocqueville captured early American democratic culture in his widely acclaimed book *On Democracy in America*, published in two volumes, respectively, in 1835 and 1840. In his treatise, Tocqueville commented on the distinctive American tendency toward democratic integrity and self-help, building on the separation of state powers, reliance on voluntary associations and initiatives, the activism of a free and unfettered press and an engaged populace.

The Foundations of American Democracy: Equality and Liberty, Civic Education and Activism

The political leaders who founded our country understood the importance of the American people being endowed with certain inalienable rights, equality and liberty being the most fundamental among these. The founders recognized the essential need for citizens to become educated and informed about civic affairs in ways that would strengthen their capacity for self-government. Numerous leaders of the early American Republic issued statements confirming the founders' belief in the central importance of education, as well as the free press in the process of educating and informing the people. As Jefferson stated, "Where the press is free, and every man able to read, all is safe." Jefferson's fellow Virginian, William H. Cabell, similarly wrote in 1808 that education "constitutes one of the great pillars on which the civil liberties of a nation depend."[2]

From its beginnings, the American experiment in democracy was based on notions of institutional checks and balances, civic education and activism, as well as certain fundamental rights that were—at least in principle—available to all. To be sure, the early American experiment in democracy was fraught with imperfections and contradictions. It held no meaningful place or rights for women, the native indigenous and Spanish-speaking populations, African-origin slaves and freedmen, or Asians, nor would it during its nineteenth-century expansion. LGBTQ Americans' and disability community rights were also not recognized under early US law. But the essential foundations for each of these groups ultimately to seek and secure federal legal rights and protections were written into our Constitution and Bill of Rights. Consequently, each generation has seen extensive and largely successful efforts by various aggrieved groups initially lacking full citizenship to seek and secure more equal rights and privileges. These pursuits of equity and equality have often required many decades of dynamic organizing and protest, legal challenges and electoral activism led by interested individuals and groups largely made up of average Americans.[3]

The False and Misinformed Patriotism of the Far Right

The right of common people, rather than royals or aristocrats, to have the final say about public priorities and decision-making is taken for granted nowadays, so much so that today a large and growing number of Americans, with considerable help from far-right ideologues and their media, have become highly misinformed about the nature of their civic rights and responsibilities in our democracy.[4] To be sure, right wing media and ultra-conservative political leaders in the Trump era have contributed mightily to this phenomenon, under the guise of "patriotism" and extreme and often inaccurate readings of America's foundational history and the Constitution.[5] In the process, they have done anything but educate and inform average Americans about the essence of our democratic rights and responsibilities; and they have increasingly sought to disqualify objective facts and logical analyses as legitimate aspects of democratic discourse by denying (or questioning) scientific consensus and berating mainstream journalistic reporting as "fake news." But, in fact, it is Donald Trump and the extreme conservative ideologues who support him that have most egregiously forwarded falsehoods in contemporary debates on public policy and governance.[6]

Even Many Longtime Conservatives Are Concerned

Mine is not just some random, unfounded swipe at the right by a biased progressive observer. Over the past two years, a growing number of longtime conservative political leaders and operatives with experience at the highest levels of governmental and civic discourse have themselves expressed these concerns about the nation's direction under Trump's and the Republican Party's increasingly extreme and angry rule. Republican US Senator Jeff Flake of Arizona wrote an entire book, *Conscience of a Conservative* (2017), dedicated to expressing concern about the Trump-led right wing's increasingly unhinged and fact-free outlook on America and the world. David Frum, former speechwriter for President George W. Bush, published his own scathing, book-length critique of the Republican Party's recent flight from facts and reality under the title, *Trumpocracy: The*

Corruption of the American Republic (2018). And like Flake and Frum, longtime Midwest-based conservative talk-radio host Charlie Sykes also recently published a book starkly examining the Republican Party's widespread unraveling during recent years: *How the Right Lost its Mind* (2017).

Flake's Republican colleague, Tennessee Senator Bob Corker, Chairman of the Senate Foreign Relations Committee, expressed his own concerns on the issues, commenting on the record in an October 2017 CNN television interview that President Trump was guilty of asserting recurrent "provable untruths" and further opining that he "is not a good role model for kids, owing to his knowing dishonesty, and is ultimately 'debasing' our country." Also, over the public airwaves, Steve Schmidt, the former presidential campaign manager to Republican Senator John McCain in 2008 and now a high profile political pundit, has gone on record almost nightly on national television news broadcasts to express concern about the wayward track his party has taken under the Trump banner. Nicolle Wallace, former White House communications director under ex-President George W. Bush, has also become a daily on-air personality on the left-leaning MSNBC television platform, where she has regularly lamented Trump's and his administration's actions. And most tellingly, perhaps, even longtime conservative icons such as columnists George Will and Peggy Noonan have publicly-acknowledged their disapproval of the Republican Party's recent direction and leadership with Trump at the helm. Indeed, in June 2016, Will announced his formal disassociation from the Republican Party for which he had been a formidable thought leader over nearly forty years.[7]

The negative impact of modern conservative extremism on American democracy and civic discourse, however, is not new. The right's ideological overreach and rejection of fact-based civil exchange has been well-documented over some years now.[8] Former Republican campaign strategist and noted political economy commentator Kevin Phillips, an early engineer of the Republican southern and sunbelt strategies of the 1970s and 1980s, has written extensively since the 1990s about the growing hypocrisy and excesses of right-wing politics in America.[9] And "Media Matters" founder David Brock, a former conservative, has also long-criticized the far right's increasingly toxic effects on American politics and intellectual integrity, dating back to his widely-discussed book, *Blinded by the Right: The Conscience of an Ex-Conservative* (2002).

The Dumbing Down of America

There can be no doubt that years of increasingly angry and unhinged Republican discontent, trumpeted by obfuscating far-right wing media, have left many Americans frothing at the bit with profoundly passionate but highly misinformed views about the major issues and concerns of the day. Over time, this has led to a growing willful ignorance on the right, an increasingly visceral disdain for intellectuals and the inconvenient truths they have to tell, as well as a substantial glossing over of how our democracy actually works, or should work. In so many ways, the right's increasingly anti-intellectual bent has imposed a high price on the American body politic. The right's entrenched disdain for facts and intellectual rigor has left contemporary Americans misinformed about the essential mechanics of our democratic system of governance. According to a national survey of American adults undertaken by the Annenberg Public Policy Center in 2014, for example, only about one-third of those interviewed could name all three branches of the US government; and only about one-fifth could successfully articulate the essential properties of America's legislative and judicial processes. Moreover, only about 40 percent reported knowing which political party controlled the US House of Representatives and the Senate.[10] Such dismal indicators of civic and political awareness have created the conditions for the often misplaced social discord we have seen over recent decades concerning the role of government in modern American society.

Declining civic and political awareness across the nation has coincided with and contributed in turn to a disturbing downward trend in civic engagement that has been well-documented in Robert Putnam's bestselling book, *Bowling Alone* (2000), in which he finds Americans increasingly individuated, disconnected from their communities and less inclined than ever to engage in civic and voluntary organizations. Instead, most US households have focused less and less on public engagement and more and more on basic economic security and survival. Given these realities, it should come as little surprise, frankly, that our democracy has waned. Today in America, nearly half of all eligible voters do not even bother to participate in our elections.

Conservative America's Growing Anti-Democratic Impulses and Practices

In addition to the worrisome decline in voter participation owing to growing public apathy, American democracy has been undercut substantially in recent years by conservative forces all across the nation through a broad range of intentional efforts to suppress voter participation in many states.[11] Using gerrymandering and other nefarious tactics, they have especially targeted populations of color and urban populations that tend to vote overwhelmingly for Democrats as a way of enhancing the prospects of conservative candidates prevailing in local, state and federal elections.[12] In a growing number of instances, they have introduced new voter identification laws requiring people to produce certain documentation to prove their standing to vote, claiming the intent to combat massive voter fraud.[13]

Expanding Structural Barriers to Democratic Participation

In addition to suppressing voting through the raising of barriers based on voter ID laws, conservatives have systemically shuttered voting stations in heavily Democratic districts and regions, forcing likely Democratic voters into fewer and fewer polling stations on election days, resulting in long lines and delays intended to discourage voting that might help non-conservative candidates or measures to succeed.[14] In some instances, conservative policy makers have limited the time legally allotted for early voting (which tends to expand voter participation and the likelihood of a Democratic turnout). They have also supported disturbing efforts to purge standing voter lists containing disproportionate representation of non-conservative voters in many states (thus disqualifying affected voters from participating in subsequent elections). And through recent expanded efforts to deny prisoners and ex-convicts the right to vote, conservatives have further diminished voter capacity, especially among the overrepresented people of color in the justice system, who would otherwise be inclined to vote against Republican candidates and measures.[15] All of these efforts combined have served to severely discourage or impede non-conservative voters from participating in too many recent US election cycles.

History Tells Us We Have to Fight Back

Under these conditions, it is easy to comprehend why people give up and tune out. It is easy to think there is nothing the average person can do to improve our situation. But it is a mistake to think that our present circumstances are unique or unprecedented; and it is surely a mistake to think that opting out will help to make things better in the future. In fact, just the opposite is true. American history is fraught with intense political passages like the one we are currently experiencing. It is replete with reactionary resistance that would have forever suppressed forward social progress, if certain visionary agents of change had not been willing to fight. In fact, in spite of what may appear to be a certain inevitability in connection with the kind of social evolution our nation has seen since its founding, when one examines history it quickly becomes clear that no gain or advancement of consequence has ever been achieved in America without dedicated and lengthy struggle.

In our political life, there have been recurrent ebbs and flows, steps forward and then backward, then forward again. Dr. Martin Luther King, Jr. reminded us in his short but important life that "the arc of the moral universe is long, but it bends towards justice." There are no guaranteed outcomes, and change can be slow to come; but, to Dr. King's point, our history as a nation has shown us over and over again that democracy progresses most rapidly when both faith and action are put to work in order for the common good to prevail. It takes the pull and haul of deeply committed people engaging in all aspects of civic and democratic life to make meaningful change in America. And, because this turns out to be a never-ending process, the necessity for vigilance in opposition to reaction and injustice is a permanent requirement of

American democratic life. But so too is the ever-present imperative with each passing generation to evolve new and better ways of improving and perfecting our democratic culture in America. Constantly pushing towards solutions and change through active civic engagement is the only way to advance and succeed as a free and open society.

Activism and Optimism Are the Keys

Activism and optimism are the inevitable drivers of American progress. As such, these are the essential tools of civic and societal advancement, especially during dark and daunting moments that challenge our basic confidence in our system and ourselves. Only the vigilance, commitment and work of the people can ultimately preserve and advance democratic life and governance. This has been the case throughout American history. As US Senator Elizabeth Warren has astutely observed, the health of our democratic society rests with the impulse of common people to participate, regularly and wholeheartedly, in the matters of state and civic life that affect their daily lives. According to Warren, "[Democracy is] about getting involved and staying involved."[16] It's about regular, everyday people becoming activists. This, it turns out, is what American democracy depends on to survive, thrive and drive towards the "more perfect union" our founders hoped their progeny would pursue.

We Must Push Forward

Today, perhaps more than at any time since the late 1960s and early 1970s, it is only logical to question the integrity and value of American democracy. But in the scheme of things, even with the unexpected turns of our recent political experience in America, the long term future of our nation still leans forward towards many new and exciting opportunities to advance progressive social, economic and environmental justice. For all of its evolving problems and tensions, our nation is still uniquely endowed with the human and natural resources, as well as the giving spirit, required to right our course. But the enormous potential of our nation to seize the day and overcome our many current challenges does not mean that we will. What will eventually happen—or not—is entirely up to us. Our present democracy is not as healthy as it should be and needs serious care and feeding, if the future ahead is to be peaceful and productive. We need far more people to be actively informed and involved in our civic culture. We need better ideas, new perspectives and expanded energy to restore our democratic way of life in America. To these ends, unprecedented grassroots and institutional efforts are called for to create new pathways and incentives for the American people to participate more fully and with far greater direct influence in the shaping of our public priorities and policies. It is a gross understatement to say there is much work to be done. All of us have a role to play in helping to resuscitate our waning democratic culture in America; virtually no one who wants progressive change and improvement for our nation and world is exonerated from this reality. Indeed, it would take something like walking in our sleep not to recognize the imperatives presently before us.

Perhaps the Situation Is Not as Bad as First Anticipated

Progressive voters can take solace from the realization that, however unappetizing and significant is Trump's ascent to the presidency and the Republican Party domination of Congress in 2016, their triumph did not amount to a sweeping new mandate for the conservative right, as the Trump campaign claimed after the vote. Since the election, in fact, progressive forces have had much to cheer about that they could hardly have foreseen on election night in November, 2016. Trump's many personal shortcomings and decidedly abnormal, unpresidential behavior both prior to and since taking office have increasingly underscored for most people the considerable limits of his political leadership and judgment. In so many ways, Trump and his Republican congressional allies have quickly proven themselves to be surprisingly ineffective and unprepared to lead. To date, owing to their own turmoil and constitutional constraints invoked by the federal courts, the Trump Administration and the Republican Congress have been largely unsuccessful at imposing the most drastic changes they promised in federal policy, despite controlling the White House, both federal legislative chambers and the Supreme Court.

Indeed, the sole significant legislation passed during Trump's first year in office was the highly controversial Republican tax bill of 2017, which both in its House and Senate forms mainly involved a large, permanent rate cut for the wealthy and large corporations. Only 29 percent of American voters said they supported the measure at the time of its passage, with fully 49 percent saying they opposed it.[17] In the end, the controversial Senate vote on the 2017 tax bill—which independent reviewers like the Congressional Budget Office and the Joint Congressional Committee on Taxation have reported would add as much as $1.5 trillion to the federal deficit and only help to generate about 1 percent in domestic GDP gains—barely succeeded. The combined House and Senate legislative proposal came to a straight party line vote that saw virtually no Democrats support the Republican proposal, and numerous last minute White House and Senate leadership concessions to various hesitant Republican senators in order to buy their support.[18] The fact that Republicans, for whom tax breaks are always a mandate, effectively struggled to get the bill over the line reflects the high degree of conservative disarray and dysfunction that has increasingly overtaken the nation. Such ineffectiveness and disarray create openings for progressive organizing and action. Indeed, all is not lost.

The Tide is Quickly Turning

From a progressive perspective, Trump's performance in office has been so underwhelming and poisonous that liberal and progressive candidates are suddenly more well-positioned to win in forthcoming elections than has been the case at any time in recent years. The indications of this are already manifest. During 2017, Trump's first year in office, many Democratic progressives in local and state elections across the nation prevailed over conservative opponents aligned with the Trump agenda. Indeed, the November 7, 2017 election outcomes in Virginia and New Jersey were most revealing. In those states, Democratic gubernatorial candidates won decisively over their Republican opponents; there and elsewhere, exciting new progressive candidates won seats that previously may have been difficult for them to secure. For example, in Montana, Wilmot Collins, a progressive former

African refugee from Liberia was elected mayor of Helena, the state's overwhelmingly white capitol city, making him the state's first-ever African American mayor. Vi Lyles became the first African American woman ever elected to serve as mayor of Charlotte, NC. Ravi Bhalla of Hoboken became the first Sikh mayor ever elected in the state of New Jersey. Jenny Durken was elected the first openly-lesbian mayor of the City of Seattle and the first woman to serve in that office in nearly 100 years. Larry Krasner, a progressive civil rights attorney, was elected to serve as District Attorney for the City of Philadelphia. Andrea Jenkins of Minneapolis was elected to serve as the nation's first transgender black woman on the city council of a major US city. Similarly, in Virginia, Danica Roem was elected to serve as the nation's first openly transgender woman state legislator. At the same time, Justin Fairfax was elected Lt. Governor of the Commonwealth of Virginia, making him only the second African American ever elected to statewide office in that state's long history. And Elizabeth Guzmán and Hala Ayala became the first Latinas ever elected to the Virginia state house. In fact, currently there are more women running for office at every level than ever before in our nation's history.

Furthermore, in various traditionally Republican strongholds, Democrats have fought hard to gain victories that would have been entirely unforeseen in previous years. In Oklahoma, which distinguished itself for delivering virtually every voting county in the state to Trump in 2016, a young Democratic state party chairwoman, Anna Langthorn, and her scrappy statewide team produced four highly unexpected Democratic victories in local and state races in 2017. In one of those races, the Democratic victor, Allison Ikley-Freeman, a young lesbian first-time candidate beat Republican Brian O'Hara in the state senate race, in a district that Donald Trump had won by some forty points in his presidential bid only one year earlier. In Wisconsin, Democrat Patty Schachtner won a state senate race in a district that Trump won by nearly 20 points in 2016. Six months later, in an April 2018 Wisconsin statewide Supreme Court election, moreover, liberal Milwaukee County Circuit Court Judge Rebecca Dallet won handily over a Republican contender to gain a seat on the state's high court that previously had been occupied by conservative Judge Michael

Gabelman. And, in another early 2018 special election in Pennsylvania, Democrat Conner Lamb closely edged out his Republican opponent Rick Saccone to win an additional Democratic seat in Congress in a district considered by many to be one of the nation's most conservative. In New Hampshire and New York, as well, women Democrats, Edie DesMarais and Christine Pellegrino, respectively, prevailed in districts that had voted for Trump in 2016.

By far, however, the most significant recent electoral victory for progressives occurred in December 2017 in the most unlikely place of all: Alabama. In a special election to fill the open US senate seat, Democratic candidate Doug Jones edged out one of the most conservative Republican senate candidates the nation has recently seen: twice-benighted former Alabama Supreme Court Justice Roy Moore. Moore, whose candidacy was ultimately disqualified by a series of alleged sexual abuse allegations involving minors when he was in his thirties and serving as a local assistant district attorney in Etowah County, is easy to characterize as a badly flawed candidate who should have predictably lost the highly contested campaign. But Moore's defeat was nevertheless significant for Alabama, one of the most conservative states in the nation, especially given that the entire weight of the Republican power structure came to his support (including the president and the Republican National Committee). Underlying Jones' victory, on the other hand, was an unexpected tidal wave of African American voters, especially African American women voters.

An Emerging New Roadmap to Victory

The Democratic victories in late 2017 and early 2018 have created great momentum and have begun to plot a new roadmap for Democratic candidates across the nation. As in Doug Jones's success and those of other candidates, a significant reason for their triumph was the efforts of women and voters of color that party officials too often ignore or take for granted. The people's voting power was more important than conventional investments in campaign research, consultants and advertising. These victories showed that a Democratic candidate with a clear and compelling commitment to inclusion and grassroots outreach could defeat a powerfully-positioned ultra-conservative candidate in the Deep South.

These winning strategies are most important for moving the progressive agenda forward. They tell us that in our next efforts we will do best to support more bottom-up, people-centered strategies (as opposed to top-down, purely money- and campaign-ad-driven approaches). Somewhat ironically, and until now counter-intuitively, it is increasingly high-touch, retail (rather than wholesale) campaign modalities that are the key to successful progressive political leadership in the early twenty-first century. To be sure, these recent victories offer grounds for hope, as well as lessons for future progressive political wins against the troublesome backdrop of the Trump presidency. But for progressive and liberal leaders to assume that all we have to do now is wait for the Trump ship to sink while we essentially travel down the same path we have been on would be sorely misguided and counterproductive.

Not a Time to Be Over-Confident or Complacent

The recent wins of progressive and liberal candidates—many of them being first-time office holders who are young, women, people of color and/or otherwise culturally diverse, are surely cause for celebration. More effort and resources will absolutely be needed to advance similar wins in coming elections. But these initial signs of a revived Democratic Party are not necessarily the product of enthusiastic votes for American liberalism. More than anything, they are the result of progressive, liberal and moderate Americans rejecting the obvious excesses and pathologies of Trumpism and the far right. These campaigns have been important, but ultimately they are defensive, or default, wins. They will help to limit the immediate harm Trumpism can impose on society and nature, but by themselves they will not necessarily advance better outcomes for humanity and the planet over the long term.

We Need to Double Down on Vision and Core Principles

To be successful in the long term and to do the greatest good for our people and correct our nation's wayward course, progressive Americans must come together to develop and aggressively champion a compelling and affirmative vision for the future. We cannot just be against Trump and the heinous ideas and policies we see coming from right-wing America. Nor can we just assume that we will regain power and win elections merely by doing what we have done since the Reagan Revolution of the late 1970s. We cannot continue to champion politicians and policies that promise to mitigate the right's excesses while failing to advance fundamentally different and better policies and outcomes. We must reject hyper-capitalism and neoliberalism in order to advance democracy.

Progressive Americans need to fully and unequivocally reject the prevailing hyper-capitalistic and neo-liberal policy framework under which we have been governed over the past decades. We need instead to advocate for fresh and bold new ideas that reflect longstanding progressive values and aims while building on new frameworks, technologies and modalities that advance those values and aims. In order to succeed in the evolving new reality before us, it is imperative that we use the present moment to identify, hone and fight for our ideals and create the foundations on which to make them a reality.[19]

First and Foremost, We Need to Fix Our Broken Democracy

In pursuing these ends, as progressive Americans we need to direct our effort and resources to meaningfully shift the American political and economic landscape by advancing badly needed reforms in our nation's basic democratic workings. These must be reforms that encourage and enable average people more fully to participate and prevail in our governance. With the advent of growing voter suppression efforts on the right and huge new structural challenges affecting our civic culture—such as the already mentioned *Citizens United* Supreme Court ruling and hyper-partisan redistricting schemes—it is imperative that progressive voices concentrate strategic efforts and investments on re-establishing the responsiveness of our electoral system to the voice of our people. This is the only way our nation can ultimately realize a more balanced and honest reflection of the people's actual political will, as envisioned by America's founders.

We need to advance comprehensive democratic reforms for the twenty-first century. We need to enhance voting capacity and address the education, engagement and empowerment deficit facing contemporary Americans, especially those who are struggling to secure the most basic elements of a decent life. While extending the vote, we need to enhance next generation citizenship and support activism in community and civic affairs. Such efforts need in turn to be well supported and widespread, be they focused on action research and civic education, public media, community organizing and activism, progressive legal advocacy, voter registration and mobilization, creative culture and/or coalition building. Gratefully, one of the many strengths of America's progressive community today is the vast array of smart, dynamic and increasingly well-resourced leaders and organizations that are driving efforts for essential change in the political economy.

Notwithstanding the obvious challenges we face, progressive advocacy organizations such as the ACLU, Planned Parenthood, the Center for Community Change and MoveOn.org are well-financed and growing.[20] In the labor movement, the Service Employees International Union (SEIU) and the AFL-CIO are regaining membership and energy after decades of decline in American manufacturing and weakened union protections resulting from conservative and neoliberal policies. Leading progressive think-and-do-tanks, such as the Center for American Progress, Demos, PolicyLink, the Roosevelt Institute and Indivisible, along with such leading progressive intellectuals as Michelle Alexander, Jared Bernstein, William "Sandy" Darrity, Jr., Darrick Hamilton, Saru Jayaraman, Naomi Klein, Paul Krugman, Manuel Pastor, john a. powell, Robert Reich, Tom Shapiro and Joseph Stiglitz, to name just a few, are producing vitally important new conceptual frameworks and thought for progressive politics and economics. Environmental advocacy and green justice leaders, such as the Sierra Club and the Greenlining Institute are building important new capacities to advance sustainability reforms that better reach and benefit multicultural people and communities.

In addition, impressive, emergent racial, gender and labor justice networks and organizations, such as the Movement for Black Lives, United We Dream, the Native American-led Water is Life Movement and the Fight for Fifteen Campaign are all helping to bring to the surface essential new policy imperatives and opportunities to achieve greater social and economic justice for people of color, immigrants, indigenous peoples and workers. And creative culture leaders, such as Lin-Manuel Miranda, originator of the groundbreaking Broadway musicals "In the Heights" and "Hamilton, and organizations and initiatives such as the Art, Culture and Social Justice Network and the Art for Justice Fund are increasingly engaging progressive multicultural writers, painters, rappers and other public arts professionals in constructive dialog on democracy and the common good.

Other important groups not named here are doing allied, similar or supporting work at the local, state and national levels in these and other essential domains. Indeed, American progressives have arguably never been so well endowed with intellectual, financial and ground-game capacity. What matters most now is how we use our growing resources and capacity to affect change. That in turn implicates how well or poorly we align around our shared interests and integrate our next efforts which, far-reaching and impressive as they may be, too often remain disconnected and siloed in ways that ultimately undermine our shared interests and aims. To be most effective and successful in the coming evolution of American democracy, progressive groups and leaders will have to become much more intentional about creating a more integrated and mutually reinforcing architecture in developing collective strategies and action.

To truly make the enduring differences we seek in the ways our society treats people and the planet over the long term, it is essential that progressive Americans unite around a shared generational campaign to establish stronger consumer and environmental protections, subsidized child care and free K-14 education, living-wage employment, quality single-payer healthcare benefits and affordable housing; these should all be protected as federal rights. American progressives need to begin now to rally around safeguarding the US Bill of Rights and extending the New Deal policies of the 1930s in ways that help to shape a new social contract for our nation's evolving needs. Such are the topics that will be addressed in upcoming pages of this book, beginning with a focus on the most strategic ways progressive Americans can join forces to tackle our nation's desperate need for structural reforms that can lead in turn to more active, robust and productive civic engagement in our national democracy.

Endnotes

[1]Warren, E., "Sen. Elizabeth Warren: 'Democracy Is about Getting Involved and Staying Involved,'" *Cosmopolitan,* 20 June 2017: http://www.cosmopolitan.com/politics/a10011181/senator-elizabeth-warren-persistence/.

[2]See, e.g., Chrystal, W. G., "What is a Good Citizen: Thoughts From Some of the Founding Fathers," The Federalist Papers Project, May 18, 2013 at: http://thefederalistpapers.org/current-events/what-is-a-good-citizen-thoughts-from-some-of-the-founding-fathers citing Jefferson's January 6, 1816 correspondence to prominent Virginia legislator Charles Yancey; and Hamilton, L., "Why We Need an Informed Citizenry," November 15, 2003, Indiana University Center for Representative Government at: https://corg.indiana.edu/why-we-need-informed-citizenry. According to Hamilton: "The truth is, for our democracy to work it needs not just an engaged citizenry, but an informed one. We've known this since this nation's earliest days. The creators of the Massachusetts Constitution of 1780 thought the notion important enough to enshrine it in the state's founding document: 'Wisdom and knowledge, as well as virtue, diffused generally among the body of the people,' they wrote, are 'necessary for the preservation of their rights and liberties.'"

[3]For a brief and informative but comprehensive overview of the main social change movements that have shaped American history and policy development, see Halperin, J. & Cook, M., *Social Movements & Progressivism*, Center for American Progress, Washington, DC, April 2010: https://cdn.americanprogress.org/wp-content/uploads/issues/2010/04/pdf/progressive_social_movements.pdf.

[4]In recent years, the growing reach of dubious and outright fallacious right-wing "news" sources, from Fox News to Breitbart, and from AM talk radio to Conservative Christian Media, have been widely reported in the mainstream media. See, e.g., Gertz, M., "Right-Wing Media 'Scandals' Never End, They Just Fade Away," October 5, 2017, Media Matters for America: https://www.mediamatters.org/blog/2017/10/05/right-wing-media-scandals-never-end-they-just-fade-away/218141; Brock, D., *The Republican Noise Machine: Right-Wing Media and How It Corrupts Democracy*, Crown Publishing, 2004; and Perry, R., "The Rise of the Right-Wing Media Machine," Fairness & Accuracy in Reporting (FAIR) March 1, 1995,: http://fair.org/extra/the-rise-of-the-right-wing-media-machine/.

[5]One of the most unfortunate trends in American political culture has been the political right's growing tendency to suggest that more left-leaning

Americans are somehow less patriotic or authentic Americans, based on biased assertions of what patriotism consists of. See Lowery, R., "Yes, Liberals Are Less Patriotic," *The National Review,* 24 February 2015: http://www.nationalreview.com/article/414287/yes-liberals-are-less-patriotic-rich-lowry and, by contrast, Chernus, I., "Who Says Conservatives Are More Patriotic?" July 3, 2013: https://www.commondreams.org/views/ 2013/07/03/who-says-conservatives-are-more-patriotic.

[6]See Flake, J., *Conscience of a Conservative: A Rejection of Destructive Politics and a Return to Principle* (NY: Random House, 2017). Flake, a conservative US senator from heavily Republican Arizona, is hardly an expected critic of the right's increasing impulse to lie and divide people for political gain. But his honest concerns about the destructive direction of his modern conservative colleagues in the Republican Party and his decision to go public with those concerns speaks volumes about the nature and extent of contemporary challenges to American democracy created by the present tenor of conservative leadership.

[7]Kaplan, S., "George Will Exits the Republican Party over Trump," June 25, 2016: https://www.washingtonpost.com/politics/george-will-exits-the-republican-party-over- trump/2016/06/25/2b6cdcaa-3b09-11e6-9ccd-d6005beac8b3_story.html?utm_term=.2e2a3ce1ccc2.

[8]See Spence, G. L., *Bloodthirsty Bitches and Pious Pimps of Power: The Rise and Risks of the New Conservative Hate Culture.* NY: St. Martin's Press, 2006 and Phillips, K., *American Theocracy: The Peril & Politics of Radical Religion, Oil and Borrowed Money in the 21st Century.* NY: Penguin, 2007, especially Chapter 7.

[9]A list and brief summaries of Phillips' various books and themes since 1990 can be found in *The New York Times*: http://www.nytimes.com/ref/books/author-phillips.html. N.D.

[10]See "Americans Know Surprisingly Little about Their Government, Survey Says," Annenberg Public Policy Center, University of Pennsylvania, Philadelphia, September 17, 2014: https://www.annenbergpublicpolicycenter.org/americans-know-surprisingly-little-about-their-government-survey- finds/.

[11]See Weiser, W. R., "Voter Suppression, How Bad? (Really Bad)," The American Prospect October 1, 2014: http://prospect.org/article/22-states-wave-new-voting-restrictions-threatens-shift-outcomes-tight-races.

[12]See Daley, D., "How the GOP Made Your Vote Useless,", *The Daily Beast*, October 7, 2017: https://www.thedailybeast.com/how-gop-gerrymandering-made-your-democratic-vote-useless and Harriott, M., "This Secret Form of Voter Suppression Might be the Civil Rights Issue of Our Time," *The Root*, April 12, 2017: https://www.theroot.com/this-secret-form-of-voter-suppression-might-be-the-civi-1794239379.

[13]Voter fraud has been shown to be a remarkably exceptional occurrence in US elections, but notwithstanding the evidence, Donald Trump established a Presidential Advisory Committee on Election Integrity in March 2017. The commission, which was disbanded in January 2018, has produced no credible evidence demonstrating that voter fraud is a significant problem in America. See "Background on Trump's Voter Fraud Commission," The Brennan Center, New York: https://www.brennancenter.org/everything-you-need-know-about-trumps-voter-fraud-commission.

[14]See., e.g., Berman, A., "There Are 868 Fewer Places to Vote in 2016 Because the Supreme Court Gutted the Voting Rights Act," *The Nation*, November 4, 2016: https://www.thenation.com/article/there-are-868-fewer- places-to-vote-in-2016-because-the-supreme-court-gutted-the-voting-rights-act/.

[15]Mock, B., "The Battle over Voting Rights for Former Felons," *CityLab*, August 22, 2016: https://www.citylab.com/equity/2016/08/confusion-could-keep-former-felons-in-virginia-from-exercising-voting- rights/496877/.

[16]See note 1.

[17]See "Nearly Half of All Americans Oppose the Republican Tax Bill, Poll Finds," CNBC, November 30, 2017: https://www.cnbc.com/2017/11/30/nearly-half-of-all-americans-oppose-the-republican-tax-bill-poll-finds.html.

[18]See Salisbury, I., "People Are Outraged about the GOP Tax Bill's 'Corker Kickback.' This Is Why," *Money Magazine* December 18, 2017: http://time.com/money/5068840/gop-tax-bill-corker-taxes-kickback/.

[19]For more in-depth and persuasive argumentation along these lines see Klein, N., *No Is Not Enough: Resisting Trump's Shock Politics and Winning the World We Need*, Haymarket Books, Chicago, 2016.

[20]See "ACLU and Planned Parenthood See 'Unprecedented' Rise in Donations after Donald Trump's Election," *Time* November 14, 2016: http://time.com/4570796/aclu-planned-parenthood-donation-increase-donald-trump/. For background on recent robust new giving to the Center for Community Change, see Durden, T., "Soros, Kellogg, Ford: Donor List Of Anti-Trump 'Resistance' Group Revealed," *ZeroHedge* October 5, 2017: http://www.zerohedge.com/news/2017-10-04/soros-kellogg-fordelite-donor-list-anti-trump-resistance-group- revealed.

CHAPTER 3
Next Stage Strategies for Restoring Our Democracy and Civic Vitality

It's time for America to get right . . .
> —Fannie Lou Hamer

Today in America, it is more important than ever for progressive people to harness our best emerging practices and innovations in civic revitalization in order to help make public policy and investment more responsive to the needs of average people and our planet. It is imperative that we promote models and approaches that show promise in resuscitating our nation's low levels of democratic and electoral participation. It is vital that we join forces to democratize our uneven and over-manipulated election, voting and campaign finance systems. We must also bolster the basic preparation of average Americans to engage in civic and global affairs in more informed, responsible and meaningful ways than we have seen in recent decades.

Achieving these aims will require us to advance badly needed structural reforms in important areas of current American law and public policy. These include supporting significant changes in our current ways of apportioning political representation, administering our elections and promoting civic education and engagement, as well as massive improvements in policy and practice in order to humanize our nation's badly broken criminal-justice and immigration systems. In all of these areas, conservatives have recently advanced policies and ideas that seek to limit people's participation in our democracy. They have erected structural barriers to citizen and community engagement in public decision-making processes and, through willful misinformation, they have skewed the very integrity of our democratic way of life.[1] Through strategic gerrymandering alone, conservative politicians across the nation have turned American democracy on its head.

In response, we need to fight as hard as ever to open up our systems of public governance to more robust and inclusive representation. We must unite to bring forward whole new innovations in democratic practice that can help to dramatically expand public engagement in our elections and other civic processes. And we must actively facilitate the electoral and policy successes of leaders of grassroots movements that are now emerging across our nation, leaders that are unequivocally committed to real change in service to common people and the common good. It cannot be denied these will be substantial undertakings under the present circumstances we face, but taking a long view, neither are they hopeless or impossible aims to achieve, given what past generations of progressive Americans were able to accomplish against even more formidable odds.

The Struggle for Democracy and Justice: Looking Back & Looking Forward

Consider for example the landscape facing progressives in the racist American South during the early post-WWII era, and the courage of African American leaders and citizens of that time in demanding and gaining their rights. Their industriousness and righteous efforts dramatically improved subsequent race relations and democracy in America. In 1964, at the height of the civil rights movement, the legendary Fannie Lou Hamer spoke in protest at that year's Democratic National Convention,[2] recounting in stark and straight-forward terms the vast array of legal and physical barriers African American citizens like her faced in the South when trying to exercise their basic voting franchise. Such barriers—all intended to substantially suppress black leadership and power—included, among other strategies, the selective imposition of poll taxes and literacy tests on black voters, as well as racially exclusive "white only" voting primaries and all-white state party convention delegations.[3]

Included among the many impediments to African American civic participation were the customary intimidation, violence and even killing of prospective black voters for merely attempting to register to vote. Up to and in that moment of American political history, even the most peaceful appeals by African American leaders and communities to support expanded black rights and voting opportunities were met with violence and rejection by ruling white elites across America. In the process of addressing the issues, many painful sacrifices and losses were imposed on those who persevered. Faith, righteous indignation, smart and sustained coalition building and collective protest were the essential means by which progressive people fought to resist America's most racist and reactionary forces. The activism of young people was particularly noteworthy at that time. The widespread movement ultimately prevailed. Overall, it was the civil rights advocates' shared conviction that, for America to be true to its principles and promises, its people—and especially its poorest and most excluded people—had to mobilize to secure fundamental changes in law, policy and practice. As Fannie Lou Hamer put it, it was "time for America to get right"—right with itself, right with its values, and most importantly, right with its most downtrodden and discriminated people. This call to "get right" in America coincided with a generation of activism that finally resulted in marked improvements in social, political and economic opportunity across the nation during the balance of the 1960s and well into the 1970s.

As a result, voter participation and representation, educational opportunity, home ownership, household income and new public contracting opportunities for small business owners all reached historically high levels for African Americans and other populations of color during the fifteen year period between 1965 and 1980.[4] While the new approaches and social investments introduced in that era hardly ended inequality in America, they helped to reduce poverty and increase the representation of communities of color in our nation's evolving governance. They demonstrated that more responsive government leadership, innovation and investment could indeed help to improve the nation's quest for social, political and economic progress.

Today, it is a time for similarly bold efforts to take shape. An expanding chorus of diverse Americans is demanding a new and better way to conduct our collective affairs as a nation and to create and distribute wealth. While there are many battles to be waged on multiple fronts as we pursue this modern-day call to action, in order to be most strategic and effective, we first and foremost need to revive our democratic culture in America. We need to awaken our populace in unprecedented ways that make fundamental progressive political change the only logical way forward.

What Has to Happen Now

To revive the nation's civic culture, progressive Americans must promote a series of structural reforms and new organizing strategies. This means focusing most on systemic, rather than merely incremental or marginal changes, and supporting more concerted efforts to fundamentally democratize the nation's current voting system and rules, campaign finance architecture, redistricting practices and civic education and engagement. It means empowering average people through the advancement of substantially new ways of making their voices heard and participating in our democracy.

Important new possibilities and ideas are increasingly available to us, many building on the evolving potential of digital technology and replicable innovations that have emerged over recent years in community organizing and coalition building. During the coming years, it is essential that we aggressively push forward to normalize, harmonize and build on these powerful potentialities at every level of democratic engagement. The following are leading examples of the kinds of reform efforts and innovations progressive activists and organizations need to rally around to reboot American democracy in new directions that are more inclusive, productive and sustainable.

Advancing Innovations in American Voting and Political Representation

Because conservative resistance to shifting voter demographics has focused on mitigating eligibility, turn out and representation in poor, multicultural and other liberal-leaning districts, we must unify as never before to contest these practices. We must advance every effort to make barrier-free, fair and representative voting a practical reality in every jurisdiction and election across the land. By drawing on the power of evolving innovations and digital technologies, we can vastly improve our future elections in ways that are at once more efficient, fair and reflective of voter will than traditional election protocols allow. Automatic Voter Registration, independent redistricting commissions and ranked choice voting are innovations that can enhance voter participation rates, representation and satisfaction. They can also save money, encourage new voices to emerge in official public policy discourse and better address the interests and needs of the vast majority of the American people.

Automatic Voter Registration

The concept of Automatic Voter Registration (AVR) has been endorsed by leading progressive organizations, such as the Brennen Center for Justice and the Roosevelt Institute,[5] and has already been adopted into law in nine states and the District of Columbia. In recent years, moreover, legislators in some thirty states have proposed measures to introduce or improve AVR plans in their jurisdictions. Automatic registration has been shown consistently to facilitate voter engagement and reduce the costs of election administration where it has been tried. Current models in play focus on a two-step process that actively facilitates citizen engagement in elections. According to the Brennen Center:

Automatic voter registration makes two transformative, yet simple, changes to voter registration: Eligible citizens who interact with government agencies are registered to vote unless they decline, and agencies transfer voter registration information electronically to election officials. These two changes create a seamless process that is more convenient and less error-prone for both voters and government officials. This policy boosts registration rates, cleans up the rolls, makes voting more convenient, and reduces the potential for voter fraud, all while lowering costs.[6]

In the State of Oregon, which has led the way in introducing this approach to voter registration, some 100,000 additional state residents voted in the 2016 election as a direct result of its automatic registration policy.[7] If AVR was adopted nationwide, it would have a profound impact on increasing voter registration and participation. According to a November 2017 Center for American Progress report,

> [We project] that if every state adopted Automatic Voter Registration like the effective system used in Oregon, more than 22 million people across the country would join the voter rolls in the first year of the program alone. These new voters would then be poised to participate in making America's political decisions. Of those 22 million new voters, almost 9.5 million are unlikely to have become registered without . . . AVR.[8]

Automatic registration is a growing trend whose more widespread adoption would further enhance voter reform measures, such as Election-Day Registration and mail-in voting, practices that progressive leaders across the nation have increasingly advocated. Such measures would serve to augment voter eligibility and participation, while also reducing administrative burdens and costs associated with traditional paper elections, as well as traditional date- and place-bound voting. According to an October 2017 report of the National Conference of State Legislatures,

> Thirteen states plus the District of Columbia [now] make same day registration available on Election Day; this is sometimes called Election Day Registration (EDR). Two states— North Carolina and Maryland—make same day registration possible for a portion of their early voting periods but not on Election Day. Additionally, Hawaii has enacted same day registration, which will be implemented in 2018.[9]

In addition, twenty-two states presently enable voters to participate to varying degrees in their elections by mail; and three states—Colorado, Oregon, and Washington—now conduct all of their in-state and federal elections principally by mail-in ballot. In 2018, the nation's largest state, California, will also conduct its elections by mail-in ballot.[10] A March 2016 assessment of Colorado's results by the Pew Charitable Trusts revealed that state tax payers saved substantially on the new mail-in voter law, with lower expenses applying to five categories of spending and the per capita cost during the 2014 cycle coming to less than $10 per vote cast, as compared with nearly $16 per vote cast under the prior in-person voting system.[11] Overall, this resulted in state savings of roughly $12 million in Colorado. In Oregon, the savings from a similar voting reform approach came to $3 million.[12]

The Colorado and Oregon experiences also show a significant increase in voter turnout since the introduction of mail-in voting. According to NonProfit Vote, a national coalition of nonprofit pro-democracy advocates, "In 2014 Colorado (72 percent) and Oregon (71 percent) led the nation in voter turnout of active registered voters—[with] both states 20+ points above the national average of 48 percent." In Oregon, during the 2014 election cycle, the turnout of 18-34 year olds (a perennially-elusive voting bloc) was double that of other states; and disability population turn-out was nearly 15 percent higher than in states not employing vote-by-mail election options.[13] Finally, the undependability of provisional ballots (a perennial problem in traditional election protocols) has been mostly eliminated by mail-in voting. Between 2010 and 2014, the year Colorado's new voting law took effect, provisional ballots in the state declined from more than 35,000 to less than 1,000.[14]

Because new measures of this kind already show clear, positive voter trajectories in the still relatively few but growing number of places where they have been employed, it is imperative for progressive activists and leaders to prioritize efforts to expand their reach to every state of our nation. The introduction of more modern, flexible, convenient and cost-effective voting practices would dramatically enhance voter engagement and especially help to enable the participation of groups that have too often been underrepresented in our nation's elections.

Independent Redistricting and Ranked Choice Voting

Other emerging pro-democracy innovations that progressive champions need to embrace and fight for are Independent Citizens Redistricting Commissions and Ranked Choice Voting (RCV). In the best-case scenario, the coordinated implementation of both of these innovations in representative government would combine to produce far more responsive political representation for Americans across the nation, irrespective of political philosophy or party affiliation. Indeed, the Fair Representation Act, a bill recently introduced in Congress by Democratic House member Don Beyer (D-VA) would do just that at the federal level. Under Beyer's proposal, voters who have been the principal subjects of recent hyper-conservative efforts to extend, rather than reduce, exclusionary barriers to voting and representation would be the greatest beneficiaries. The Fair Representation Act would reform congressional elections by building on the redrawing of larger and more representative districts in each state by independent redistricting commissions.

Beyer's proposal would further enable proportional district representation based on "ranked choice voting," a system in which voters select more than one candidate based on their respective priority preferences. Votes are immediately accumulated in cycles of review that ultimately determine the election outcome based on a far more in-depth expression of voter will than applies in traditional single vote, winner-take-all elections. Despite expanding districts and enabling multi-member representation of the districts, Beyer's bill would maintain the current size of Congress, but it would imbue each newly-formed district with a far broader representation of local views and perspectives than is presently possible under current winner-take-all congressional elections. By building on district lines drawn by independent citizens' panels, rather than sitting politicians who have an interest in protecting their incumbency, the Fair Representation Act would substantially re-center the rules of political representation in favor of the people.

In 2008, and then again in 2010, statewide ballot initiatives made California the first state in the nation to rely on a truly independent citizens' commission, rather than self-interested political incumbents, in drawing state and federal representational lines.[15] The initial positive impact of California's novel approach was fairly substantial. In the 2012 election cycle, the first major contest following the new state laws, five congressional incumbents were defeated in the course of seeking re-election under the more representative and competitive scheme designed by California's commission members. More significantly, nine incumbents chose not to run for re-election under the new California system. Thus, the immediate effect of California's change in approach was to create space for new voices to enter the congressional field. The general outcome of the move to an independent citizens' commission has been increased transparency and public confidence in state elections.[16] In addition to California, six other states now use nonpartisan or bipartisan citizen commissions to draw their electoral district lines. These include Arizona, Hawaii, Idaho, Montana, New Jersey and Washington. Going forward, progressive activists need to aggressively expand on these efforts to normalize the inherently fairer and more democratic district mapping offered by independent citizens' commissions.

The notion of promoting proportional representation in congressional elections based on ranked choice voting would further benefit American political culture.[17] It would result in enlarged, multi-member congressional districts that would be more inclusive of a range of political viewpoints and thus more representative and competitive than is presently the case in our current, highly partisan and gerrymandered system. Ranked choice voting reflects voters' second, third and possibly fourth priority candidate selections, with built-in cost savings in the process. It eliminates the need for primary elections; and, in all but the most unusual circumstances, it precludes expensive run-off elections to arrive at a definitive winner.[18] According to Fair-Vote, the rationale for ranked choice voting is:

Too often, candidates can and do win election to offices like Mayor and Governor despite being opposed by most voters. With ranked choice voting, if no candidate has more than half the vote in first-choices, candidates finishing last are eliminated round-by-round in an instant runoff until two candidates are left. The winning candidate will be the one with majority support when matched against the other. In a multi-winner election, ranked choice voting promotes majority rule because the majority of voters will always be able to elect a majority of seats, without fear that an entrenched minority has used gerrymandered districts to ensure they stay in office.[19]

In every way, the approach advocated under Congressman Beyer's proposed legislation would enhance congressional representation and good governance. Ultimately, this sort of electoral reform could also be broadly advanced nationwide at the state and local levels. Already, San Francisco and Minneapolis have adopted this more progressive form of electoral decision-making with positive results; Memphis, Santa Fe and Sarasota have recently passed local legislation to move their future elections in this direction.[20] According to FairVote, one of the nation's leading proponents of ranked choice voting procedures, the benefits of this novel approach to electoral administration at any level are manifold:

> Compared to winner-take-all elections, ranked choice voting in multi-winner contests allows more diverse groups of voters to elect candidates of choice. This promotes diversity of political viewpoint as well as diversity of candidate background and demographics. Even in single-winner races, ranked choice voting can promote the representation of historically under-represented groups like racial and ethnic minorities and women. A report co-authored by FairVote and the New America Foundation found that racial minority populations prefer ranked choice voting and find it easy to use, and that ranked choice voting increased turnout by 2.7 times in San Francisco.[21]

Recalibrating Campaign Finance Practices

One of the most vexing structural problems facing progressives today is the significant change in campaign finance rules resulting from the 2010 Supreme Court decision in *Citizens United v. FEC*. By a close 5-4 vote, the court ruling in that case equated the rights of large corporations and institutions with those of individuals to make campaign contributions under federal constitutional law. The essential court finding was that corporate and institutional entities have the same legal standing as individuals to express their political views in public elections and can, like individuals, donate unlimited funds to advance or oppose political candidates and causes, as they choose. The ruling imposed only very minimal obligations on donors in making their political giving transparent through mandatory reporting. The only significant constraint applied by the court was its decision to prohibit large-scale donors from making direct campaign donations to individual candidates for federal elective office.

The decision in *Citizens United* was a major boon to corporations and their controlling shareholders. In one fell swoop, it allowed them to spend unlimited sums on ads and other political tools to elect or defeat individual candidates, so long as they did so through approved pass-through entities whose donation activities were not directly coordinated with any particular campaign. Not surprisingly, the ruling has since resulted in a plethora of new Super Pac giving entities and a flood of new money being infused into elections from largely hidden sources—often millionaires and billionaires with giving capacities that dwarf the average citizen's.[22]

The patently undemocratic nature of the *Citizens United* ruling has created substantial new hurdles for progressive leaders and candidates who want to fundamentally change American law and policy, while it has redoubled establishment politicians' incentives—even among liberal and moderate Democrats—to maintain the status quo benefitting monied interests. Without efforts to address these massive structural barriers to entry in our nation's most important political campaigns, it is hard to imagine any meaningful pathway to the policy changes progressive leaders and activists seek. Because of the current conservative majorities in Congress and on the US Supreme Court, and the consequent unlikelihood that further federal legislation or litigation can soon reverse *Citizens United*, progressives and liberals who oppose its perverting impacts on our democracy have few options at the moment.

We can only hope to ride growing public consternation with the many unnerving pathologies of the Trump administration and run smarter campaigns with more dynamic candidates that effectively help to offset the still predominant role of money in American politics. We can also support various progressive initiatives that have recently emerged across the nation in response to *Citizens United,* including ways to increase campaign giving transparency and public-funding options at the municipal, county and state levels.[23] Otherwise, in this context, we have very few strategic options upon which to bank our electoral future.

American Promise

There is now, however, one interesting strategy emerging that all progressive people should consider: the undoing of *Citizens United* through a Constitutional amendment. This very proposal is presently being forwarded by leaders of an ambitious new group called American Promise, which is led by an impressive bipartisan council of advisors that includes such leaders as former Ohio state representative Nina Turner, presidential historian Doris Kearns Goodwin, former Massachusetts governor and US presidential candidate Michael Dukakis, former Iowa congressman Jim Leach and former US Senator Alan Simpson of Wyoming, among others.

American Promise seeks to gain sufficient votes across the various states of the nation in coming years to create a 28th Amendment to the US Constitution that would establish individuals, rather than corporate entities, as solely entitled to determine and administer our nation's legal rights and public elections. Among the operational goals of American Promise are the following: to inspire, empower and organize Americans from across the political spectrum to build support for a 28th Amendment; to help set reasonable spending limits for

US political elections, so that all Americans–regardless of net worth—can take responsibility for their lives, governance and national destiny; and to shepherd a winning Amendment out of Congress that can successfully be taken to the states for ratification.[24]

American Promise staff and supporters are advancing this work through an online petition, civic engagement and consensus building campaigns in regions and localities across America, as well as through public information and advocacy efforts in the major media. To date, nineteen states and some 800 localities in most parts of the nation have formally endorsed this work in some form or fashion, including public entities in both blue and red states. In February 2017, congressional Democrat Richard Nolan of Minnesota introduced a House Resolution to provide that the rights extended by the US Constitution are the rights of natural persons only. Clearly, given the Republicans' recent control of both the US House and Senate, proposals like the one recently advanced by Congressman Nolan to undo the essential logic of *Citizens United* are not going to proceed. Nevertheless, there is growing momentum behind this work, and progressive leaders and networks should build on it.

Constitutional Amendments are hardly light undertakings, as progressive women and their allies learned bitterly during the unsuccessful efforts in the 1970s and 1980s to gain approval of the Equal Rights Amendment that would have embedded gender equality in all of the nation's laws and policy. Nevertheless, the campaign for a 28th Amendment offers an unusual opportunity to further educate Americans about the remarkable inequities and anti-democratic values conservative forces have embedded in our contemporary campaign laws. And it can help to mobilize an active and meaningful response from concerned Americans.

Promoting Digital Democracy

It has been said time and again that "all politics is local." Indeed, a central aspect of dynamic democracy is the nature and quality of interactions between the people and their government, especially where the exchange of essential public services and benefits are concerned. Nowhere is that relationship more defined and important than in municipal and regional governance, where people actually live and work. Sadly, in recent decades, largely as a result of conservative government-bashing and/or willful ineptitude,[25] public confidence in government has declined precipitously. As a result, too many Americans today, including many who are natural constituents for progressive causes, feel disconnected from—and even hostile to—civic institutions and democratic processes. Left untreated, this crisis of confidence in government institutions and processes presents important problems for progressive efforts to forge needed change. It diminishes the readiness and predisposition of too many Americans to advocate for change by promoting apathy and the related assumption that change is simply not possible.

Gratefully, powerful new technologies are increasingly available to help improve government engagement of and responsiveness to grassroots Americans in the provision and administration of vital public services. Progressive leaders should be at the forefront of efforts to advance this evolution during coming years. New modalities in digital democracy are helping to bolster public confidence and input regarding the nature and direction of government and civic culture. Such new ways of advancing the public's business draw on the power of Internet technology, social media and viral communications to more broadly engage average Americans and policy leaders in addressing the shared problem of how to meet human and community needs.

Building on 3-1-1 City Services Platforms to Engage and Activate Local Residents

In 1996, the City of Baltimore, MD revolutionized the possibilities for improved public services by introducing a 311 call service for residents. The 311 platform allowed local people to seek quick, cost-free information and referrals to non-emergency city services they often could not otherwise locate. The 311 offerings have made public services more transparent and accessible, particularly for low-income, non-English-speaking and elderly city-dwellers who often have the greatest needs for services. Baltimore's innovation has been replicated by other cities, large and small, now numbering more than one hundred. Increasingly, 311 services are operative on such digital platforms as municipal websites, email, mobile apps and social media outlets like Twitter, Facebook, and others. They offer vital applications through these new media that can further help to strengthen local democracy and civic culture by more dynamically engaging citizens and community residents in interactive problem-solving. In this emerging digital landscape, socially-minded enterprises—including San Antonio-based City Flag and UK-based FixMyStreet—are advancing promising new interactive programs for municipal leaders and residents.

Presently, the public benefits offered by these emerging centers of civic technology are fairly mundane, though important to their growing number of users. Typically, they involve securing pothole repairs, treating uncollected trash build-up or replacing a missing street sign. But emerging trends in municipal digital engagement offer opportunities for revolutionizing the ways in which local governments engage with and serve their constituents. In the not-too-distant future, the public interface with these systems will increasingly replicate the kind of experiences consumers are now experiencing through commercial applications in digital gaming and virtual reality. The platforms will be increasingly fun and interactive for users, making them not merely more user-friendly and responsive, but also more magnetizing[26].

More and more local governments are resorting to digital engagement strategies to both better serve and learn from their constituents. According to Spencer Stern, a leading, Chicago-based technology expert interviewed recently on Microsoft's CityNext platform:

> Los Angeles and Boise, Idaho, are trying to build these very rich citizen profiles so they can better engage, better interact with the citizens than they have in the past. San Francisco has done a great job of leveraging social media to communicate with their citizens. Boston is one of the leading communities, especially around using mobile to engage their citizens. The City of Chicago is another that's using texting and Facebook very well (for example) to help with snow removal and plowing. In some instances, they're trying to pair up people who

can't shovel with citizens that are willing to volunteer to shovel. I think it's an innovative way to engage citizens, to build a sense of community.[27]

With the right support driving it, more than merely reacting to individuated and disconnected problems, future engagements with local residents through amplified 311 services will enable municipalities and their inhabitants to proactively identify more strategic opportunities to serve the people. As Spencer Stern suggests, this will mean not merely responding to problems, but also inviting and advancing proposed solutions and innovations provided by local residents, and even assembling whole communities of volunteer problem-solvers in direct exchange with public officials to achieve more broadly responsive local policy and practice.[28] Kansas City, Missouri is already setting the table for this new approach to engaging with and serving the public by aligning its community 311 input with annual resident surveys to help drive local resources and attention across city agencies and jurisdictions in the most responsive ways possible.[29]

By more broadly encouraging movement in these directions among local government leaders and their constituents (especially those who have the greatest need for public services), progressive leaders can help to re-establish public trust in government and institutions. They can also lay a foundation for parallel forms of digital democracy and activism that can further leverage policy and practice improvements benefitting underserved people and communities all across the nation. These additional innovations could include, among other things, developing robust, real time, online opinion polling on local issues and concerns as they arise, advancing emerging innovations in community-informed public budgeting and eventually enabling widespread digital voting in local, state and national elections.

Amplifying and Harmonizing Social Media Organizing Efforts

In the months and years to come, progressive groups can achieve important collective gains by more effectively mobilizing and orchestrating large numbers of social media users to weigh-in simultaneously on evolving local and regional policy debates. For groups that face structural barriers to participating fully in electoral and civic activities—such as undocumented Americans, young people not yet of voting age, poor people, people with disabilities and senior citizens—innovations in digital democracy are especially important. Such innovations offer a vital means for disaffected and underserved Americans to express their political views and will at little or no cost and with relative ease. This is true even in areas of concentrated poverty, where local residents lack access to desk top computer technologies outside of local schools or libraries that offer them limited, occasional access. With the advent of smart phones and the relatively low cost of communications techology, people in even the most economically challenged communities now have increased capacity to communicate, exchange information and organize quickly, effectively and cheaply.

Such means offer an amplified capacity to affect progressive policy and practice; they could be game-changing for the nation's evolving civic culture. Already, tech-savvy progressive groups such as the Color of Change, United We Dream, the ACLU, MoveOn.org, Indivisible and PolicyLink support active social media and phone texting campaigns that engage literally millions of progressive Americans, mainly at the national level of political and policy discourse. But these and other organizations and networks are increasingly making strides in applying these new approaches to state and local actions as well. We can and must now build aggressively on these capacities to more strategically mobilize people in places where the barriers to democratic participation remain most pronounced.

Aligning with these opportunities would increase participation in civic decision-making and governance. It would result in quicker, more inclusive and more robust grassroots responses to policy proposals and developments, and also enable the broader strategic coordination of activist campaigns and networks. Too often, our efforts and actions in the field operate in silos. As a result, these efforts too seldom add up to something more than their component parts. The resulting reality is that our collective voice is unduly muted, thus weakening our impact and success. The strategic use of digital technologies to harmonize and amplify our advocacy efforts and organizing actions wherever possible would substantially augment our current capacities to prevail in public debate and decision-making.

Encouraging Digital Voting

More widespread digital voting in public elections of the future would offer the most revolutionary benefits for our modern democracy, both in terms of facilitating voter participation as well as strengthening the impact of progressive voters on election outcomes and resulting policy. Digital voting options that would allow voters to register and cast their ballots electronically from a home computer or mobile phone would fundamentally transform voting as we know it. It would substantially lower the barriers to entry that currently apply in our traditional paradigm of place- and time-based voting. Above all, the use of digital democracy in our voting systems would markedly increase the participation of voters whose voices have been all-too-conveniently pushed aside by the egregious voter suppression strategies of the right over recent years.

While cyber-security risks are surely real and present dangers, in time there will be a safer and clearer path to enable digital democracy to extend to voting as a matter of course in America. Already in Canada, more than eighty municipalities now use online voting, and digital voting in Canada has markedly increased voter participation across that nation. Since 2003, Estonia has conducted its elections entirely via online voting, with no major problems; and other foreign nations, including Switzerland and India have also recently introduced Internet-based voting in select local and regional settings following extensive testing and the incorporation of security measures to mitigate the prospects of mistake or foul play in their electoral outcomes. In addition, important global policy research and leadership groups, such as the Atlantic Council have acknowledged the inevitability of Internet democracy and called for expanded efforts by American and global leaders to adequately prepare for and secure electronic voting measures and means.[30]

Strong advocacy efforts by progressive leaders and activists today can help to accelerate online democracy's introduction and adoption in the United States in ways that would significantly increase voting and the representation of people and groups that have too long been underserved by our current, outdated voting system. Achieving success in this area would create opportunities for growing constituencies of young people, people of color, seniors, Americans with disabilities and poor people to vote more easily.

Advancing Criminal Justice and Immigration Reform

The past several years have revealed gross contradictions between America's fundamental commitments to democracy and fairness on the one hand and its evolving criminal and immigration law practices on the other. As documented in Chapter 2, since the mid-1990s, US detention policy has led to major increases in the nation's prison inmate and incarcerated immigrant populations, and the growing use of for-profit security corporations to house and oversee both sets of detainees. Also mentioned earlier, America's inmate and detainee populations have become even more racially imbalanced, with a significantly disproportionate representation of black and brown people being incarcerated across the justice system. Our current system of justice also increasingly encourages the incarceration of people crossing our borders without permission as economic refugees as well as asylum seekers; they too are racially profiled and discriminated against, especially given the name-calling and targeting of immigrants from Mexico and Central America by President Trump. According to recent reporting by *USA Today* (5 December 2017), "The number of immigrants apprehended for non-criminal violations . . . skyrocketed (by 42 percent) in the first year of the Trump administration, even as the number of people arrested at the border for entering the U.S. illegally has dropped to its lowest level in decades." Moreover, the Spring 2018 introduction of Trump's "Zero Tolerance" policy affecting Central American asylum seekers at the nation's southern border—including the intentional separation of detained infants, toddlers and minors from their parents—has taken our nation to new lows in terms of our legal and moral integrity.

What Is at Stake

All of these developments have disturbing moral implications, to be sure, but also very practical consequences for our democracy, because neither felons who comprise a large portion of the nation's growing inmate population, nor non-citizens who make up the nation's sizable immigrant detainee population are afforded important basic rights, including especially the right to vote.[31] Considering the relatively fast growth of communities of color as a proportion of our national population, recent trends in criminal and immigration law should inspire concern among all progressive-thinking people in America. They reveal a systematic effort to thwart the voice and will of our nation's increasingly diverse body politic.

Given the recent glaring inequities we have seen in American criminal justice and immigration policy during the past two decades, it is especially incumbent on progressive leaders and activists to redouble our efforts to seek fundamental reforms in these areas. Many of our leading advocacy and issue groups, including the ACLU, Asian Americans Advancing Justice, the Sentencing Project, the Center for Community Change, the Ella Baker Center, UnidosUS and the National Immigration Law Center, among others have centered much of their recent efforts on key aspects of these issues and raised important awareness of them in community, the media and policy circles. Other progressive groups, such as the Ban the Box Campaign, California-based Barrios Unidos and robust and active immigrant rights coalitions in various states and cities have also advanced important work in the field.

Unfortunately, with only a few exceptions, these groups have increasingly been limited to playing defense in much of the public policy space over recent years.[32] Their forthright attempts to seek needed reforms through formal procedural changes in US legal policy and practice have been significantly limited by the recent success of ultra-conservative political leaders in gaining control of Congress, the courts and the federal government, as well as many of the nation's state houses. In the present context, advocacy efforts in criminal and immigration law reform are often met with disdain, despite clear and continuing institutional and private injustices impacting communities of color and immigrants in these systems. All the while, American prisons and private detention centers are warehousing now more than 2 million prisoners and immigrant detainees—a vastly-disproportionate share of whom are people of color.[33]

Rather than being discouraged by these disturbing trends, leading champions of change have been developing more aggressive collective actions to advance the cause of justice in America in creative and affirmative ways. Among the leading efforts have been the Black Lives Matter and Dreamer movements of recent years. Together, the exemplary grassroots efforts of the primarily young Americans of color who are most directly affected by these issues have moved the dial for the entirety of Progressive America. Their leadership and priorities offer vital guideposts for all who seek to promote democratic change in the nation's failing systems of criminal and immigration law. Indeed, both Black Lives Matter and the Dreamer Movement have advanced their organizing and advocacy work in ways that are refreshingly creative, engaging, collaborative and decentralized. Each one has built its early success on well-defined and well-communicated aims, a culture of inclusion and a willingness to place young people in leadership positions. Both movements have also been remarkably savvy in their use of social media and text technology to educate and inform the public on their issues, to mobilize their bases and to orchestrate their activities with followers and allies. There is much that other progressive activists, organizations and networks can learn from these groups in order to further embolden and enrich the entire field of progressive politics and organizing across America.

Black Lives Matter

Black Lives Matter (BLM) has quickly developed into a global, chapter-based and member-led organization that seeks to build local power and end the violence inflicted on black communities. BLM was co-founded by three powerful women—Patrisse Khan-Collors, Alicia Garza and Opal Tometi—following a rash of police and vigilante executions of unarmed African American citizens. Since its formation in July 2013, BLM has been complemented by hundreds of social justice organizations (including among others the Advancement Project, Color of Change and Freedom Inc., as well as other groups and networks operating under the umbrella organization, the Movement for Black Lives.

BLM's core activities are based on comprehensive justice and community empowerment efforts achieved through broad, grassroots organizing and public engagement activities. At the heart of BLM's proposed justice reforms is the growing call to replace current repressive policing, criminal sentencing and detention policies with restorative justice innovations, including the end of such inhumane practices as solitary confinement, shackling and capital punishment, and a reintroduction of more rehabilitative practices for individuals in state custody. BLM and its allies have also challenged state practices like those in Florida, Iowa, Kentucky and Virginia that do not automatically restore the voting rights of felons after they have completed their sentences. Along with the larger Movement for Black Lives, BLM seeks to redirect state resources from prisons to schools and communities with a strong focus on prevention and opportunity investments. Drawing on model legislative proposals and extensive research, their reform objectives range from ending the criminalization of black youth to reforming the current extractive money bail system that robs so many poor and minority Americans of their own and their family's limited resources, while virtually incarcerating them because they are poor.[34] BLM additionally calls for immediate and substantial efforts to demilitarize local police forces, to end prison privatization and, perhaps most importantly, to shut down the nation's prison-industrial-complex.[35]

BLM has distinguished itself in ways that exemplify the kind of progressive action and organizing that should be prioritized and replicated in the years ahead. While remaining unapologetically focused on the condition, hopes and needs of black Americans, BLM has advanced an organizational culture forging alliances with other racial and ethnic groups, young people and LGBTQ and immigrant community members. In the online description of its goals and aims, BLM offers the following declaration of its commitments and approach:

> We are expansive. We are a collective of liberators who believe in an inclusive and spacious movement. We also

believe that in order to win and bring as many people with us along the way, we must move beyond the narrow nationalism that is all too prevalent in Black communities. We must ensure we are building a movement that brings all of us to the front. . . . We affirm the lives of Black queer and trans folks, disabled folks, undocumented folks, folks with records, women, and all Black lives along the gender spectrum. . . . [36]

While BLM has advanced a core set of strategic activities building on certain programs—such as a media training program to assist current and emerging black activists in communicating effectively and an educational program around Black History Month—most of its efforts have been viral and locally driven by volunteer leaders in the network's extensive number of grassroots strongholds. BLM's current online community exceeds 325,000 users on Facebook, and its Twitter account has been followed by at least 40 million users around the nation and world over the course of its short history. The allied Movement for Black Lives and its partner entities, Color of Change and OrganizeFor.org, explain their approach to social change and social media in the following terms:

We know that change at a national level is not possible unless we build power locally. We also know that petitions, online organizing, social media and anything digital can only create long-term systemic change when it is used to support and uplift existing work on the frontlines. That is why we have [decided] to create a digital space to launch campaigns, share strategies, build relationships, and the trans-local power needed to advance new transformative policy. A #Vision4BlackLives.[37]

The recent evolution of Black Lives Matter and the associated Movement for Black Lives has helped to refocus public attention and grassroots action on the issues facing African American communities, and especially youth, in vital and inspiring ways. Using social media and phone texting, BLM and its many allies have developed extensive remote education and mobilization capacities. Drawing on these emerging modalities and more traditional community organizing techniques, they have supported well-attended marches, flash protest actions, learning exchanges and active documentation of abuse by police and others against black people—all of which have significantly enriched and helped to further the civic engagement of African Americans in the United States.

BLM has expanded its reach by forming coalitions to take up issues ranging from immigration advocacy to reproductive rights. In addition, BLM has actively collaborated with Native American leaders protesting federally approved oil extraction on sacred tribal lands in North Dakota and with Muslim American leaders whose communities are under duress because of the Trump administration's demonizing of Muslims and banning travel to the United States from certain largely Islamic nations.

BLM's aims are emblematic of the types of justice system reforms progressive Americans generally should be uniting behind. They comprise an ambitious, yet concrete and actionable, set of proposals that properly supported would help to dramatically realign our nation's democratic ideals with actual policy and practice.

United We Dream

United We Dream (UWD), co-founded and led by Cristina Jiménez, an Ecuadorian-born Dreamer, is a robust national organization of more than 400,000 members and supporters organized in 48 chapters, across 26 states. The organization seeks to secure permanent legal status and a pathway to citizenship for young non-citizen immigrants who have been raised in the United States, as well as members of the nation's large and growing undocumented population in general.[38] UWD is the largest, youth-led immigrant advocacy group currently active in the United States. Its online community now totals more than 4 million users. UWD seeks to empower its members and followers to develop their leadership, their organizing skills and their own campaigns to fight for justice and dignity for immigrants and all people.

UWD pursues its work principally through immigrant youth-led campaigns that are active at the local, state and federal levels. Since its formation in 2009 with support of the Los Angeles-based National Immigration Law Center and the Center for Community Change, UWD has been a major driver of national political pressure on Democratic and Republican leaders alike to seek a permanent, favorable resolution to the highly vulnerable legal status of young foreign-born Americans who were brought to the United States as minors without immigration documents, but who have effectively lived their entire lives as Americans. UWD has become a major force for comprehensive immigration reform.

While Latino Dreamers comprise the largest share of the organization's constituency, especially those from Mexico, UWD is a largely multi-racial and multi-ethnic organization. It reflects the reality that Dreamers are a diverse group originating from many countries and cultures. According to a recent informative report by Matthew Hildreth, political director at America'sVoice, "Seven of the top 24 countries for Dreamers are in Asia, Europe, or the Caribbean. Tens of thousands of young Dreamers come from South Korea, the Philippines, India, Jamaica, Tobago, Poland, Nigeria, Pakistan [and] Brazil . . ."[39] Owing largely to its robust multicultural make-up and progressive orientation, UWD, like Black Lives Matter, has publicly committed itself to broadly inclusive values and common cause with other groups and communities facing institutional exclusion or other forms of discrimination. UWD expresses these core commitments in the following specific terms:

We understand that, in order to achieve [our] vision, how we do our work must be reflective of the kind of society we aim to create: multi-ethnic, interdependent, intersectional, and inter-generational, all connected and reliant upon one another to achieve the highest standards for our collective humanity and liberation. We embrace the common struggle of all people of color and stand up against racism, colonialism, colorism and xenophobia. We stand against sexism, misogyny and male-centered leadership while uplifting womxn leaders and the leadership of LGBTQ people. We work to make our spaces accessible to people of all abilities and seek to stand in solidarity and partnership with all who share our values.[40]

Drawing on the lessons of recent successful efforts by LGBTQ leaders to gain long-overdue marriage equality rights for their community, UWD has had success in large part by branding its public appeals for support through the real-life stories of at-risk Dreamers themselves.[41] Countless public actions have featured Dreamers as the principal spokespersons and protagonists for their cause. They have mobilized people to participate in marches and protests in numerous cities across the country, to engage in hunger strikes and to raise awareness through aggressive and highly effective social media efforts. Most importantly perhaps, they have proactively invoked core American ideals to support the case for their larger policy goals.[42] In an in-depth May 2011 Dissent Magazine examination of the Dreamers' strategies based largely on interviews with UWD co-founder José Luis Marantes, Daniel Altschuler observed:

[Through efforts like UWD,] immigrant youth activism got the country's attention. Dreamers developed a compelling iconography to highlight their stories. Graduation caps and gowns became ubiquitous at DREAM events, where students not only protested but also donated blood, prayed alongside religious leaders, and in one case held a "study-in" in a Senate cafeteria. Those Dreamers who wish to serve in the armed forces also played their part, dressing in fatigues and donning flags while they marched and saluted their way through the Capitol. These actions reinforced a persuasive narrative of young people who simply want to study and serve.[43]

Importantly, Altschuler's closing observation in the quote above was not the product of mere political optics. Indeed, evidence shows that the Dreamer population, like much of younger America, is highly inclined to civic and public engagement.[44] It is not an overstatement to assert that UWD's efforts to date, and the Dreamer Movement generally, have underscored a high degree of civic interest among affected youth that is both socially significant and affirming.[45]

Despite much recent policy discussion and debate on the issues, and polls showing overwhelming public support for the Dreamer cause,[46] UWD leaders and allied immigrant rights organizations have been unsuccessful to date in their ultimate quest to secure a federal legislative resolution to the Dreamer community's precarious status.[47] Nor have they succeeded in securing badly needed comprehensive immigration reform for broader community members who face criminal apprehension, detention and deportation on a daily basis. But the organization has succeeded in forging a clear pathway forward towards future success; and in the process it has awoken significant new awareness and leadership within one of the nation's most active and growing communities of interest.

Supporting new leadership initiatives in pro-democracy and civic engagement work, to build on and complement the compelling recent efforts of grassroots activist groups like BLM and UWD, is of paramount import to progressive America. Progressive leaders must redouble their common cause with these groups and apply the important lessons of their work in broader organizing and mobilization efforts. It is especially important that we develop supportive new political leadership and policy change capacity that can help to turn the goals of activists into policy and legislation. Many new and exciting opportunities are emerging in that space that warrant more widespread attention and support as well. We turn now, accordingly, to an examination of some of the leading examples of those potentialities with an eye to encouraging increased support for their advancement and replication in other places and contexts.

Supporting Emerging Multicultural Political Leaders and Activists

Looking ahead, it is essential that more established progressive activists and groups support the next generation of compelling and informed political leaders and grassroots advocates who can help right the nation's wayward course during the years and decades to come. The emerging progressive leaders of the future represent greater diversity of race, ethnicity, gender, sexual identity, class and disability than past and present cohorts of progressive leaders. Based on the style and disposition that this emerging leadership has displayed so far, it will rightly embrace more intergroup coalition-building and bridging strategies. These are all vital strengths that we need to build on going forward.

Promoting New Modalities in Civic Activism and Leadership

America has long benefited from important independent-sector civic leadership and community-building organizations, such as the National Civic League and the League of Cities, as well as more recent organizations, such as Everyday Democracy and the Community Democracy Workshop. These organizations have helped maintain the focus within and across America's diverse communities on our shared interests in advancing good government, inclusive problem solving and civic participation. Their efforts remain vital in the evolving context of American civic life. At the same time, a new generation and way of advancing this work with a stronger eye to community organizing and activism is taking shape that has the aim of markedly accelerating the rate of social change in our times.

As we have seen from exemplary and largely youth-driven efforts, such as Black Lives Matter and United We Dream, the emerging leaders and activists are already showing us the way forward. They are highly informed, dedicated, smart, creative and collaborative. They are not waiting for permission to engage, to express their heartfelt views or to lead. And they are ardently committed to advance multi-racial, multi-issue and multi-stakeholder campaigns that intentionally unify progressive causes, which often in the past have co-existed at best, but in too many instances collided in misplaced competition and conflict. This predisposition to unite is all to the good, since it should be more clear than ever that to succeed, progressive and liberal elements comprising the nation's evolving resistance to Trumpism must come together as never before.

Not surprisingly, some of the most exciting models of new civic leadership formation and grassroots activism are located in communities that have been among the most derided in recent years by the far right and their standard bearer, Donald Trump. These include especially communities comprised of young people of color, immigrants, Americans with disabilities, Native Americans and women. In solidarity with these groups, we need to redouble our efforts to nurture and advance next generation progressive multicultural leadership in ways that help to make possible the many political and economic reforms we all seek. Numerous projects and evolving civic engagement strategies emanating from diverse communities are underway and ready to scale up and/or be replicated for broader impact.

Among the leading examples are the Alliance for Boys and Men of Color, coordinated by Marc Philpart of PolicyLink;[48] the African American Civic Engagement Project led by California Calls director Anthony Thigpen;[49] #AAPIResist—a broad-based coalition of more than 200 progressive Asian American and Pacific Islander organizations committed to resisting the Trump administration's divisive policies; the RevUp Project of the American Association of People with Disabilities, led by Helena Berger; the Native Voice Network, coordinated by Chrissie Castro; and Mom's Rising, led by Joan Blades and Kristin Rowe-Finkbeiner. More than ever, in the current environment we all face, each of these efforts and leaders—and so many others like them—warrants redoubled financial and moral support from social investment organizations, forward looking corporate donors and interested individuals.

Encouraging Next Generation Political Leadership

Our capacity to develop more effective civic leaders and alliances is growing and healthy. But, until only recently, the advancement of next-generation political leadership has been an afterthought in progressive and liberal circles. To be sure, progressive movements have produced various promising new political figures in recent years, ranging from US Senators Elizabeth Warren of Massachusetts and Kamala Harris of California to recently elected congressional members Tulsi Gabbard of Hawaii, Ro Khanna of California, Joaquín Castro of Texas and Pramila Jayapal of Washington, among others. But, for the most part, relatively little investment has been committed to developing new political—and especially elected—leadership from the emerging generational cohort of progressive young people that groups like Black Lives Matter and United We Dream have drawn on so inspirationally in recent years.

Recognizing this problem, the Women's March Movement that began in early 2017 with the nation's most significant single-day protest ever has begun to move decidedly into the business of rallying women to run for elected office in unprecedented numbers, and these efforts have begun to pay dividends. Since the initial Women's Marches around the nation and the world in January 2017, the long-active organization Emily's List, which supports women Democratic candidates, has had more than 25,000 women express interest in running for public office.[50] And even more erstwhile organizations like the nearly 100 year old League of Women Voters have seen marked new interest in their work to expand female voting in U.S. elections.[51] In response, the Women's March organizers framed the 2018 March in decidedly electoral terms, focusing on efforts to promote women's political empowerment under the banner "Power to the Polls."

Organizers of the January 2018 Women's Marches accordingly initiated a massive call to action for even more women to seek political office in local, state and national contests. They also announced a coordinated voter registration drive to support this push towards expanded women's electoral representation, encouraging 1 million first-time female voters to register in time for the 2018 campaign season.[52] The Women's March's focus on civic leadership development, and particularly their support for new elected and appointed officials as well as groundbreaking civic activists, can help bridge our evolving efforts to achieve concrete legislative and policy wins. Indeed, we must come together to support emerging leaders that will actively advance the democratic and new economy reforms we all agree are so badly needed.

To this end, a number of vital efforts are also worthy of our focus and support. These include the Washington DC-based New Leaders Council; New American Leaders based in New York City; nationally focused but Washington, DC-centered APIVote; New Mexico-based Americans for Indian Opportunity; the Women's Policy Institute of the

Women's Foundation of California; New York-based Higher Heights for America; and the Denver-based disability rights action group, ADAPT. While some of these public leadership and advocacy entities have been around for decades and others only a few years, all of them align with important grassroots analogs, such as Black Lives Matter and United We Dream. All have produced compelling bodies of work, strategy, data and innovation. All underscore the importance of promoting purposeful, informed, accountable and outcomes-oriented political leadership that is culturally versatile and fundamentally responsive to grassroots will and intersectional concerns. And all are committed to advancing concrete political wins, either with respect to successful electoral campaigns or direct actions leading to desired legislative, policy and practice reforms. The following are brief accounts of these leading groups' work.

New Leaders Council

The New Leaders Council (NLC), founded in San Francisco and now based in Washington, DC, trains broadly multicultural cohorts of emerging professionals from across the United States in the skills needed to run for public office, start a non-profit or launch a social enterprise. Nearly 60 percent of NLC's alumni are non-white; and nearly 55 percent are women. In addition to receiving vital training in policy analysis, political organizing and communications skills, NLC fellows are paired with mentors in their select fields of interest to advance action projects and campaigns in their local communities. All told, NLC supports a robust and active alumni community of more than 6,000 individuals (organized in nearly 50 local chapters across the nation).

One of NLC's flagship programs is its Millennial Policy Initiative (MPI), which supports fellows in developing and publishing policy briefs and pursuing projects designed to promote the common good in various areas of focus. Recent MPI projects have focused on opportunities to support undocumented students, new labor organizing strategies and open-source technology innovations. In addition, MPI recently commenced an effort to develop a comprehensive "Millennial Compact with America" that seeks to encourage and build consensus around novel thinking and policy concepts intended to advance new-economy opportunities, community building and innovations in American democracy. Among NLC's distinguishing features is its ultimate goal of contributing to the formation of a new governing coalition in America: one that is progressive, multicultural and gender-balanced. It seeks to establish itself as a hub for new thinking and action in the progressive space and as a bridge between diverse communities, regions and industry sectors. Furthermore, while the organization is nonpartisan, it customarily takes progressive policy and political positions related to issues that its participants consider important. In these ways, NLC embodies the sort of purposeful, activist approach that frontline champions need to advance in order to secure progressive political change.

New American Leaders

New American Leaders (NAL) was founded in 2010 by Sayu Bhojwani, an Indian-born and Belize-raised immigrant to the U.S. Bhojwani was appointed in the early 2000s by the then-current New York mayor, Michael Bloomberg, to serve as New York City's first Commissioner of the Mayor's Office of Immigrant Affairs. From its start, NAL has supported robust education and training programs designed to prepare qualified and highly-motivated American immigrants and refugees, as well as their offspring and descendants to seek and succeed in elected offices across the United States. In collaboration with partner organizations, such as Wellstone Action, NAL programs offer introductory and advanced issue and candidate training, leadership conferences that bring together elected immigrant officials for informative and tactical exchanges on policy development and public engagement strategy, and awards programs that recognize the innovations and contributions of successful immigrant policy makers.

NAL's unique candidate training programs are designed by immigrants for immigrants. Participants learn how to use their immigrant experience as an advantage in their quest for public office. They gain strategic currency on issues, become adept at connecting with voters, master political fundraising skills and develop strong messaging capacities that challenge racist and xenophobic sentiments. In fact, one of the organization's principal aims is to change the narrative about immigrants from one rooted in the notion of them being needy individuals and communities on the take, to one underscoring their remarkable, still untapped talents and assets to contribute to America's forward progress. Efforts such as NAL's are vital to enabling not only American immigrants, but also more longstanding communities of Americans, to benefit from the voices, votes and vantage points of immigrants and immigrant elected officials.

The need to promote more diverse political leadership is especially pressing, given the nation's fast-changing demographics; experts predict that for the first time in history, there will be more Americans of diverse backgrounds than not at about the mid-point of the current century.[53] But broader political representation of the nation's burgeoning racial, ethnic and immigrant communities is already a pressing moral and practical imperative. In fact, there remains a huge gap between the cultural make-up of Americans in elected office, who are overwhelmingly white, male and privileged, and the nation's increasingly diverse population. According to Bhojwani, "There are more than 500,000 local and state offices in America [but] fewer than 2 percent of those offices are held by Asian Americans and Latinos—the two largest immigrant groups in our country."[54]

In order to begin changing the direction of our politics, as of Spring 2018, New American Leaders has offered training to more than 500 emerging immigrant and refugee community change-makers to pursue key elected offices across America. It has also established formal partnerships with some thirty organizations, including the National Education Association, People for the American Way and the New York Immigration Coalition. Already, in just the few years since its inception, an impressive number of NAL program alumni have achieved success, notwithstanding the anti-immigrant public discourse which has persisted over the past several election cycles. According to a recent article featured on the Moyers & Company website, Bhojwani reported:

We know [our] model works because even in 2016, one of the most hate-filled election cycles in recent memory, 67 percent of our 39 alumni won their races for local and state office in Arizona, California, New York and Michigan. Now, these leaders from the newcomer communities most under attack in our society today—American Muslims, the formerly undocumented, children of refugees—are serving on school boards, city councils and state legislatures.[55]

Among NAL's recent program graduates who successfully ran for elected office in 2016 are many young first- and second-generation Americans who are serving for the first time, including Lan Diep, a first-generation Vietnamese American now sitting on the San José, California City Council; Stephanie Chang, the daughter of immigrant parents from Taiwan who is the only Asian American woman ever to be elected to the Michigan State House; and Ylenia Aguilar, a Mexican immigrant woman who now sits on the Phoenix Osborn School District Governing Board in Arizona. Indeed, the organization's multicultural reach is substantial. In 2017, NAL's program cohort of future immigrant and refugee elected leaders consisted of 49 percent women, 42 percent Latinos, 28 percent Asian Pacific Americans, 12 percent Arab or Middle Eastern Americans and 13 percent LGBTQ participants.[56]

APIVote

APIVote is the national Asian American and Pacific Islander (AAPI) community's leading democracy and civic engagement organization. Asian Americans and Pacific Islanders comprise the fastest growing demographic group in America today, with the largest populations in New York, California and Hawaii. According to a mid-2016 NBC News report based on Census Bureau data,

The nation's Asian population grew at 3.4 percent between July 2014 and 2015, with migration responsible for the majority of the growth, government officials said Thursday. There are now 21 million Asians in the United States—1.7 million of which live in California.[57]

Importantly, the states that have seen the fastest-growing populations of Asians in recent years, such as Nevada, Arizona and North Carolina, are increasingly among the nation's most important swing states for presidential elections. Since 2000, Nevada has seen a 140 percent increase in Asian Americans and Pacific Islanders. In Arizona the rate of increase since 2000 has been 123 percent; and in North Carolina, it has been 115 percent since the turn of the new century. Nationwide, moreover, roughly one in four congressional districts now include more than 5 percent Asian residents; and Asian community members exceed 5 percent of the local populations of nearly 600 cities and municipalities across the country.[58]

APIVote seeks to encourage the country's emerging and increasingly significant Asian American and Pacific Islander populations to vote in local, state and national elections. Presently, despite their significant numbers and established potential to contribute robustly to American society and institutions, this population remains one of the nation's most overlooked groups in politics, the media and even higher education and technology (where Asian Americans are disproportionately represented).[59] While recent gains in Asian community political leadership across the nation have been substantial in recent decades, still today with only slightly more than 4,000 office holders nationwide, Asians Americans remain grossly-underrepresented in policy-making and institutional life.[60]

In response, APIVote supports nonpartisan training for electoral campaigns and civic organizing, education and engagement activities at major party political conventions, aggressive media engagement to educate the public about Asian American issues, election monitoring activities to ensure fair access to the ballot box for Asian Americans and Pacific Islanders, voter technical assistance and partnerships with local and regional groups. APIVote also runs a youth ambassadors project that encourages college-based Asian American and Pacific Islander students to vote. Since 2006, APIVote's Norman Y. Mineta Leadership Institute has provided in-depth, nonpartisan training for several thousand Asian American and Pacific Islander community and political activists on issues and strategies, next generation leadership development and coalition building. At a Summer 2016 Presidential Town Hall convened by APIVote, the organization hosted more than 3,000 community leaders and youth in an effort to examine the various major party campaigns' platforms to secure Asian American and Pacific Islander votes. The event was attended by former US President Bill Clinton (speaking on behalf of Democratic candidate Hillary Rodham Clinton), Utah attorney general Sean Reyes (representing Republican candidate Donald J. Trump) and Libertarian and Green Party standard bearers Gary Johnson and Dr. Jill Stein, respectively.

Forty-five partner organizations help to support APIVote's important work across the nation, including Asian Americans Advancing Justice, the Japanese American Citizens League, the Asian American Organizing Project and the Asian Pacific Islander Americans for Civic Empowerment Project, among others. Forming partnerships and alliances has made APIVote one of the most significant Asian American advocates in the country.

Americans for Indian Opportunity

Created by LaDonna Harris, a founding member of Common Cause and an enrolled citizen of the Comanche nation, Americans for Indian Opportunity (AIO) was formed in 1970. Its work in American Indian community advancement and activism draws on traditional indigenous philosophies in fostering values-based leadership, inspiring stakeholder-driven solutions and convening visionary leaders to probe contemporary issues that undergird the continuing challenges facing native communities and the planet. Governed by a board of international indigenous leaders, AIO also seeks to create innovative international exchanges that contribute indigenous worldviews to the global discussion.[61]

Run today by LaDonna Harris' daughter, Laura Harris, AIO is one of the nation's foremost civic leadership and activism incubators focused on tribal peoples and indigenous values. AIO's program centers on efforts to advance appreciation of traditional native communal history, sacred gatherings and community-building endeavors and the purposeful development of young and emerging native leaders, ages 25 to 34, who are interested in representing Native American perspectives on public issues. Recent AIO priorities have included supporting solidarity efforts with the Water is Life Movement, initiated in late 2015 by Standing Rock Sioux tribal leaders and other indigenous community activists protesting federally-approved drilling on sacred native lands in North Dakota.

Through its community-centered leadership programs, AIO has engaged nearly 250 young native leaders in programs designed to encourage their "giving back" to indigenous communities and groups as they pursue education, careers and life opportunities. Laura Harris, the organization's chief executive, is passionate in her view that what is needed in Indian Country and elsewhere is not more conventional, materialistic and accumulation-focused leadership, but rather leadership that is committed to serving people and the planet. As she puts it, "We need more proactive, values-based leaders."[62]

AIO promotes stronger efforts by leading American institutions, such as schools and the media, to more honestly educate and inform non-native groups about the important and often tragic history of American Indians, and the need to build stronger trust and ties across all racial and ethnic communities in the interest of community peace and mutuality. The organization is committed to multicultural, multi-racial and multi-issue coalition building activities involving diverse native and non-native groups. It is also deeply committed to racial healing and anti-racism training across as its organizational and programmatic goals.[63]

One of AIO's most significant recent undertakings has been a groundbreaking collaboration with other leading Native American advocates to produce a first-of-its-kind study and action plan on opportunities to enhance Native political representation in America. Presently, only two members of the US House of Representatives are of Native American origin and both are conservative Republicans.[64] The study, entitled *Advance Native American Leadership*, was produced in late 2016 and co-written by Laura Harris, Native Voice Network weaver Chrissie Castro and former Democracy Alliance investment advisor Anathea Chino, with the advisory support of nearly 45 leading, mostly Native American experts.[65] Among other things, the study co-authors found that Native American political representation continues to be hindered by structural factors and thus remains unacceptably low. Their report defines the issues in lucid terms, citing recent survey research showing that in states with large Native American populations, "of more than 41,000 elected officials from county to federal levels . . . 90 percent . . . are white, while only .03 percent of elected officials are Native American."[66] In response, the study authors offer actionable recommendations intended to establish new pathways and opportunities for prospective Native elected leaders to serve, especially in such key states as California and New Mexico. The urgency of encouraging enhanced Native political representation through efforts like those of AIO are amplified by recent significant growth in the Native American population, especially youth, with those under age 18 now making up fully one-third of the nation's tribal communities. Between 2000 and 2010, the US indigenous population grew by a whopping 27 percent (almost three times the national average).[67]

Women's Policy Institute

The onslaught of uncovered misogyny that America has recently witnessed in its national life is anything but new. Rather, it is merely more out in the open than ever before. In fact, in so many areas of modern life, cisgender and trans women, especially from communities of color, continue to be abused in male-dominant institutions and workplaces. Women continue to earn substantially less than their male counterparts in comparable employment. They are grossly underrepresented on corporate boards of directors and in political positions of consequence. And women continue to experience poverty and powerlessness in degrees that men rarely do, irrespective of race or educational attainment.[68]

A leading example of concrete ways to expand women's voice in society and their impact on policy is offered by the Women's Policy Institute (WPI) in California. WPI is an anchor project of the Women's Foundation of California, one of the nation's most successful alternative philanthropies, which is focused on empowering women and girls in the state's cultural, political and economic life. The WPI was established by the Foundation in 2003 under the leadership of former CEOs of the Women's Foundation, Patti Chang and Judy Patrick, and the Institute's longtime director, Marj Plumb. Over its now decade-and-a-half of activity, the WPI has solidly established itself as an extraordinarily effective, replicable and timely model of program innovation. Each year since its founding, the WPI has trained as many as thirty-five California community leaders to become skilled agents of statewide policy change. The year-long program is offered at no cost to participants or the organizations with which they are affiliated.

Fellows represent a highly diverse group by design. Each class reflects the geographic, racial, age, class and sexual orientation and gender diversity of California. Some 80 percent of WPI's participants are people of color and a third are queer or identify as something other than heterosexual. Fellows bring varied advocacy experience to work on a range of issues, including health, reproductive rights, environmental justice and economic justice. Under Plumb's leadership, a skilled faculty equips fellows with expertise on the inner-workings of the public policy process. Fellows learn how to research and draft legislation, testify at hearings and influence the state budget process. Participants also receive intensive skill training in collaboration and team building.

The Women's Policy Institute model is unique because it does not just invest in the development of established and rising leaders, but in addition bolsters the work of their home organizations. In fact, most of the fellows that WPI trains go back to their organizations and train their colleagues, as well as lead public policy and advocacy initiatives in their local communities. As a result, this work is fueling the larger gender, racial and economic justice movement, not just particular leaders in the movement. In addition, the program is structured around intersectional work that seeks to bridge and unify the interests of participating fellows. Accordingly, all of the WPI teams focus on public policy strategies that support historically-oppressed communities across California, including low-income, immigrant, LGBTQ communities and communities of color.

During the WPI fellowship, participating women work in teams to develop and lobby for California state legislation of their choosing with a mentor who is experienced in public policy work. Over the years, the institute has yielded tremendous success. To date, fellows have contributed significantly to the passage of thirty-two new laws in the areas of women's health, safety and economic prosperity. One of the landmark laws successfully brought forward by WPI participants, the Domestic Worker Bill of Rights of 2017, extended legal labor and overtime pay protections for the first time to 500,000 low-wage workers in California, the majority of them women.[69] Other laws successfully advanced by WPI participants during the 2017 legislative session supported important gains for California women in the state's subsidized child care system, in relation to accessing renewable energy benefits and, in cases of formerly incarcerated transgender Californians, securing expedited new gender markers on state records.

In 2015, under the leadership of its current chief executive, Surina Khan, the Women's Foundation of California expanded its groundbreaking WPI-State program to the local level. That work focuses on building strong grassroots women's policy and budget advocates. WPI-Local is made up of pre-formed teams from Riverside, Los Angeles, San Bernardino, Monterey and Alameda counties. The classes are generally composed of twenty fellows working in five teams, 80 percent of whom identify as women of color. WPI-Local is open to both English- and Spanish-speakers. In recent years, WPI principals have also worked with organizations in five other states (New Jersey, Rhode Island, Georgia, Illinois and Wisconsin) to replicate the WPI model.

Higher Heights for America

Higher Heights for America was formed in 2011 by Glynda C. Carr and Kimberly Peeler-Allen, two young African American women striving to elevate black women's voices in American progressive politics. By strengthening black women's civic participation in grassroots advocacy campaigns and the electoral process, Higher Heights seeks to create an environment in which more black women, and other candidates who are committed to supporting black women, can be elected to public office. Recent data on the voting propensity of black women in America suggests the organization has fertile ground to build on. Black women had a whopping 64 percent voter turnout rate in the 2008 national election cycle and an even more impressive 74 percent turnout rate in 2012—the highest voter turnout rates of any racial or gender subgroup in those elections.[70] Making national news, the overwhelming number of votes cast by black women proved decisive in the important 2017 Alabama special election race that put Democrat Doug Jones in the US Senate—the first Democrat in twenty years to win a senate seat in that state.

Unfortunately, despite the political involvement and voting proficiency of black women, relatively few succeed in politics as candidates and officeholders. The problem Higher Heights seeks to address, therefore, is the continuing paucity of African American female representation in elected office. A *Colorlines* magazine report in 2016 underscored the significant continuing barriers facing black women in politics:

> Despite being 7.4% of the US population, Black women are just 3.4% of Congress, less than 1% of statewide elected executive officials, 3.5% of state legislators, and 1.9% of mayors in cities with populations over 30,000. Four Black women serve as mayors in the 100 largest cities in the United States. Historically, only 35 Black women from 15 states have ever served in the US Congress, only 10 Black women from 9 states have ever served in statewide elected executive offices, and three states have still never elected a Black woman to their state legislature.[71]

Since its founding, Higher Heights has focused on building a national infrastructure to harness black women's political power and elected leadership potential. Headquartered in New York, the organization is structured in two parts. Higher Heights for America trains and funds black women to run for elected office at various levels. Its sister organization, the Higher Heights Leadership Fund, develops long-term strategy to expand and support the black women's leadership pipeline at all levels and to strengthen black female civic participation beyond just election day. Higher Heights sponsors engaging and actionable program activities to achieve its mission. It supports intensive trainings and webinars designed to prepare and assist black women political candidates to successfully run for office. It also supports a salon and brunch series that informally brings together black women office-seekers for peer learning exchanges on strategy and best practices. And, through strategic communications, the organization broadly educates and informs the general public about the underlying rationale and aims of its work.

Higher Heights for America is committed to multi-party and multi-racial collaboration in most of its work and strategies, in order to advance progressive political gains for women and communities of color. In 2017, for example, Higher Heights joined forces with Democracy in Color and the Collective PAC to rally financial and other support on behalf of Georgia legislative house leader Stacy Abrams, one of the nation's leading African American female elected officials, in her quest to become Georgia's next governor. Among Higher Heights' training and campaign management partners are Emily's List, VoteRunLead.org, Wellstone, the Midwest Academy, BossedUp and BRAVA Investments.

ADAPT

ADAPT is the nation's oldest and most aggressive community organizing and activism network, engaging and giving expanded voice to Americans with disabilities. It was formed as an outgrowth of the early 1970s disability rights activism of Wade Blank and Mike Auberger, Denver-based leaders affiliated with the Atlantis Community, an independent living facility.[72] Blank, Auberger and other disability rights leaders in Denver were concerned about the near-total absence of accessible transportation and services for the local disabled population. In response, they staged dramatic civil disobedience actions, including blocking public thoroughfares during rush hour and sledgehammering sidewalk curbs that were impossible for wheelchairs to navigate. In 1983, with renowned organizing strategist Shel Trapp and other activists, these leaders incorporated ADAPT to advance independent organizing campaigns on behalf of the national disability community.

Initially, because of the incipient mobility and public access issues that informed its work, ADAPT's acronym stood for Americans Disabled for Accessible Public Transit. In 1990, as disability community concerns had expanded to include cognitive as well as physical disabilities, the meaning of the acronym was reframed to stand for the American Disabled for Attendant Programs Today, and since then, the organization has focused increasingly on efforts to augment disability community access to public services generally and expanded home- and community-based housing and support options for people with disabilities. From its founding, ADAPT established itself as a national, grassroots, nonviolent direct-action organization focused on aggressive community organizing, legislative advocacy and public education.

The organization is largely credited, along with other leading disability rights groups, such as the Disability Rights Education and Defense Fund (DREDF), as having made possible the landmark Americans with Disabilities Act (ADA) of 1990.[73] That legislation radically transformed US policy to accommodate the historically-unmet accessibility and other rights of people with disabilities; and it led to subsequent important policy breakthroughs benefiting Americans with disabilities under the 2009 Affordable Care Act (ACA).[74] Presently, ADAPT is especially committed to passing the Disability Integration Act (DIA), which was introduced in Congress by Senate Minority Leader Chuck Schumer (D-NY) in 2017 to address the needs of people with disabilities for long-term services and supports when they are forced into institutional housing facilities, rather than being given the option to choose affordable community-based housing.

During the heated national debate of Spring 2017 over efforts by the Trump White House and Republicans in Congress to undo the Affordable Care Act through a legislative repeal, ADAPT staged widely-reported actions that many credit for the ultimate failure of the conservative onslaught.[75] They held sit-ins in the offices of various members of Congress, both in Washington, DC and in district offices in places as varied as Kansas, Louisiana and New York. They held flash rallies, stopped street traffic and peppered social media with action updates and commentaries. They flooded the US Senate chamber with their members on the eve of the vote, loudly chanting "kill the bill, not me!" as national television cameras rolled. In the end, ADAPT's efforts paid off, as the final Republican challenge to the ACA failed to gain the votes needed to pass.

Throughout its history, ADAPT has distinguished itself not only for its uncompromising and relentless organizing, but also for its unusual organizational culture. To begin with, because disability is a shared experience that crosses lines of race, ethnicity, gender, religion, class and geography, ADAPT, like the larger disability movement, is highly multicultural and multi-faceted. This enables the network to draw from a large pool of talent that less diverse movements too often lack. Moreover, unlike most leading national change organizations and networks, ADAPT is fundamentally unencumbered by leadership and control concerns, issues about who gets credit for the work, or who gets to be interviewed in the press. Rather, ADAPT is a movement of many faces, in many places. Its organizing priorities are not established in a headquarters, but rather on the ground wherever and however its members feel their voices need to be elevated.

Lessons and Imperatives for the Future

The lessons of ADAPT and all of the model civic and political empowerment efforts reviewed here are significant. They offer timely, informative and actionable guidance for social justice activists and communities of all kinds that are committed to democratic change in America. They underscore the continuing power of creative and conscientious community organizing efforts, suggesting new strategic directions and modalities for progressive America. They speak to significant emerging imperatives, including the need for greater integration and alignment of progressive community building and political empowerment efforts.

More specifically, these lessons reveal the need for less conventional emphasis on issues of campaign centralization, control and credit, with much greater focus on real public engagement and institutional change. They urge us to focus more on actions and outcomes, rather than processes and personalities. They remind us that, whatever our origins or issues, at the end of the day, as a progressive community, we need each other—as well as people of every background and persuasion who share our vision of a better future. In this connection, emerging lessons from the field demonstrate our growing need for greater unity and mutual support in all of our efforts to advance more progressive politics and values in America. They remind us that, given the many formidable and unprecedented challenges we now face, more than ever, we need to come together as one movement and one voice for the common good.

Investing in Public Art and Civic Education

Finally, as we think about consolidating our national unity and common cause in the next phases of our work together, it is vital that our national progressive community fight to advance a shared vision of a truer and more inclusive democratic society through expanded public art and civic education. We badly need to reintroduce these cultural and community-building assets into our public spaces and dialogs following now decades of efforts by conservative leaders to mute their impact on American values and progress. Public art is a large part of our history in America, dating back to Franklin Roosevelt's heavy investment in the Works Progress Administration (WPA); and, up until very recently in our national history, civic education had been a significant and largely unifying aspect of our shared educational experience.

The WPA funded a wide variety of public arts projects in order to employ artists during the Great Depression, and also to create cultural works that could help Americans unite in difficult times. Mexico, France, Canada and China have long benefitted from state-supported public art programs in ways that have had unifying and positive impact on their societies and cultural heritage.

As for civics education, since the days of John Dewey in the early twentieth century, American K-12 education has historically included robust democracy and civic education content in the standard curricula. Sadly, over recent years, we have experienced a disturbing retrenchment relative to this longstanding practice.

Recent Issues and Trends

Indeed, recent decades have seen quite effective efforts by conservative forces to censor or defund public art, culture and civic education. The most noteworthy specific targets have been the National Endowment for the Arts (NEA) and the Corporation for Public Broadcasting (CPB), not only for defunding but also elimination. Whereas these arts and media agencies have survived, civic education has virtually been excised from the high school curriculum.[76] Moreover, industry-focused conservatives have propelled workforce training and Science, Technology, Engineering and Math (STEM) studies into the forefront of our public educational priorities, largely at the direct expense of teaching civics, liberal arts and other subjects bearing on the rights and responsibilities of American citizenship and self-government.

Conservatives fear the potential for controversial content to subvert so-called "traditional American values"; they also privilege the needs of the economy and the marketplace over those of public citizenship, community and the common good. Over the years, such fears and biases have increasingly permeated our civic consciousness as schools and other public institutions have scaled back or defunded their own arts and civic education programs, both in response to conservative-inspired budget cutting and content concerns. These are hypocritical compromises for a nation that prides itself on its commitment to democracy and free expression. They are especially problematic for the message they send to our youth, whose voices and views are not being heard on the issues of greatest concern to their generation.

Emerging Opportunities for Change

The recent enthusiastic public response to socially- and politically inspired theatrical productions, such as Lin-Manuel Miranda's Broadway hits "In the Heights" and "Hamilton," and rapidly growing interest in funding public art projects through social media platforms, such as Kickstarter, reveal the latent appetite of so many Americans—and especially younger Americans—for more active civic dialogue and purposeful artistic expression. It is more important than ever that progressive leaders across America join forces to build on this newfound civic and creative energy. In doing so, it is essential that we re-establish civics and culture as fundamental platforms for promoting our nation's democratic advancement and values.

We can ultimately do this best by identifying and supporting exemplary efforts in the field and positioning those examples for broader national scaling when future, more progressive government leaders are able to take the helm and expand their benefits through federal policy and funding. In the meantime, we can more aggressively advocate at the state and local levels of public decision-making for increased funding and policy support for cultural arts that celebrate diversity, elevate our shared humanity and educate and inform especially younger Americans about evolving issues affecting our democracy and the world. Many proven leaders, programs and initiatives are already active in these spaces and ready to show us the way. These models range from the performing arts to public art, and from expanded, quality civics education to more extensive national service offerings. The following are notes and reflections on some of the leading efforts we can draw on in this context and why this work is so timely and necessary.

Community and Performing Arts

Theatre companies and arts centers have evolved in recent years to reflect the nation's changing culture and demography. Their work helps to bring new understanding and appreciation to the varied experiences of diverse American communities and the ways in which mutual respect and common cause are vital to our future success as a society. During recent decades, ensemble companies ranging from Theatre Rhinoceros in San Francisco to About Face Theatre in Chicago, and from the 20% Theatre Company in Minneapolis to Richmond Triangle Players in Virginia[77] have led the way in bringing LGBTQ identity and rights issues onto the main stage in key regions and centers across the country. Similar efforts have emerged from other leading community and performing arts groups focusing on African American experiences and perspectives—such as the Harlem Repertory Theatre in New York, Chicago-based Black Ensemble Theatre,

True Colors Theatre Company in Atlanta, the Ensemble Theater in Houston and the Ashé Cultural Center in New Orleans.

Latino community cultural centers have also emerged to produce increasingly important institutional leadership and content bearing on issues of American identity and democracy; these include Teatro Repertorio Español in New York City, Company of Angels theatre group and Tía Chucha's Centro Cultural in Los Angeles, the Houston-based media and publications center Arte Público Press and, more recently, via the largely viral Latinx Theatre Commons Movement. So too have leading Asian Pacific American groups contributed mightily to our national civic discourse over recent decades through the work of such performing arts centers as East West Players in Los Angeles, New York-based Pan-Asian Repertory Theatre and Minneapolis-based Mu Preforming Arts. And powerful disability community arts leaders, such as the Oakland, CA-based AXIS Dance Company and Bodies of Work in Chicago, have further added to the nation's increasingly rich cultural content.

In addition to these important diverse institutional leaders in culture and the performing arts, an exciting emerging population of individual public performance artists, many of them women, has made important contributions to American civic discourse about democracy and our rights and responsibilities as citizens. Progressive creators of important concept and public engagement art, such as North Carolina-based artist and activist Sheryl Oring, Detroit-based multi-media innovator Maya Stovall and New York performance artist Emma Sulkowicz, have also advanced the impact of art on our evolving civic culture. Each of these cultural leaders has supported highly innovative, engaging and interactive works in recent years that are emblematic of an emerging new focus on contemporary social issues in the arts. Important recent works by these artists actively provoke their viewers to ponder contemporary issues and new possibilities related to our civic identity and democratic values.

I Wish to Say—Sheryl Oring's "I Wish to Say" project (some would call it guerrilla theater) has encouraged new opportunities for Americans of diverse backgrounds to comment on the issues and concerns of the day all across the nation. Oring and, in some cases, select other women who she assembles in teams sit at desks stationed in well-trafficked rush hour locations, dressed as 1960s office secretaries. Positioned in front of manual typewriters, Oring and her colleagues type up and mail single paragraph postcard messages to the President of the United States that passersby are invited to dictate as they see fit. This engaging, interactive work has been performed in more than 100 sites over the past decade, including Oakland, Reno and Ann Arbor; and in 2012, Oring took the project to the Democratic National Convention in Charlotte. Following on her 2012 election-related events, in April 2016, Oring staged a day-long "Type-In" at Bryant Park in New York, where she set up 20 typing stations behind the New York Public Library and worked with more than 100 volunteers who took dictation of postcards to the various presidential candidates. The event was presented as part of the PEN World Voices Festival and received widespread attention from the media. To date, "I Wish to Say" has resulted in thousands of postcards being directed to the White House with messages reflecting a broad range of views on any number of current issues. In an age of hyper-electronic and impersonal communications, Oring's use of old technology and direct human contact offers a refreshing framework for more meaningful civic discourse.

Liquor Store Theatre Performance and Films—Maya Stovall works across the disciplines of dance, theory, anthropology, ethnography, film and contemporary art. In Liquor Store Theatre, she stages impromptu dance performances on public parking lots, sidewalks and streets in front of liquor stores in the largely African American McDougall-Hunt neighborhood of Detroit, where she lives. In the absence of more robust neighborhood commerce, the liquor stores have become the de-facto centers of local shopping activity, a place for residents to socialize. Stovall's flash performances include herself and other select artists who perform a meditative-style of ballet and jazz, with the occasional bystander joining in the movement. After each performance, Stovall engages her audience in conversation and documents their personal experiences, musings and predictions on Detroit's socioeconomic condition and future. Dance is not the objective but a conduit for communication and reflection. Stovall's work has received increasing acclaim. Portions of the Liquor Store Series were recently presented as part of the 2017 Whitney Biennial and exhibited at Cranbrook Art Museum in Broomfield Hills, Michigan.

Mattress Performance: Carry That Weight—Emma Sulkowicz's "Mattress Performance: Carry That Weight," and allied works it has inspired,[78] examines rape and sexual assault issues, especially on college campuses. Reflecting the burdens that far too many women carry as a result of being raped or otherwise sexually aggressed, Sulkowicz traverses public spaces carrying a mattress. As observers see fit, they can approach the artist to help her carry the mattress. In effect, by doing so, participating audience members help Sulkowicz—and symbolically all women who have experienced rape—to carry the memories and loss associated with sexual transgression and violence. In recent years, the artist's work has inspired more than 10,000 women at various campuses across the country and abroad to participate in analogous events intended to support survivors of sexual and domestic violence. Participating campuses have included Columbia University, Stanford University, the University of California at Berkeley, Syracuse University and the University of Michigan, as well as various overseas institutions such as the University of Budapest in Hungary and the University of East Anglia.

Each of the impressive creative collectives and innovators highlighted above (and others like them all across the country) have added immeasurably to our democracy and civic culture over recent decades, but with precious little public support. According to a recent report by the University of Maryland's Institute of Arts Management, such groups and authors have been notoriously underfunded in comparison to larger, mainline cultural centers and more highly established performing artists. As recently reported by the Los Angeles Times, commenting on the study's findings regarding the particular underfunding of Afro- and Latino-centric arts and culture:

> Although many of these organizations produce important work, 'the majority are plagued by chronic financial difficulties that place severe limits on what can be produced, how

much can be produced, how many artists are trained, and how many people are served . . .'[79]

Funding and Staffing the Cultural Arts

The problem is not lack of management ability or insufficient talent on the part of multicultural arts organizations or community arts groups. Rather, there are longstanding biases held by organized philanthropy and individual donors towards funding ethnic and multicultural arts. As the *Los Angeles Times* (12 October 2015) revealed, racially and ethnically diverse performing arts and cultural institutions—and, by extension, the artists who drive their work—are systematically underfunded compared to their larger mainstream counterparts:

The median annual spending for the big arts groups . . . was $61.1 million in 2013, compared with a $3.8 million median budget for the 20 largest African American and Latino arts groups in the study. Median means half the organizations in a category are above that figure and half are below . . . The report said that minority-focused arts organizations' most debilitating weakness has been difficulty in attracting private, individual donors, a demographic whose charitable giving far exceeds the grant making of foundations, corporations and government . . . Wealthy individuals typically make the big gifts that can transform an organization, but . . . it's also important to develop a large base of individual backers who loyally give smaller amounts. A survey to which 29 of the 60 black and Latino arts groups in the study replied showed that the median percentage of donations coming from individuals was 5%. The norm is about 60% for big mainstream arts organizations.

By most accounts, funding for other racial and ethnic, women's and LGBTQ and disability centered arts groups is at least as problematic.[80]

To be sure, negligible support for multicultural institutions and talent is a large, continuing problem in the arts. In November 2017, for example, the Houston Museum of African American Culture

(HMAAC) released a "White Paper on Racial Disparities in Cultural Funding."[81] The report underscored the difficulty organizations like HMAAC face in securing adequate city and private financial backing to fulfill their timely and important missions, notwithstanding strong facilities, management, and programming. Moreover, a January 2016 report by the New York City Department of Cultural Affairs revealed that across some 1,000 museums and cultural organizations now active in the City of New York, fully 62 percent of their staffs were white.[82] Recent reports by the American Association of Museums in 2008[83] and 2010 acknowledged continuing field imbalances. The association's findings underscore the fact that the nation's populations of color have more than doubled since the 1970s and are expected to grow still more, as previously cited, from presently about one-third of the nation's population to nearly half by 2035. Yet, despite the clear, dramatic trend lines reflecting this epic demographic change, large mainstream museums that constitute the bulk of the Association's membership are demonstrating little progress in attracting diverse donors and visitors. According to the Association's 2008 "Museums and Society 2034: Trends and Potential Futures" report: "The fundamental challenge is that while the population is already one-third minority, heading towards majority minority, today only 9% of the core visitors to museums are minorities and approximately 20% of museum employees are minorities."[84]

All across the country, notwithstanding their many continuing challenges, multicultural arts institutions specializing in visual works by exciting past and contemporary artists of various backgrounds are highly active in efforts to advance public appreciation and support of their collections and shows. Such organizations include, among others, the Japanese American National Museum in Los Angeles, the National Museum of Mexican Art in Chicago, the National Civil Rights Museum in Memphis, the National Museum of the American Indian in Washington, DC, and the GLBT History Museum in San Francisco. Given the great wealth of leadership and cultural heritage that exists at these leading institutions, and the expanding imperative for Americans of all persuasions to gain greater understanding of our nation's many diverse cultural assets, it is more vital than ever for progressive leaders to support the reach and financial sustainability of these and comparable institutions. If indeed mainstream cultural organizations are to have continuing public and civic relevance in the future to come, and to use public funds, they will need to build their audiences, programs and content to create a new and enlarged following among the nation's more diverse Americans. But that cannot fully happen without major new investments now in America's grossly-underfed multicultural arts institutions and leaders. Local and national government agencies and philanthropy, as well as individual donors, can no longer fund the "major" cultural institutions at the expense of the smaller, diverse culturally specific institutions which, more and more, represent the largest portions of the overall population.

Progressives who care about the future of our communities and democratic society must come together in more concerted ways to help establish the case for greater public and private funding of community and multicultural arts that bring to the fore our history, our present and the future we hope to realize together. We must speak more loudly than we have in recent years about the importance of our communities having first-voice opportunities to speak for themselves through the arts and culture. Private organizations and initiatives, such as the Art for Justice Fund (a recent, $100 million collaboration to fight mass incarceration involving Agnes Gund, the Ford Foundation and Rockefeller Philanthropy Advisors) are increasingly engaging progressive multicultural writers, painters, rappers and other public arts professionals in constructive dialog on democracy and the common good.

Looking ahead, more leading private efforts like these are needed, as well as much stronger community advocacy to compel public arts funding institutions to match them. Given the relentless and consciousness-numbing buzz of growing commercial encroachments on people's minds and in the public square, it is more important than ever for progressive leaders and communities to fight for vastly increased opportunities to enable diverse community expression and exchange through the arts. This means challenging the quiet exclusion and censorship of too many current public and private funding streams where multicultural creative leadership and work are involved. It also means advocating for a more robust opening of conventional arts institutions and patrons to the new canons that are emerging across multicultural America regarding the very role and purpose of modern creative culture.

Expanding Civic Education and Service in America

Last but not least, in order to restore the vitality of our democracy and the active engagement of everyday people that we ultimately depend on in that regard, it is essential for progressive leaders and organizations to unite behind two important and allied efforts. First, across every state of the nation, we need to push hard for expanded public funding to reintroduce quality civic education and fact-based democratic exchange in our schools and other public institutions. Recent data and events reveal that we have been too-long asleep at the wheel on this front in ways that have now begun to produce disturbing consequences for our national civic and political culture. Second, we need to work hard to increase public and private incentives to promote community service, especially for younger Americans, building on but extending beyond the current offerings of the Corporation for National and Community Service (CNCS).

Under current circumstances, it is essential to expand public support for enhanced civic education and community service in order to rebuild national cohesion and unity in a period of growing social division. As previously noted, recent years have seen considerable concerns emerge in national education circles about decreasing attention to civics in American teaching at all levels, including among college and university students and graduates. Many studies from diverse reputable sources over the past years reveal that growing numbers of Americans are remarkably uninformed about the basic workings of American democracy and government. Indeed, organizations ranging from the Pew Research Center to the American Political Science Association have released timely reports on the issues underscoring Americans' declining knowledge of basic civic processes.[85]

According to a 2016 report of the American Council of Trustees and Alumni (ACTA), an independent, nonprofit organization committed to academic freedom, excellence and accountability at America's colleges and universities, "When surveys repeatedly show that college graduates do not understand the fundamental processes of our government and the historical forces that shaped it, the problem is much greater than a simple lack of factual knowledge. It is a dangerous sign of civic disempowerment."[86] A similar downward trend threatens our democracy as well in relation to national and community service, which has faced growing opposition in conservative thought circles over recent years.[87] President Trump's initial policies reflect as much. Indeed, his first budgetary submission to Congress called for CNCS's elimination in 2018, providing funding in 2017 only for purposes related to ensuring the agency's orderly shutdown. This is precisely the wrong direction for our nation to be taking.

By reintroducing civic education as a priority component of our public education system and by augmenting the capacity and interest of younger Americans to give back through service, we can do much to regain our sense of collective purpose and identity as a democratic nation. In the process, we can underscore both our shared history and fate through added investments in these areas, encourage the next generation of Americans who have already shown strong desire and inclination to do more to advance needed improvements in the public space, and address in more meaningful and durable ways many lingering social and economic problems that continue to afflict our communities. In pursuing these paths, we can re-establish a more proper relationship between the American people and their government. In effect, we can achieve this by actively connecting more of our people's energy and creativity to the important business of public decision-making and problem-solving in times that fundamentally call for new thinking and more active civic participation. In fact, active civic engagement, based on the initiative and ideas of the people, is precisely how the nation's founders envisioned advancing democratic self-government in America. Thus, our history suggests a rich array of potential pathways forward when it comes to creating a more highly-shared sense of what it means to be an American through expanded civic education and community service.

New Opportunities for Promoting Civic Education

Gratefully, there exists a healthy number of models, many of them digital, and multi-media, that American institutions and communities of all types can draw on to increase public understanding of the basic workings of democracy and the responsibilities and rights of Americans. Among the most noteworthy are the following: UCLA's Center for Civic Education and the Tufts University Center for Information and Research on Civic Learning and Engagement (CIRCLE); the Southern Poverty Law Center, whose digital Teaching Tolerance program helps students talk constructively about democracy and intergroup conflict resolution; Facing History and Ourselves, with online, multi-media training programs for teachers and students on how to think about and address the lingering consequences of past and continuing social injustice; the California YMCA, whose annual "Youth and Government Model Legislature and Court Programs" offer participating high school and middle school students role playing experiences as legislators and justices at the state capitol; and icivics.org, which introduces students to substantive content in US civic history through computer-based learning.

The very act of advancing civic education based on fact-based analyses of both historical and contemporary issues may be one of the most important investments we can advocate today. Over time—and hopefully sooner than later—renewed investment in active civic education and engagement will ultimately encourage a normalization of democratic procedures and practices sufficient to challenge the anti-democratic impulses we see emanating from the Trump White House and from far right-wing conservatives around the country. Progressives must lead the charge to confront and combat these tendencies in America; and expanded investment in civic education is where we must begin.

Increasing Opportunities in National and Community Service

Finally, it is equally vital that progressive Americans unite behind expanded community building efforts in the form of more robust investment in national and community service. Over the course of modern American history, Democratic presidents from Roosevelt and Kennedy to Clinton and Obama have enthusiastically endorsed federal investment in community work and service, such as the Works Progress Administration programs, the Peace Corps, AmeriCorps and the Corporation for National and Community Service. These programs have cost the federal government relatively little, yet they have resulted in remarkable talent development and notable improvements in community and human relations, public infrastructure and global esteem.

Most of our nation's efforts in this arena have especially focused on young Americans as a means of encouraging their development as active citizens and effective leaders at various levels of our civic culture. And they have additionally leveraged significant corporate and private contributions to the field of national and community service. According to a September 2013 report by Teachers College at Columbia University, for example:

> Service—intensive and formal programs to support communities—is an important commitment to the nation's social well-being. It also has important economic consequences. Communities with more extensive service initiatives have better civic infrastructure, stronger labor markets, and more human and social capital. The initial benefit—services provided—leads to future benefits as participants build skills and move toward economic independence. National service is an investment in future prosperity.[88]

The Columbia study also reports that for every dollar invested in national service by the taxpayer, more than two dollars is returned in taxpayer savings. In addition, for every $10 of public funds directly committed to national and community service, an additional $15 is generated from corporate and individual donors, making the cost-benefit ratio of such programs even more discernibly positive. According to the study,

> The total social cost of youth national service—including federal funding, matched funding, and tax burdens—is $1.7 billion annually. The total social benefit of youth national service—including the value of output produced and the longer-term gains from greater human and social capital—is

$6.5 billion. For society, the benefit of national youth service is 3.95 times greater than the cost.

With so many benefits clearly resulting to our youth and our nation from programs like these, it is hard to imagine why conservative politicians would be increasingly against supporting them. Recent decades have seen a vast diminishment of the common spaces in which Americans of diverse backgrounds can join hands to make our country stronger, more inclusive and more prone to weather crises and challenges. We have ended compulsory military service, vastly diminished our public education system and privatized almost all other forms of public exchange over the past half century. In the process, we have seen a notable decline in our sense of national cohesion and unison. Incentivizing more robust national and community service by Americans of all backgrounds would constitute an actively patriotic and common-sense way to move forward as a more harmonious and successful nation.

Honoring Legacy

In the mid-1960s, when the great civil rights elder Fannie Lou Hamer and others like her across the land challenged the powers that be in America "to get right," she and her partners in the struggle envisioned an America that would one day lower the barriers to participation in our so-called democracy. They prayed and sang with the highest of hopes for an America that would one day actively facilitate, rather than hinder, each individual's capacity to engage, to contribute and to benefit from our nation's unique commitment to freedom and equality. Now more than fifty years later, rather than more fully approaching the dream Hamer and her contemporaries envisioned, we find ourselves perhaps moving further away from America's promise than at any time in our collective memory and experience.

We can and must do better if America is to continue to stand as a beacon of hope and possibility for the people of our nation and the world. We can and we must do better if we are to honor the past sacrifices and suffering of those who came before us to advance the cause of equality and freedom. By organizing and activating ourselves and our communities to move public policy in a new and better direction, we can do better in the months and years to come. By coalescing around efforts to aggressively modernize our systems of voting, apportionment and public governance, by substantially reorganizing our law enforcement and immigration policy, by lifting up and unleashing the talents of emerging multicultural progressive leaders, community organizers and producers of creative culture, and by resuscitating our commitments to quality civic education and community service, we can revive our waning democracy. And in the process of doing these things to help America get right, we can honor the legacy of pioneers, like Fannie Lou Hamer, who inspire us still today to champion the cause of democracy in our contemporary times.

Endnotes

[1]See Roth, Z., *The Great Suppression: Voting Rights, Corporate Cash, and the Conservative Assault on Democracy*, NY: Crown, 2016.

[2]Hamer's testimony before the DNC Credentials Committee challenged the Party's empanelment of an all-white delegation at the Party's 1964 convention.

[3]Comparable voter suppression strategies were also directed at Latinos in much of the southwestern United States. See Sepulveda, Jr., J., *The Life & Times of Willie Velásquez: Su Voto es Su Voz*, Houston: Arte Público Press, 2003.

[4]See "Civil Rights: The Second Revolution, 1965-1980," National Park Service, Washington, DC: https://www.nps.gov/subjects/civilrights/secondrevolution.htm; and Thernstrom, A. & Thernstrom, S., "Black Progress: How Far We've Come and How Far We Have to Go," Brookings Institution, March 1, 1998: https://www.brookings.edu/articles/black-progress-how-far-weve-come-and-how-far-we-have-to-go/. For insight into how Latinos also benefitted from the Great Society, see Ramos, H.A.J., *The American GI Forum: In Pursuit of the Dream (1948-1983)*, Houston: Arte Público Press, 2003.

[5]See Kim-Lee, A., et al., "The New York Votes Act Would Expand Democratic Access," April 18, 2017: http://rooseveltinstitute.org/new-york-votes-act-expand-democratic-access/ and Baines, E., "Fighting Young Voter Apathy: Automatic Voter Registration for College Students in Virginia," 2017: http://rooseveltinstitute.org/wp-content/uploads/2017/05/113-FINAL.pdf. See, also *The Hidden Rules of Race: Barriers to an*

Inclusive Economy, 2017, Cambridge University Press, 161-162, where the Roosevelt Institute supports a new system of universal registration and voting, including incentive measures that would make not voting punishable by a modest fine.

[6]See "Automatic Voter Registration," Brennan Center for Justice, December 4, 2017: https://www.brennancenter.org/analysis/automatic-voter-registration.

[7]See Chokshi, N., "Automatic Voter Registration a 'Success' in Oregon," *The New York Times*, December 2, 2016: https:// zwww.nytimes.com/ 2016/12/02/us/politics/oregon-voter-registration.html.

[8]See Kennedy, L. & Griffin, R., "Close Elections, Missing Voices, and Automatic Voter Registration Projected Impact in 50 States," Center for American Progress, November 30, 2017: https://www.american-progress.org/issues/democracy/reports/2017/11/30/443333/close-elections-missing-voices-automatic-voter-registration-projected-impact-50-states/.

[9]See "Same Day Voter Registration," October 12, 2017, National Conference of State Legislatures: http://www.ncsl.org/research/elections-and-campaigns/same-day-registration.aspx.

[10]"All Mail Elections (aka Vote by Mail)," National Conference of State Legislatures, January 12, 2017: http://www.ncsl.org/research/elections-and-campaigns/all-mail-elections.aspx. For clarification, while mail is the preferred and central means of voting in states utilizing this approach, they all afford alternative in-person voting centers in designated parts of the state that voters who prefer to do so can access, either to complete and cast their ballot on-site or to deliver their already completed ballot in person.

[11]"Colorado Voting Reforms: Early Results," The Pew Charitable Trusts, March 2016: http://www.pewtrusts.org/~/media/assets/2016/03/coloradovotingreformsearlyresults.pdf.

[12]See "Voting by Mail in Colorado, Oregon and Washington," NonProfit Vote: http://www.nonprofitvote.org/get-ballot-home-2-weeks-election-day/.

[13]"Colorado Voting Reforms: Early Results," The Pew Charitable Trusts. On youth voter turnout issues, see also, Malone, S., "Negative Tone of White House Race Sours Younger Voters," Reuters, 24 October 2016: https://www.reuters.com/article/us-usa-election-millennials/ negative-tone-of-white-house-race-sours-young-voters-idUSK CN12O1X8 and File, T., "Young-Adult Voting: . . . Presidential Elections, 1964–2012," U.S. Census Bureau, April 2014: https://www.census.gov/prod/2014pubs/ p20-573.pdf.

[14]"Voting by Mail in Colorado, Oregon and Washington," and "Provisional Ballots," National Association of State Legislatures, June 19, 2015: http://www.ncsl.org/research/elections-and-campaigns/provisional-ballots.aspx.

[15]California Proposition 11 was passed in 2008, mandating the establishment of the California Citizens Redistricting Commission as the Golden State's sole authorized agency for determining the drawing of state district political lines. In 2010, Proposition 20 was approved by 61 percent of state voters, extending the state Citizens Redistricting Commission's powers to the drawing of congressional district political lines as well. See the Commission's website: http://wedrawthelines. ca.gov/. It should be noted that, with passage of Proposition 106, Arizona voters approved a predating plan to promote citizen-led redistricting in that state, starting in 2000. However, unlike California's approach, which offers the only redistricting system in the nation that entirely separates redistricting from legislative influence, Arizona's commissioners are appointed by select Arizona elected officials and thus not entirely independent of their appointers' respective political interests.

[16]See Sonenshein, R.A., "When People Draw the Lines," League of Women Voters of California2013,: https://cavotes.org/sites/default/files/jobs/RedistrictingCommission%20Report6122013.pdf and Meyers, J., "Political Roadmap: How California Went From Worst to First in Drawing Fair Political Maps, *Los Angeles Times* 7 October 2017: http://www.latimes.com/politics/la-pol-ca-road-map-california-redistricting-supreme-court- 20171008 story.html.

[17]The genesis of proportional representation proposals dates back to the early 1990s and the legal thinking of Lani Guinier, then a University of Pennsylvania law professor whose appointment to serve as President Bill Clinton's civil rights leader in the US Justice Department was withdrawn as a result of conservative backlash concerning her views on these issues. See Guinier, L., *Lift Every Voice: Turning a Civil Rights Setback Into a New Vision of Social Justice*, NY: Simon & Shuster, 1998, and Amy, D. J., "Proportional Representation: A Tool for Empowering Minorities and the Poor," Poverty & Race, Poverty & Research Action Council (PRRAC), September/October 1993: http://www.prrac.org/full_text.php?text_id=494&item_id=4885&newsletter_id=10&header=Race+%2F+Racism.

[18]For more background on the principles and possibilities of ranked choice voting in America, see "Ranked Choice Voting/Instant Run Off," FairVote: http://www.fairvote.org/rcv#rcvbenefits.

[19]"Ranked Choice Voting/Instant Run Off," FairVote.

[20]See "Ranked Choice Voting," Ballotopia, November 2017: https://ballotpedia.org/Ranked- choice_voting_(RCV).

[21]"Ranked Choice Voting/Instant Run Off," supra at n. 33.

[22]See Blumenthal, P., "Super PAC Megadonors Are Giving More Than Ever In 2016," *Huffington Post*, October 10, 2016: https://www.huffingtonpost.com/entry/super-pac-donors-2016_us_57fc068de4b0e655ea b6f34e.

[23]See, e.g., Blumenthal, P., "Here's Where Campaign Finance Reform May Move Ahead As Congress Dithers," *Huffington Post,* 20 December 2014: https://www.huffingtonpost.com/2014/ 12/20/campaign-finance-reform- states_n_6357182.html.

[24]See the American Promise: http://www.americanpromise.net/.

[25]See Fried, A., "Distrust in Government as a Political Weapon," Scholars Strategy Network, March 2012: http://www.scholarsstrategynetwork.org/brief/distrust-government-political-weapon on issues related to conservative government-bashing.

[26]Telephone interview with Alberto Altamirano, Founder and CEO, City Flag, November 7, 2017.

[27]See Friedman, J., "A 'Stern' View of What's Next in Citizen Services," Microsoft/CityNext March 8, 2017: https://enterprise.microsoft.com/en-us/articles/industries/citynext/a-stern-view-of-whats-next-in-citizen- services/.

[28]Friedman, J., "A 'Stern' View of What's Next in Citizen Services."

[29]Newcombe, T., "311: From a Hotline to a Platform for Citizen Engagement," June 1, 2017, govtech.com at: http://www.govtech.com/dc/articles/311-From-a-Hotline-to-a-Platform-for-Citizen-Engagement.html. Last year's municipal survey showed that over 60 percent of Kansas City residents participating approved of their local 311 service and its responsiveness to users.

[30]See McCormack, C.B., *Democracy Rebooted: The Future of Technology in Elections*, The Atlantic Council, March 2016: http://publications.atlanticcouncil.org/election-tech/assets/report.pdf. According to the Council's Director, Peter Schechter, in the report's Foreword, "The Atlantic Council believes that technology's forward march is inevitable and its use in elections will accelerate. Our role as a policy think tank is to ask how best to insure that its implementation in countries large and small enhances access, expands participation, and strengthens democracy's credibility."

[31]In fact, many felons are denied basic voting and employment rights even well after serving their court designated prison terms. See "Felon Voting Rights," National Conference of State Legislatures, November

28, 2017: http://www.ncsl.org/research/elections-and-campaigns/ felon-voting-rights.aspx.

[32]Among the exceptions have been California's passage of Proposition 47 in 2014, which dramatically reduced the state's prison rolls and redirected considerable public corrections resources into prevention programs that seek to mitigate inmate recidivism. Other successes have included efforts by Ban the Box and its allies to secure policy accords with more than 150 cities, 29 states and such major corporations as Target, Walmart and Home Depot to end their practice of seeking information on employment applications regarding past criminal records. In addition, nine states have taken legal action to preclude private employers from inquiring about past criminal records in their recruitment and employment practices. See Avery, B. and Hernández, P., "Ban the Box: U.S. Cities, Counties, and States Adopt Fair Hiring Policies," National Employment Law Project, August 1, 2017: http://www.nelp.org/publication/ban-the-box-fair-chance-hiring-state-and-local-guide/.

[33]See Wagner, P. & Rabuy, B., "Mass Incarceration: The Whole Pie," Prison Policy Initiative (PPI), March 14, 2017: https://www.prisonpolicy.org/reports/pie2017.html. PPI reports, for example, that while African Americans make up only 13 percent of the national population, they comprise fully 40 percent of the nation's prison population. Latinos, who make up 16 percent of the national population, are also overrepresented in US prisons and detention facilities, comprising 19 percent of the nation's inmate population.

[34]See, e.g., DeVuono-powell, S., et al., *Who Pays? The True Cost of Incarceration on Families*, 2015, Ella Baker Center & Forward Together, Oakland, CA at: http://ellabakercenter.org/sites/default/ files/downloads/who- pays.pdf and *BAIL FAIL: Why the U.S. Should End the Practice of Using Money for Bail*, September 2012, Justice Policy Institute, Washington, DC at: http://www.justicepolicy.org/ uploads/justicepolicy/documents/bailfail.pdf.

[35]See "End the War on Black People," Black Lives Matter at: https://policy.m4bl.org/end-war-on-black-people/.

[36]See BLM's website "About" section at: https://blacklivesmatter.com/about/.

[37]See https://campaigns.organizefor.org/efforts/m4bl for background on the relationships and work pertaining to A Vision for Black Lives (#Vision4BlackLives).

[38]See, e.g., Foley, E., United We Dream: We Won't Settle for Just the Dream Act," *Huffington Post*, December 3, 2012, at: https://www.huffingtonpost.com/2012/12/03/united-we-dream_n_2233425.html.

[39]See Hildreth, M., "What is DACA? What is the Dream Act? . . . " America's Voice, July 20, 2017: https://americasvoice.org/blog/what-is-a-dreamer/.

[40]See "About" on the United We Dream website: https://unitedwedream.org/about/.

[41]See Ball, M., "What Other Activists Can Learn from the Fight for Gay Marriage," *The Atlantic*, July 14, 2015: https://www.theatlantic.com/politics/archive/2015/07/what-other-activists-can-learn-from-the-fight-for-gay- marriage/398417/,

[42]See Altschuler, D., "The Dreamers' Movement Comes of Age," *Dissent Magazine*, May 16, 2011: https://www.dissentmagazine.org/online_ articles/the-dreamers-movement-comes-of-age. For an in-depth self-reporting of UWD's extensive activities and pursuits over recent years since its founding see, also, *Demanding Dignity by Speaking Truth to Power*, 2015, PDF PowerPoint Deck, United We Dream, Washington, DC at: https://www.unboundphilanthropy.org/sites/default/files/UWDN%20Case%20Study%202015_Final%20for%20Public%20Dissemination.pdf.

[43]Altschuler, D., "The Dreamers' Movement Comes of Age," *Dissent Magazine*.

[44]See Terriquez, V., "Anything But a DREAM: Legal Status, Civic Organizations, and Political Participation among Latino Young Adults," Dornsife Center for the Study of Immigrant Integration, University of Southern California, Los Angeles, June 13, 2017: https://dornsife.usc.edu/csii/veronicaterriquez-youthorganizing/.

[45]See Nicholls, W.J., *The Dreamers: How the Undocumented Youth Movement Transformed the Immigrant Rights Debate*, Palo Alto: Stanford University Press, 2013.

[46]See Gómez Licon, A. & Swanson, E., "Majority of Americans Support Dreamers Staying in the US, Poll Says," *Christian Science Monitor*, citing Associated Press (AP) survey, October 11, 2017: https://www.csmonitor.com/USA/Politics/2017/1011/Majority-of-Americans-support-Dreamers-staying-in-the-US-poll-says. The AP poll, conducted in collaboration with the NORC Center for Public Affairs Research found that only 1 in 5 Americans support deporting Dreamer community members back to their respective nations of origin.

[47]It should be noted, however, that United We Dream and other DACA recipient supporters won a major federal court case on February 26, 2018, when the United States Supreme Court helped to temporarily prevent federal authorities from deporting Deferred Action for Childhood Arrivals (DACA) status-holders. The Court effectively enabled a continuation of DACA recipients' right to remain in the United States to

work and/or study until the end of 2018 by refusing to hear the Trump administration's appeal for a quick affirmation of the President's right to end the special protections originally extended to such individuals by the Obama administration in 2012.

[48]To date, nearly 100 legislative measures in restorative justice endorsed by the Alliance have been enacted into law. http://www.allianceforbmoc.org/.

[49]See the following website for more information on the African American Civic Engagement Project and other important corollary efforts to advance black political empowerment nationwide under the umbrella of the Association for Black Foundation Executives (ABFE): http://www.abfe.org/wp-content/uploads/2014/04/Building-a-Strong-Infrastructure-for-Black-Civic-Engagement-Political-Giving.pdf.

[50]North, A., "How the Women's March Made Itself Indispensable," January 19, 2018, Vox at: https://www.vox.com/identities/2018/1/19/16905884/2018-womens-march-anniversary.

[51]See, e.g., Itkowitz, C., "Why This Nearly 100-Year-Old Organization is Seeing a Resurgence Thanks to Trump's Election," February 9, 2017, The Washington Post at: https://www.washingtonpost.com/ news/ inspired-life/wp/2017/02/09/league-of-women-voters-seeing-sudden-surge-in-membership/?utm_term=.eb11215bd14b.

[52]Totten, K., "How the Women's March Is Turning Protesters into Politicians," *Rolling Stone Magazine*, January 22, 2018: https://www.rollingstone.com/politics/womens-march-2018-protesters-turn-politicians-w515703.

[53]Wazwaz, N., "It's Official: The U.S. Is Becoming a Minority-Majority Nation," *U.S. News & World Report*, July 6, 2015: https://www.usnews.com/news/articles/2015/07/06/its-official-the-us-is-becoming-a-minority-majority-nation.

[54]Bhojwani, S., "Recruiting More Diverse Candidates Creates a Stronger, More Inclusive Democracy," Spotlight: Activism, Moyers & Company, May 31, 2017: http://billmoyers.com/story/a-democracy-for-all/.

[55]"Recruiting More Diverse Candidates Creates a Stronger, More Inclusive Democracy."

[56]Telephone interview with Sayu Bhojwani, January 30, 2018.

[57]Lam, C., "Asians Remain Fastest Growing U.S. Group…" NBC News: https://www.nbcnews.com/news/asian- america/asians-remain-fastest-growing-us-group-pacific-islanders-mixed-race-n597711.

[58]See the APIVote website for more background on recent trends in AAPI population and voting data at: http://www.apiavote.org/why-aapi#fastest-growing-population.

[59]See Chris Lu's compelling commentary on this issue in *Time,* October 20, 2017: http://time.com/4992021/asian-americans-pacific-islanders-representation/.

[60]See Vasquez, R., "Number of Asian American Public) Officials has Reached Historic Levels, UCLA Study Shows," UCLA Newsroom, June 2, 2014: http://newsroom.ucla.edu/releases/number-of-asian-american-public-officials-has-reached-historic-levels-ucla-study-shows and Zheng, E., "Asian American Underrepresentation: Political Consequences and Policy Reform," January 22, 2016, The Claremont Journal of Law & Policy at: https://5clpp.com/2016/01/22/asian-american-underrepresentation-political-consequences-and-policy-reform/.

[61]Telephone interview with Laura Harris, December 18, 2017. See also: http://aio.org/.

[62]Telephone interview with Laura Harris, December 18, 2017.

[63]Telephone interview with Laura Harris, December 18, 2017.

[64]See Hillary, C., "Why Aren't More Native Americans Members of the US Congress?" Voice of America News , August 3, 217: https://www.voanews.com/a/why-arent-more-native-americans-members-of-congress/3971053.html.

[65]See Castro, C., et al., *Advance Native American Political Leadership: Addressing the Strengths, Structural Barriers and Opportunities to Getting Native Americans Elected to Office*, October 2016 at: https:// advancenativepl.org/wp-content/uploads/2016/10/ANPL-Political-Power-09-22-16.pdf.

[66]The reporting on disparities in racial and ethnic representation among elected officials was drawn from data assembled in 2015 by the Women Donors Network: https://womendonors.org/.

[67]See Kareem Little, N., "Interesting Facts and Information about the Native American Population," ThoughtCo. (DotDash), July 8, 2017: https://www.thoughtco.com/interesting-facts-about-native-americans-2834518.

[68]See Warner, J. & Corley, G., "The Women's Leadership Gap," Center for American Progress, May 21, 2017: https://www.americanprogress.org/issues/women/reports/2017/05/21/432758/womens-leadership-gap/.

[69]See "The Domestic Worker Bill of Rights (AB 241)": https://www.dir.ca.gov/dlse/DomesticWorkerBillOfRights.html.

[70]Zoila-Pérez, M., "This Duo Wants to Turn the Most Reliable Voters—Black Women—Into Candidates," Colorlines Magazine, RaceForward, June 9, 2016: https://www.colorlines.com/articles/duo-wants-turn-most- reliable-voters—black-women—candidates.

[71]Zoila-Pérez, M., "This Duo Wants to Turn the Most Reliable Voters—Black Women—Into Candidates." See also, Harris, M., "Women of

Color: A Growing Force in the American Electorate," Center for American Progress, October 30, 2014: https://www.americanprogress.org/issues/race/reports/2014/10/30/99962/women-of-color/.

[72]See, e.g., "ADAPT Celebrates 25 Years of Disability Rights Activism," SKIL Resource Center, Winter 2008: http://skilonline.com/index.php/recent-news/63-feburary-a-march-2009/274-adapt-celebrates-25-years-of- disability-rights-activism.

[73]See "A History of the Disabilities Movement," Individual Abilities in Motion (I AM), June 3, 2015: http://individualabilities.org/blog-posts/a-history-of-the-disabilities-rights-movement/.

[74]See "Fact Sheet: The Affordable Care Act and the Disability Community," National Council on Independent Living, January 26, 2017: http://www.advocacymonitor.com/fact-sheet-the-affordable-care-act-and-the-disability- community/.

[75]See, e.g., Wanshel, E., "Persons with Disabilities Deserve the Credit for Saving Obamacare," *Huffington Post,*July 28, 2017: https://www.huffingtonpost.com/entry/activists-disabilities-adapt-healthcare-bill_us_597b5508e4b02a4ebb751e2e.

[76]"Civics Education Testing Only Required In 9 States For High School Graduation: CIRCLE Study," Huffington Post/Education, October 12, 2012: https://www.huffingtonpost.com/2012/10/12/circle-study-finds-most-s_n_1959522.html.

[77]See Grunfeld, A., "15 Regional Companies Leading the Charge in Gay Theatre," *Playbill,* June 21, 2016: http://www.playbill.com/article/15-regional-companies-leading-the-charge-in-gay-theatre.

[78]See Davis, B., "Columbia Student's Performance Art Catalyzes a Full-Fledged Protest Movement," ArtNet News, September 13, 2014: https://news.artnet.com/exhibitions/columbia-students-performance-art-catalyzes-a-full-fledged-protest-movement-102061 and Skovos, A., "Students Bring Out Mattresses In Huge 'Carry That Weight' Protest against Sexual Assault," Huffington Post, 6 December 2017: https://www.huffingtonpost.com/2014/10/29/carry-that-weight-columbia-sexual-assault_n_6069344.html.

[79]See Boehm, M., "Study Sends 'Wake-Up Call' About Black and Latino Arts Groups' Meager Funding," *Los Angeles Times*, 12 October 2015: http://www.latimes.com/entertainment/arts/culture/la-et-cm-diversity-arts-study-devos-black-latino-groups-funding-20151009-story.html.

[80]See Mauldin, B., et al., "Los Angeles County Arts Commission Cultural Equity and Inclusion Initiative: Literature Review," March 30, 2016: https://www.lacountyarts.org/sites/default/files/pdfs/ceii_litrev_final.pdf.

[81]See "HMAAC to Hold Meeting on Racial Disparities in Cultural Funding," Defender Network, November 13, 2017: http://defendernetwork.

com/art-entertainment/hmaac-hold-meeting-racial-disparities-cultural-funding/.

[82]Voon, C., "Staff at NYC Arts Organizations Is 62% White, City Report Shows," Hyperallergic, January 29, 2016: https://hyperallergic.com/271609/staff-at-nyc-arts-organizations-is-62-white-city-report-shows/.

[83]See "Museums & Society 2034: Trends and Potential Futures," December 2008, American Association of Museums/Center for the Future of Museums, New York at: http://www.aam-us.org/docs/center-for-the-future-of- museums/museumssociety2034.pdf.

[84]See "Museums & Society 2034: Trends and Potential Futures."

[85]Matto, E. C., et al., Teaching Civic Engagement Across the Disciplines, 2017, American Political Science Association: http://web.apsanet.org/teachingcivicengagement/wp-content/uploads/sites/9/2016/10/Teaching-Civic-Engagement-Across-the-Disciplines_opt.pdf, as well as "Politically Apathetic Millennials," Fact Tank, Pew Research Center, November 23, 2010: http://www.pewresearch.org/fact-tank/2010/11/23/politically-apathetic- millennials/ and Wong, A., "Why Civics Is about More than Citizenship," *The Atlantic,* September 17, 2015: https://www.theatlantic.com/education/archive/ 2015/09/civic-education-citizenship-test/405889/.

[86]*A Crisis in Education,* American Council of Trustees & Alumni, January 2016: https://www.goacta.org/images/download/A_Crisis_in_Civic_Education.pdf.

[87]See Mataconis, D., "Just Say No To 'National Service' Schemes," Outside the Beltway, June 28, 2013: http://www.outsidethebeltway.com/just-say-no-to-national-service-schemes/.

[88]Belfield, C., *The Economic Value of National Service,* Teachers College, Columbia University, September 2013: http://cbcse.org/wordpress/wp-content/uploads/2013/09/belfield.FranklinProject_EconomicValue_final-1.pdf.

CHAPTER 4
The Limits of Hyper-capitalism and Material Accumulation for the Few

> Functional societies need algorithms which reward us for being of service to those who need it most. Instead we have algorithms which reward us for being of service to those who need it least.
> —Heather Marsh
> *Binding Chaos: Mass Collaboration on a Global Scale*[1]

To most observers, the American economy appeared to be roaring back in 2017, following stagnation stemming from the 2008 Great Recession and huge losses in employment and savings for many middle and working-class households. At just over 4 percent, the U.S. unemployment rate was at its lowest in a decade and, with shares trading at over 25,000 on the Dow Index of the New York Stock Exchange to begin 2018, all seemed to be right in the universe for those whose main focus rests with standard economic performance data.

But just beneath the glow of these statistics were the lingering realities of the economic dislocation affecting most people and households across America due to stagnating wages,[2] diminishing working conditions,[3] rising health, housing, and living expenses[4] and growing household debt.[5] In spite of the questionable financial and business practices that brought on the Great Recession of a decade ago, virtually none of the them—excessive wealth concentration, over-speculation, inequality and debt—have significantly improved in the decade since. In fact, so little has changed that one wonders how far away we are from the next cataclysmic economic meltdown.

A Tale of Two Americas

Much of the data reflecting renewed economic robustness in our times camouflages a growing underclass of Americans whose economic fates have rendered them largely inoperative. Owing to the vagaries of the market, millions of working-age people across the nation have simply stopped looking for jobs in recent years;[6] and many among this cohort have essentially dropped out of society altogether. In Los Angeles County alone, the population of homeless is now approaching 60,000 people, many of whom are women and teens.[7]

In many rural communities, chronic unemployment and opioid addiction have plagued the current generation of young and working-age adults.[8] In key industries, such as food service (which accounts for nearly six million workers, about two–thirds of them women), employees are systematically undercompensated and subject to abuses ranging from wage theft to sexual predation.[9] And, notwithstanding growing anti-immigrant sentiment across much of the land, numerous sectors of the American economy—ranging from agriculture and construction to house-keeping and home care—increasingly cannot function without highly-exploitable undocumented laborers to make their products and services affordable to consumers.[10]

We see all around our cities the seemingly relentless building of new high rises for the corporate class, the appearance of exorbitantly priced new restaurants and entertainment facilities to amuse the wealthy and the privileged, and the proliferation of luxury consumer items to further engage society's haves, from the latest technological gadgets to the current lines of high-end fashion items and cars. But it is a relatively smaller and smaller cohort of Americans who can afford to access these symbols of the so-called good life, or even the basics of a comfortable middle-class existence. More and more Americans simply are not in a position to meaningfully participate in this economy; and, practically speaking, they never will be.

Growing Economic Disparities

Recent reporting by the *New York Times* reveals that America's Gini coefficient (representing the income or wealth distribution of a nation's residents), at about .045, is worse than Iran's.[11] In fact, the extremes that separate America's wealthiest from its poor are unmatched among advanced economies.[12] Racial disparities in wealth are especially pronounced in America. According to recent reporting by Inequality.org, for example,

> The billionaires who make up the Forbes 400 list of richest Americans now have as much wealth as all African-American households, plus one-third of America's Latino population, combined. In other words, just 400 extremely wealthy individuals have as much wealth as 16 million African-American households and 5 million Latino households.[13]

Not only are disparities in wealth between the races increasingly excessive, but so too are the nation's relative wealth trend lines across racial communities, which are also increasing, even for white versus minority Americans with the same levels of educational attainment. According to a *Washington Post* (28 September 2017) analysis,

> Despite gains in income and wealth, the economic chasm between black and Hispanic families and their white counterparts widened between 2013 and 2016—even when it comes to Americans with comparable levels of education, according to data released Wednesday by the Federal Reserve. . . . The median net worth of whites remains nearly 10 times the size of blacks'. Nearly 1 in 5 black families have zero or negative net worth—twice the rate of white families.

With so much of our nation's future political and economic fate depending on an increasingly multiracial population, these trend lines should be distressing to all Americans who care about the future of our nation. Demographers predict that by the midpoint of the current century more than half of the US population will be non-white. These disparities have real-life consequences not only for the people and communities of color who are so evidently disserved by this economy, but also for the longer term integrity of our national democracy and overall economy.

The Incredibly Shrinking Middle Class

Traditionally, America's strength has depended on upward mobility and a robust middle class. But today's middle class is stagnant, to the point where Canada now has a stronger middle class than we do.[14] In the 1970s, some 70 percent of Americans lived in middle-class neighborhoods; now only about 40 percent do. Increasingly, America's poor and working-class households face considerably fewer prospects for upward mobility than at any time in our country's recorded past. Indeed, as the *New York Times* (22 April 2014) recently reported,

> The struggles of the poor in the United States are even starker than those of the middle class. A family at the 20th percentile of the income distribution in this country makes significantly less money than a similar family in Canada, Sweden, Norway, Finland or the Netherlands. Thirty-five years ago, the reverse was true.

Increasingly, it seems, the very vitality of the American economy hinges on the purchasing and investment power of a relatively shrinking population of well-endowed individuals and families, who frankly cannot spend their money fast enough to fuel a recovery that would benefit working- and middle-class Americans. For this reason, significant structural impediments to a truly healing national economic recovery from the Great Recession are essentially built into our present political and economic outlook for the foreseeable future. This portends still further political and economic turmoil in America for years, and possibly even decades, to come.

The Limits of Hyper-capitalism

The problem is that the current concentration of wealth in our economy is simply too great to drive true down line prosperity sharing. As a mathematical proposition, let alone as a practical matter, the purchase of luxury goods and services by a relatively smaller and smaller group of high-end consumers can never be a prescription for broad-scale growth and upward mobility in an economy the size of America's. Such is the fallacy in logic behind the recent Trump tax cuts, which were not necessary for the economy given its recent acceleration at the time of the bill's passage.[15]

While touted by Republicans as a way to help middle-class families enhance their spending and saving power, in fact only a paltry 13 percent of the tax cuts made possible by the new legislation will actually benefit middle-class households, according to recent reporting by CNN based on analytics by the investment house Morgan Stanley; and fully 43 percent will benefit corporate shareholders in the form of stock buybacks and dividends.[16] As reported by Forbes, based on its analysis of congressional Joint Committee on Taxation data, $850 billion of the nearly $1.5 trillion price tag for the Trump tax bill will benefit businesses and corporations, rather than individuals and households.[17]

Even if our current consumer spending levels were able to sustain a semblance of economic growth and recovery for the masses, the very nature and direction of our contemporary economy effectively precludes more significant investments that would better serve the long-term common good. This is because, at its essence, our current production model is fundamentally geared to vanity consumption and an expectation of endless growth based on exponential human and environmental exploitation. It is not a sustainable model for solving people's and society's most pressing problems, from securing more affordable health care and housing to producing safer and more accessible energy and food products, to ensuring more adequate employment and care for our most vulnerable people. Nor is our current economic model one that can, over the longer term, adequately protect our natural environment from increasingly aggressive human development and carbon consumption. All of this makes our current economy and political system highly toxic and vulnerable.[18]

The Rising Costs of Inequality

It cannot be denied that inequality impacts our standard of living; this becomes more painfully manifest with each passing year. According to urban economy expert Richard Florida, wealth and income inequality in major American cities is now equivalent to levels of inequality in many of the world's poorest nations. According to Florida, for example, inequality in New York City is now similar to levels of inequality in Swaziland. In Los Angeles, it is equivalent to Sri Lanka; and in Miami, it is comparable to Zimbabwe.[19] Adding to the downward trend line in economic opportunity that we have seen in recent years, average American households have experienced significant asset losses over the past decade as a result of misguided economic policy favoring the super-wealthy.

Economist Aaron Pacitti has recently calculated the price tag of recent American economic decline stemming from the Great Recession at over $27,000 per household:

> The difference between actual GDP and its potential is what economists call the output gap. Using this measure, it is possible to calculate the monetary cost of a decade of economic stagnation. For each worker, the cost of the recession and slow recovery—the value of the output gap—was $2,722 per year, adjusted for inflation. That means that for the decade since December 2007, the average worker became $27,220 poorer in terms of the goods and services they could have purchased, or in terms of income.[20]

Institutionalized Racism's Expanding Footprint

There is also growing evidence that the disturbing, earlier reported increase in economic disparity by race is having an insidious impact on the nation's overall economic performance. This disparity has been growing for some time, according to research over recent years by leading political economists affiliated with such groups as the Insight Center for Community Economic Development, the Institute for Policy Studies and the Center for Global Policy Solutions. A recent study of the issues by the Institute for Policy Studies, entitled "The Road to Zero Wealth: How the Racial Wealth Divide is Hollowing Out America's Middle Class," found that,

The declining wealth of households of color is already taking a significant toll on the broader economy. The nation's overall median wealth decreased nearly 20% from 1983 to 2013 ($78,000 to $64,000)—a period when Black and Latino median wealth went down and White wealth slowly went up.[21]

Recent reporting by the W. K. Kellogg Foundation, moreover, underscores the significant opportunity costs to the entire nation resulting from racial disparities in the American economy. According to a foundation-supported study produced in 2013,

> . . . if the average incomes of minorities were raised to the average incomes of whites, total US earnings would increase by 12%, representing nearly $1 trillion today. By closing the earnings gap through higher productivity, gross domestic product (GDP) would increase by a comparable percentage, for an increase of $1.9 trillion today. The earnings gain would translate into $180 billion in additional corporate profits, $290 billion in additional federal tax revenues, and a potential reduction in the federal deficit of $350 billion, or 2.3% of GDP.[22]

In sum, the research shows that our nation is losing mightily and increasingly as a result of persistent institutionalized racism—both directly in terms of relative declining wealth and indirectly in terms of lost profits and revenues.

Increasing Housing Speculation and Abuses

Growing inequality is also promoting cut-throat practices in the nation's increasingly expensive housing markets with more and more dire impact on economically vulnerable populations of low wage earners, single women with children, families of color and immigrants. The rise of gig economy opportunities for landlords through transactional platforms such as Air B&B have added to the problem. But so too has the rise of "no cause" evictions, which have increasingly enabled landlords in high demand markets to seek ever-higher rents by ousting lower paying tenants, who are invariably uninformed of their rights and so are typically forced to seek more affordable alternatives in ever-more remote locations outside of our urban centers.

Making matters even more dubious in this context is the growing prevalence of distant, out of town corporate landlords behind these unfair and largely unreported practices. According to a recent report on the issues spearheaded by Derecka Mehrens of Working Partnerships USA and Silicon Valley Rising:

> . . . Since 2010, more than 2,200 'no cause' evictions have been reported in San Jose (rent controlled units are the only ones required to report such evictions). These kinds of evictions allow landlords to raise rents (including illegal rent increases in rent controlled units) and have enormous impacts on low-income families and communities. . . . It's possible that this is only the tip of the iceberg of no cause evictions, since... most such evictions go unreported. . . .
>
> The largest property owners in the city, those with forty or more rental units, own more than three quarters of all multi-family apartments. Small landlords . . . own only about one in every twenty apartments in the city. . . .
>
> . . . Of the over 6,000 companies who own properties in the city, only about 1,600 have a San Jose address . . . In fact, the five largest owners of apartments in San Jose are all based outside the city.[23]

Legalized Usury, Debtor Incarceration, Consumer Exploitation and Wage Theft

An additional disturbing sign of how far afield we have gone in this economy is the growing incidence of heavy-handed monetary and legal penalties, as well as hassles and abuses that increasingly victimize average people, consumers and workers in order for the wealthy and powerful to make still more money. The principal centers of gravity in this regard are unscrupulous payday lending institutions, the growing use of fees, fines and jail sentencing for small-scale debtors by local courts and the recent increase in overall consumer and worker exploitation we see in ways large and small across our entire economic system. All of these practices violate basic principles of fairness that have evolved since the mid-to-late twentieth century in response to earlier approaches that were finally (and most appropriately) deemed to be immoral. Such approaches ranged from institutionalized loan redlining and predatory lending in racial minority communities to systemic fraud in sales, contracting and worker compensation, as well as the widespread use of debtor prisons.

Payday Lending

One of the primary ways in which economic exploitation increasingly occurs in America is through the only very-loosely-regulated practices of payday lending institutions, which cater to vulnerable workers who otherwise do not have access to basic banking services. Over recent years, significant evidence has emerged concerning the exorbitant interest and fees that payday lenders charge their low-wage-earning and often uninformed consumers. The overwhelming majority of payday lending customers, in fact, are wage laborers who lack bank accounts and credit cards, for any number of reasons, but mainly because they are poor. Typically, these are undocumented immigrant day laborers or otherwise poor and under-educated American workers, often of color. Except for payday lending institutions, such workers have no other practical way to cash compensation checks for the sporadic work they are able to secure. And this is largely what gives payday lenders such extraordinary leverage over their consumers. According to a recent report on payday lenders by Consumerist,

> . . . the average payday borrower is not someone with a high-paying job. Only 4% of payday loans are made to consumers earning more than $60,000 per year. Meanwhile, more than two-thirds of payday borrowers have annual incomes below $30,000. The largest chunk of borrowers came from those making between $10,000 and $20,000 per year; this group accounts for nearly one-third of all payday loans. . . . More than half the borrowers in that largest group of borrowers

reported receiving some form of public assistance. Overall, nearly one-in-five payday borrowers fell into this category.[24]

Owing precisely to the economic vulnerability of payday lending clients, their capacity to repay their loans in full and on-time is often mitigated by variables in the marketplace over which they have no control. As a consequence, the incidence of delay or default in their repayment performance can be high. All too often, this serves as a justification for payday lenders to charge skyrocketing fees for late payments or loan modifications that typically re-up the loan amounts and exposure to risks for their clients, to the point literally where often borrowers can never get out of debt. According to the Consumerist analysis,

> . . . the median payday loan amount was $350 with the average being $392. . . . The median APR on a payday loan is 322%, with the average APR being slightly higher at 339%. . . .
>
> Payday loans are often thought of as 'two-week' loans, which aligns with the data's median term of 14 days. However, since the terms of these loans are often tied to the borrower's pay cycle, which can vary by employer and source of income, the average loan length is 18.3 days.
>
> And while payday loans are marketed as short-term solutions—get cash now, pay it back in two weeks—the CFPB found that over the course of 12 months, more than one-third of borrowers will take out between 11 and 19 payday loans. Fourteen percent of borrowers will take out 20 or more payday loans within this same time period. It's on these borrowers that payday lenders make the most money. . . . 76% of lenders' fees come from borrowers taking out at least 11 loans in a year. . . . The median borrower takes out 10 payday loans in 12 months and pays a total of $458 in fees on top of the original amount borrowed.
>
> One-quarter of borrowers paid at least $781 in fees over the course of 12 months.

In response to these clearly usurious practices, the Obama administration-appointed leadership of the Consumer Financial Protection Bureau issued a November 2017 requirement mandating payday lenders first to ascertain a prospective loan recipient's capacity to repay a given loan before proceeding to consider and process a loan application. However, the Trump Administration and Republican members of Congress have already moved to reverse it.

Court-Imposed Fines, Fees and Jail Terms

Another insidious way in which the current economy increasingly short changes the poor and otherwise vulnerable is through the expanding imposition of fees and fines for minor legal violations that are disproportionately imposed on poor people of color by local courts. Such violations mainly involve routine traffic tickets, failure to keep up with court-ordered child support payments and select property maintenance infractions. Recent reporting by multiple sources reveals that, when such orders are imposed on people who are unable to pay owing to limited income, they are increasingly jailed and made subject to additional financial penalties. In many instances, the imposed penalties and fees exceed the costs of the original violation. Over time, such practices have the impact of further unraveling the financial prospects of already poor people or, worse yet, criminalizing individuals for simple civil law infractions.

These are practices that should concern all of us. But the problem appears to be even more heinous than initially meets the eye. In fact, many states and municipalities are using these methods to pad their local budgets. PolicyLink published a study in May 2017 reporting that presently more than ten million individuals are facing fees and fines of more than $50 billion because of their involvement in the criminal justice system, mainly for lower level violations. As noted in PolicyLink's report,

The practice targets the most vulnerable communities, such as low-income people and children who are unwittingly pulled into various court systems through unlawful and biased policing tactics. Wide swaths of low-income communities' resources are being stripped away due to their inability to overcome the daunting financial burdens placed on them by state and local governments.[25]

Growing Consumer Exploitation

Recent years have seen additional disturbing economic abuses emerge at the expense of average Americans through corporate misconduct and unfair business practices. Once relatively well regulated, such practices are surprisingly commonplace nowadays and increasingly heavy handed.[26] On the one hand, unscrupulous businesses fleece unwitting consumers of their money in any number of ways: offering substandard goods or services they will not replace, misleading consumers on matters concerning their rights of recourse and/or indirectly enhancing their profits through price add-ons and fees that are not initially transparent. On the other hand, in each instance where consumers are subject to such treatment, the burden is increasingly on the victims to seek relief in the face of private-sector bureaucracies that are both significantly advantaged in terms of their resources and/or largely impenetrable when it comes to securing meaningful communication. In today's economy, it has become commonplace for aggrieved consumers to be subjected to impossibly long waits on customer service calls or in corporate review processes—in most cases only to gain a modicum of relief.

Few aggrieved consumers have the inclination or the means to pursue legal recourse, except in all but the most blatantly abusive cases. Frankly, many people, being too busy and preoccupied on more important fronts to stay the course, fail to achieve any fair resolution in these exchanges. As a result, the businesses and corporations that stiff average consumers are as likely as not to skate by with their profits fully in hand and without so much as even extending a meaningful apology to disaffected customers.

Recent years have seen especially egregious efforts to actively defraud vulnerable consumers—and especially elder Americans—in finance, healthcare and other areas of economic activity. CNBC recently reported that elder fraud now accounts for about $36 billion in the United States; and, according to a recent survey of the North

American Securities Administrators Association, the problem is growing. A 2017 Association study showed fully 30 percent of state securities regulators reporting increased incidents of elder abuse in their local financial and consumer markets.[27]

Some of the worst corporate abuses of consumer trust of the past several years have occurred in the banking sector, with major financial institutions being severely fined or otherwise punished by federal regulators for their misdeeds. In 2015, for example, Bank of America was forced to pay an historic penalty—over $16.5 billion in fines—for fraudulent business practices contributing to the 2008 home mortgage meltdown. More recently, Wells Fargo Bank was shown to have fraudulently falsified some 3.5 million bank and credit card accounts to grow its bottom line. The company was forced by the federal Consumer Financial Protection Bureau to pay nearly $150 million to settle a consumer class-action suit related to its malfeasance and has been subsequently sanctioned by the Federal Reserve Bank, which has capped Wells Fargo's access to growth capital until it corrects its corporate policies and practices.

Among the most common complaints cited by consumers involve auto sales according to recent reporting by Aimee Picchi of CBS News "MoneyWatch," based on data assembled by the Consumer Federation of America and North American Consumer Protection Investigators. Those sources cite everything from misrepresentations in sales to leasing disputes as significant recurring problems for consumers across the nation. The report built on a survey of 39 state and local consumer protection agencies in 23 states about the most common complaints they received during 2016.[28] In 2015, Volkswagen Corporation was found to have fraudulently sold more than 500,000 automobiles to US consumers knowing that their engines produced up to forty times the federally allowable volume of polluting exhausts into the atmosphere. The principal carcinogens implicated in the scandal contribute significantly to lung cancer in humans. Volkswagen has been fined or otherwise agreed to pay compensation totaling now over $10 billion to address the problem.[29]

Taken together, these and other fraudulent corporate practices reveal a growing culture of negligence and greed in contemporary private enterprise that increasingly threatens human and environmental interests from coast to coast.

Wage Theft

One of the most heinous and widespread abuses on the upswing across the American economy is employer wage theft that precludes society's most vulnerable workers from securing pay they are owed for time worked, both in terms of regularly scheduled hours and over-time. A February 2018 investigative report by *Politico* underscored the extent to which wage laws are grossly under-enforced. A large part of the problem is the under-resourcing of state regulatory and inves-tigative personnel. According to *Politico*'s review of the national field, six states were found to employ virtually no staff investigators to enforce standing wage laws. An additional 26 states employed fewer that ten investigators assigned to wage violation cases. Many states across the nation, moreover, including Alabama, Georgia, Louisiana, Mississippi, South Carolina and Tennessee, preclude legal filings against abusive employers through their local labor agencies, requiring aggrieved parties instead to file wage theft complaints with the US Department of Labor, which takes cases only selectively.[30]

The problem is exacerbated by the failure of the system to secure recovered funds owed to workers, even when such workers succeed in proving their claims of withheld back pay. Marianne Levine, author of *Politico*'s revealing report on these problems found that even when employers are ordered to pay back their workers by state agencies or courts, "more than 40 percent of the time the withheld wages still never make it back to the aggrieved workers." Largely as a result of such major failings in the system, Levine observes, most cases go unreported. Because of this, she estimates that "$15 billion in desper-ately needed income for workers with the lowest wages goes instead into the pockets of shady bosses."[31]

The injuries imposed on workers as a result of these violations and system shortcomings are not only to the low-wage individuals most directly affected. In fact, the resulting damage to families, com-munities and the larger economy is significant. As Levine observes in the above-referenced Politico exposé:

[The] failure to enforce the minimum hourly wage—$7.25 under federal law—and rules requiring higher pay for overtime distorts the economy, giving advantages to employers who break the law. It allows long-term patterns of abuse to take root in certain industries, especially restaurants, landscaping and cleaning. Advocates for lowest-wage workers describe families facing eviction and experiencing hunger for lack of money that's owed them. And, nationally, failure to enforce wage laws exacerbates a level of income inequality that, by many measures, is higher than it has been for the past century.[32]

Ignoring the Obvious at Our Own Peril

There are serious underlying structural problems in our economy and, if sweeping reforms are not forthcoming soon to reverse our current course, these problems will persist in our future. To be sure, modern American economy is characterized by its underlying fragility and volatility, despite the boastful claims of Donald Trump and ultra-conservatives. The White House and much of the business media enthusiastically advance claims of an emerging American economic renaissance under Trump's leadership, arguing that the fundamentals are all in place for a massive US rebound with annual growth rates approaching 4 percent.[33]

In reality, nothing could be further from the truth. There is evidence of even more serious economic problems on the horizon for America and the world. Recent reporting from credible financial industry sources, including Fidelity Investments and Dow Jones & Company's "MarketWatch," reveal multiple signs of weaknesses in the economy that could well produce another major downturn.[34] Moreover, when the next major economic recession arrives, its impact will not be limited to the poor and the vulnerable. In fact, as we saw in 2008-09, even comfortable middle-class families suffered significant losses. And there is little to suggest that the next downturn will not be as severe or worse. One need only observe recent stock market over-speculation and volatility to gain a measure of the still very real and ever-present risks that we face these days.

Between February 2 and 5, 2018, for example, the otherwise raging US stock market posted sequential trading losses of more than 650
and 1,100 points, respectively; that was, a total two-day value decline
of nearly 1,800 points. On February 5, 2018 alone, the Standard &
Poor's 500 index fell by more than 4 percent, erasing its earlier substantial gains for the year; the Dow Jones industrial average sank by
4.6 percent. The Dow's February 5 losses constituted the single largest,
one-day value decline in Wall Street history. While subsequent trading
helped to correct somewhat for these substantial declines, the underlying volatility of the market remains a point of concern for objective
observers of the American and global economies.

Indeed, during early 2018, numerous factors helped to increase
the volatility of financial markets, including but not limited to a
potential trade war with China and Europe over tariffs on imports,
growing inflation and interest rate pressures, as well as general signs
of weakness in American investment values. Owing to these and other
factors, by March 2018, even tech company stocks, the longtime
backbone of expanding market values, began to show unusual vulnerability in their market valuations. And many analysts have begun
to acknowledge the general sluggishness of major stock indices
extending beyond the tech space.[35] These and other indications have
convinced many informed observers that all is not as well as may
appear to be the case on the surface of things.

The Unwritten Rules of Modern American Political Economy

The increasingly unequal structure and benefits of the US and
global economies have been keenly assessed in recent years by
numerous progressive analysts, most notably the French economist
Thomas Piketty (author of the bestselling volume, *Capital in the 21ˢᵗ
Century* [2016]), former US Labor Secretary Robert B. Reich (author
of *Saving Capitalism: For the Many, Not the Few* [2015], among other
key works) and former Chief Economic Advisor to Vice President Joe
Biden, Jared Bernstein (*The Reconnection Agenda: Reuniting Growth
and Prosperity* [2015]). In addition, impressive reporting and analyses on issues related to America's increasingly problematic economy
have been produced over recent years by leading progressive policy

think tanks, including Demos, the Economic Policy Institute, and the Center for American Progress. But the latest work of the New York-based Roosevelt Institute, headed by Felicia J. Wong, has especially captured the underlying insidiousness of US economic policy when it comes to how it negatively impacts the vast majority of the American people. The Institute's recent volumes *Rewriting the Rules of the American Economy: An Agenda for Growth and Shared Prosperity* (produced by Nobel prize-winning economist Joseph E. Stiglitz, 2015) and *The Hidden Rules of Race: Barriers to an Inclusive Economy* (2017), offer particularly comprehensive and compelling analyses of the very real but typically masked ways in which private capital and wealth are produced and perpetuated at the expense of common people and communities.

At bottom, the Institute's evolving research underscores the fundamental causes of recent lackluster prosperity sharing and upward mobility for the vast majority of the American people—even in the context of record corporate profit-making. In the process, it reveals that these outcomes are neither incidental nor accidental. On the contrary, the diminishing opportunities most are experiencing in today's economy are deep, structural and entirely the product of policy choices that have been made over recent decades to benefit the wealthy few at the expense of the many. Because this is the case, the Roosevelt Institute's leadership argues, there are discernible things we can, and indeed must, do to correct our course. But to do so will require more progressive leadership and policy intentionality to move in a wholly different direction. Among the policy prescriptions for change urged by the Roosevelt Institute's team of experts are: substantial disinvestment from punitive criminal justice systems and policies in favor of massive new investments in under-resourced and asset poor communities; a robust enhancement of worker rights; adoption of universal healthcare coverage for all; widespread investment in child savings accounts and Baby Bonds to encourage asset accumulation for families that otherwise have no other means to achieve a modicum of economic agency; and widespread corporate and financial reforms to even the playing field for poor and middle-class workers and consumers. Many of these proposals are squarely complementary to and overlapping with the content of this book's next chapter, focused on emerging reform concepts in national economic policy and practice.

Joseph Stiglitz' analysis in *Rewriting the Rules of the American Economy*, furthermore, asserts that in order to overcome growing barriers to economic revitalization and prosperity sharing, two things have to happen simultaneously. First, we need to "Tame the Top." That is, we need to moderate and reform the current legal and regulatory rules of modern commerce and private wealth accumulation that over-privilege those who already substantially control society's investment capital. As we do that, in turn, we also need to "Grow the Middle." That is to say, we need to augment the opportunities for economic mobility available to working and middle-class Americans who are not as economically secure as they should be. In these coordinated ways, we can help level the economic playing field to create a better balance between the wealth we produce as a nation and its distribution across diverse income groups.

In the *Hidden Rules of Race: Barriers to an Inclusive Economy*, Wong and various experts affiliated with the Roosevelt Institute tackle the insidious mechanics of institutionalized bias in American systems that recreate and grow racial and other disparities in economic opportunity from one generation to the next. From the legal frameworks that govern the disposition of wealth and income distribution, to our systems of criminal justice, education and healthcare, and to our very system of democracy, the Institute's analysts found numerous examples of inequities in the core of our economy. Their conclusion is clear: without fundamentally altering the often hidden rules that allow long-embedded intergroup disparities to persist and grow over time, it will be virtually impossible to avoid unprecedented challenges to our democracy and way of life in the future. In summary, the Institute writes:

> Our framework argues that rules matter and having the power to write the rules matters. We argue that the economy is shaped by choices—choices determined by legal, regulatory, and expenditure policies, among other factors. In this way, the values and interests of the powerful (in terms of race, class,

gender, etc.) are baked into the economy and can circumscribe opportunities and outcomes for the less powerful.

When the rules are written to benefit those who already hold privilege and power, as they too often are, the incentives for preserving and reinforcing those rules increase, and more resources are devoted to shaping the rules in favor of the powerful. In this kind of 'rent-seeking' economy and society, short term gains for the privileged . . . are accompanied by long-term losses for the majority of individuals and for the economy as a whole.[36]

In effect, what the Roosevelt Institute's work reveals is that American policy is fundamentally wired to service the needs of the already wealthy and powerful, rather than the needy and the aspiring. This goes directly to the heart of human rights and Internet activist Heather Marsh's burning and ironic observation in her book, *Binding Chaos*, that our societal algorithms have gone haywire, focusing more now on serving those who already have, rather than those who still badly need the basics required to live a full and meaningful life.[37] Indeed, the core disconnects that increasingly define the modern age are manifest in the rapidly growing distances between the precious few who have access to society's political and economic benefits and the burgeoning many who do not. This is a fundamentally immoral, unnecessary and dangerous situation for us to find ourselves in.

Our Waning Social Contract: Where There Is No Justice, There Can Be No Peace

As in other Western industrial nations, the United States economy is the product of centuries-long thinking and practice in Democratic Capitalism, the roots of which date back to the Age of Enlightenment. From René Descartes to Jean-Jacques Rousseau and from Isaac Newton to John Locke, these early champions of Democratic Capitalism and science asserted a moral case for economic liberalism and notions of individual empowerment that set the stage for capitalism's robust growth across Europe and North America.

Descartes and Newton espoused both philosophical and practical notions of the individual's primacy in society and man's rightful command over nature. Rousseau and Locke articulated the earliest notions of the social contract and the concept that society and individuals could best harmonize their respective interests through democratic governance and free enterprise. These thinkers served as the precursors to subsequent figures, such as Adam Smith and John Stuart Mill, who further advanced the intellectual underpinnings of Democratic Capitalism as a major driver of world commerce and development.

Physicist and social commentator Fritjof Capra (1939-) has written that the impact of these figures on modern society was ultimately employed to advance policies and practices that helped to justify the widespread exploitation of people (by race, gender and class), as well as the exploitation of nature in service of the perceived good for the majority.[38] In essence, these ideas enabled the ruling powers of the day to rationalize exercising forceful dominion over certain classes of humanity and the natural world in the name of morality and the common good.

During the evolution of capitalism, the justification of its excesses often took on Christian religious notions of God's will. Ironically, although capitalism wrapped itself in morality, its earliest practitioners and their political sponsors ignored the free market's many subsequent transgressions. In America, under the banner of Manifest Destiny, these included, among other things, the subjugation of women and African slaves as chattel, the genocide of indigenous tribes, the taking of Mexican lands and various Caribbean and Asian territories for expansionist purposes, the general exploitation of wage laborers of all backgrounds, and the rampant exploitation of nature in the quest for development and profit.

Middle Stage Blips: The Limits of Exploitation and Paper Entrepreneurialism

Over time, as America developed into an industrial and later a post-industrial world power, we over-extended these exploitative aspects of our national political and business model. We graduated from classical capitalism and its general exploitation of human and natural capital in the process of producing basic goods and services, to a now even more highly accelerated form of capitalism that fuels growth by exploiting people and the natural world using high technology and financial capital. That is to say, we underwent a significant transition from classical capitalism to hyper-capitalism. Former US Labor Secretary Robert B. Reich assessed the earliest manifestations of this shift in his book *The Next American Frontier* (1983):

> In recent years, as America's professional managers [have proven to be] ill equipped to undertake the necessary shift from high-volume production to flexible systems, they have resorted to various ploys designed to maintain or increase their firms' earnings without new productive investment. "Paper entrepreneurialism" of this kind merely rearranges industrial assets. . . .
>
> . . . Paper entrepreneurialism is a version of scientific management grown so extreme that it has lost all connection with the actual workplace. Its strategies involve generating profits through the clever manipulation of rules and numbers that only in theory represent real assets and products. At its most pernicious, paper entrepreneurialism involves little more than imposing losses on others for the sake of short-term profits for the firm. The others are often members of the taxpaying public, who end up subsidizing firms that creatively reduce their tax liability. The others are sometimes certain of the firms' shareholders who end up indirectly subsidizing other shareholders. Occasionally, the others are unlucky investors, consumers, or the shareholders of other firms.[39]

As our economy came more and more to be built both on continued human and ecological exploitation, as well as the sort of "creative accounting" Reich critiqued in *The Next American Frontier*, we began to experience increasingly destabilizing political resistance from certain aggrieved groups by the middle to then end of the twentieth century. Recognizing the corrosive effects of these developments on our social contract—the implicit bargain that bonds society's haves and have-nots around the idea that those with power and privilege can only have such things to the extent they serve the needs of those who don't—we made various moves to correct the course of capitalist development. We incorporated women and various minority communities as property owners and voters. We granted expanded bargaining rights and workplace improvements to various worker groups. We introduced certain environmental protections in our public policy. And we made important new commitments to Americans with disabilities to facilitate their mobility and access in society and the economy.

Yet despite these efforts as a society and as a global community to establish more functional balances in these areas, our systems, institutions and leaders have continued to advance a model of political economy that remains almost universally favorable to the wealthy and powerful few, while being hardly responsive to the rest of us. We have also seen the recent continuing degradation of our global ecological systems in the form of planetary climate change, renewed efforts to expand extractive and polluting industries, and the destruction of growing numbers of animal species and natural habitats across the globe.[40]

Now, as the inevitable costs and limits of our emerging hyper-capitalistic reality become increasingly clear, we are beginning to see concerted efforts by the powerful and the privileged to reverse even the most basic mitigating policies intended to accommodate society's least advantaged interests. We are seeing a discernible, heightened renewal of racial and gender discrimination, an aggressive retrenchment of worker and consumer rights, a massive pulling back from the essential environmental protections required to sustain the planet, and renewed attacks on Americans with disabilities and other vulnerable groups.

The End of Work

As these retrenchments are occurring, society's most vulnerable populations and communities are facing still more daunting prospects related to the uncertain future of employment. Through evolving research on Artificial Intelligence (AI), growing uses of robotics and allied cost-cutting measures, the leading businesses and industries that drive our modern advanced forms of capitalism and political economy are increasingly eliminating whole categories of jobs and careers that once established the basis of sustenance and upward mobility for average people across America and the world. This problem was first identified in the mid-1990s by the ever-forward looking social commentator Jeremy Rifkin in his book, *The End of Work*.[41] In this highly prescient work, Rifkin described in stark terms the seismic labor market shifts that would ultimately result from expanding technology and economic efficiency:

The Information Age has arrived. In the years ahead, new, more sophisticated software technologies are going to bring civilization ever closer to a near-workerless world. In the agricultural, manufacturing, and service sectors, machines are quickly replacing human labor and promise an economy of near automated production by the mid-decades of the twenty-first century. The wholesale substitution of machines for workers is going to force every nation to rethink the role of human beings in the social process. Redefining opportunities and responsibilities for millions of people in a society absent mass formal employment is likely to be the single most pressing social issue for the coming century.[42]

Today, Rifkin's predictions are bearing out as growing numbers of American and other western corporations turn increasingly to job outsourcing and labor-replacing technology as competitive strategies to survive and maximize profits. Presently, US companies outsource jobs to nearly 15 million workers overseas who staff their foreign technology operations, call centers, back office administrative functions and manufacturing units.[43] In addition, corporate investments in and use of robotics and other forms of AI to advance their production processes and profitability are aggressively on the rise.

New tech finance companies, such as New York-based GlobalX, have been seeing robust growth as a result, building on the use of robotics-targeted Exchange Traded Funds to aggregate capital and profits for this rapidly emerging field of production and investment. In only the past two years, GlobalX has raised some $300 million in new market capitalization for robotics and other AI-related invest-ments.[44] And, as the *Financial Times* recently reported, it is not mere-ly US companies and workers that are implicated in the accelerating use of robots and AI in contemporary production processes:

> After growing at a compound rate of 17 per cent a year, the robot market will be worth $135 billion by 2019. . . . A boom is taking place in Asia, with Japan and China, which is in the early stages of retooling its manufacturing sector, accounting for 69 per cent of all robot spending.
>
> Although the amount of money flowing into a new robotics industry is still at a relatively early stage, all the lead indicators of the innovation economy are pointing up. Patent filings cov-ering robotics technology—one sign of the expected impact—have soared. According to IFI Claims, a patent research com-pany, annual filings have tripled over the past decade. China alone accounted for 35 per cent of robot-related patent filings last year—more than double nearest rival Japan.
>
> In another sign of the expected boom, venture capital invest-ments more than doubled last year to $587 million, according to research firm CB Insights.[45]

The prospect of robots replacing workers at a faster pace than we may be able to produce new jobs is real and daunting, though still not fully assessed by experts.[46] As a result of the emerging worldwide investment push towards new, non-human forms of production and efficiency, credible sources like CNN and TechRepublic report that nearly 40 percent of current US jobs are at risk of being replaced by technology over the coming fifteen years.[47] McKinsey & Company analysts reach a more conservative conclusion, estimating that by 2030 about 15 percent of the current job footprint in some 45 leading nations is likely to be lost owing to automation.[48] But even McKin-sey's projected lower level of impending job loss is substantial, if nothing is done now to mitigate the impact on affected workers and households. The practical and political implications of these numbers are unprecedented and profound.

The Increasingly Elusive American Dream

If western democratic capitalism ever really worked for a majority of the people who have lived by its rules over the centuries, contemporary evidence suggests that it no longer does. And sadly, as we have seen in this chapter, things are actually likely to get even worse during coming years, absent drastic changes. The social contract that enabled America to develop into the world's leading democracy and economy during the nineteenth and twentieth centuries no longer serves as a working framework for our future. In the past, Americans largely believed that if we all worked and saved hard enough, stayed out of legal and criminal troubles, and remained faithful to America's core values, there would be a fair reward in the form of opportunities to buy a nice home, send our kids to good schools and establish a comfortable retirement nest egg. This notion of America's promise was all-too-often highly attenuated for large numbers of diverse Americans over the course of our history; but until the early 1970s, the real life prospects for upward mobility were relatively more significant for all Americans, including racial and ethnic minority groups.[49] For too many Americans today, the essential promises of the American Dream are increasingly elusive, if not downright unattainable.

Our waning social contract reflects the failure of the past forty years of conservative and neoliberal politics in America. It is a signpost that our system and its leaders are no longer committed to establishing a fair and shared prosperity across our nation. It reveals that we are increasingly no longer "One nation, under God, indivisible, with liberty and justice for all," but rather a nation increasingly divided into ideological and economic camps whose differences are hard to imagine ever being reconciled. In this context, it is difficult if not impossible for growing numbers of our people—the growing majority, that is, that can never seem to get ahead—to feel a lived sense of justice. Rather, to a rapidly increasing number of us, it is self-evident that the only Americans who seem to be able to access justice in our nation today are those who can afford it or otherwise command it as a result of their political advantages.

It has often been said in poor and diverse communities, which are typically ground zero for the worst of society's hardships and inequities, that where there is no justice, there can be no peace.[50] Our society is increasingly wired to benefit only a select group of privileged individuals and families, much the way that colonial America was principally structured to produce wealth for a crown located a continent away. This is not a just and, therefore, not a sustainable situation. If it is not quickly and fundamentally addressed, there will be unfortunate consequences for all Americans with profound down line negative impact on much of the rest of the world.

Changing the Paradigm

During his first presidential bid, former President Barack Obama often reminded voters of the oft-cited saying, that the definition of insanity is doing the same thing over and over again and expecting different results. Objectively speaking, that would be an apt description of what has been happening often in America for decades when it comes to our economic policy-making. For decades our political and business leaders have been selling us a toxic formula of tax-, social spending- and regulatory cuts that have lined the wallets of a relatively small number of well-off business owners and investors while diminishing the overall economic standing and quality of life of average Americans. The cycle has become painfully predictable. Every decade or so, we experience a nasty recessionary setback, each one seemingly deeper and longer than the last one, and each one leaving more and more people behind. Yet, rather than seeking to address the fundamentals of our increasingly privilege-centric, boom and bust economy, the invariable prescription each time has been to further cut taxes, social spending and regulations. At each turn, such retrenchment has been followed by cuts in corporate re-investment and diminished benefits to workers, consumers and the larger public good. In the process, the capital assets of the wealthy have grown exponentially, to the point where a relative handful of US households now controls wealth exceeding the combined holdings of tens of millions of other American families.

In the process, our economy has been skewed to encourage expanded corporate concentration and rationalization at the expense of generating and sustaining greater numbers of locally-owned enterprises that are more responsive to grassroots consumer and community needs. This trend has multiple implications for the American economy and culture, especially as relates to the entrepreneurial values and traditions that have historically informed American business leaders. According to Derek Thompson, writing in *The Atlantic*, Entrepreneurship, as measured by the rate of new-business formation, has declined in each decade since the 1970s, and adults under 35 (a.k.a. Millennials) are on track to be the least entrepreneurial generation on record.

This decline in dynamism has coincided with the rise of extraordinarily large and profitable firms that look discomfortingly like the monopolies and oligopolies of the 19th century. American strip malls and yellow pages used to brim with new small businesses. But today, in a lot where several mom-and-pop shops might once have opened, Walmart spawns another superstore. In almost every sector of the economy—including manufacturing, construction, retail, and the entire service sector—the big companies are getting bigger. The share of all businesses that are new firms, meanwhile, has fallen by 50 percent since 1978.[51]

The hyper-capitalistic, pro-big business policies that govern our national production, moreover, have imposed nearly irreparable harm on our global environment, on our increasingly decimated urban and rural housing and job markets, and on our very spirit and integrity as a nation. After nearly half a century on this path, and facing clear and growing evidence that our present economic model is imploding, we badly need a new paradigm to guide our economic decision-making. It is time for a fundamental change in the way that we understand and manage our economic affairs. It is time to imagine a wholly new and better way forward for people and the planet. It is time to invest meaningfully in a sustainable social economy. The core elements of a sustainable social economy consist of an abiding respect for nature and the environment, an elevated attention to the needs of the poor and the vulnerable, a diminishment of materialistic values and pursuits in favor of more unifying and responsible productive priorities, and an alignment of laws and practices that can center these concerns in our public policy. These policy goals are entirely attainable in the coming years, if we are collectively committed to advance them.

In recent years, important concepts have emerged through the work of forward-thinking business and social thought leaders who have put their reputations and personal capital on the line to challenge our currently accepted means of creating and distributing wealth. For example, Paul Hawken, founder of the former high-end specialty garden shopping platform Smith & Hawken, advocated working towards a Restorative Economy in the early 1990s. His book *The Ecology of Commerce* (1993) established the core concepts and elements of such a new economy, including aligning profitability with expanded corporate social and environmental responsibility.[52] Former Morgan Stanley Managing Director John Fullerton has subsequently built on these ideas to advance the concept of a Regenerative Economy, an economic model that seeks to direct productive activities in close accord with the laws and sustainability needs of nature and local communities.[53] More recently, along similar lines, futurist Jeremy Rifkin has predicted the ascendance of a new Collaborative Commons by 2050 that will reset our economic center more in the direction of communitarianism and sharing, rather than individualism and competition.[54] Progressive leaders in Massachusetts have advanced the concept of the Solidarity Economy, one that is built on multicultural community-based visions and strategies leading to a more just, sustainable and democratic society.[55] And National Domestic Workers Alliance principal and intergenerational caregiving advocate Ai-jen Poo has recently joined forces with Riane Eisler and the Caring Economy Campaign to advance the concept of the Caring Economy, an economy focused on building living wage jobs, careers and human connections around the expanded provision of quality care to society's most vulnerable people.

Each of these thought leaders and the frameworks for a new economy they have advanced are helping to bring us closer to what is needed to ensure continuing human survival, evolution and harmony across the planet in the future. At the same time, a growing cadre of national and grassroots innovators are putting key elements of these frameworks in motion all across America. That work, in turn—much of which is highlighted in the next chapter—can help us all to achieve even more widespread benefits for America and the world than conventional capitalism has made possible over the past several centuries. It can help us ensure that progress and prosperity are more widely shared, more driven to the service and needs of all humanity and friendlier to nature and the planet.

Indeed, notions of the Collaborative Commons and of a more restorative, regenerative, solidarity-driven and caring economy—the essential elements of a sustainable social economy—are the templates upon which new economic decision-making must be based in the decades to come. This is the exciting future that awaits us. Let's turn now to what it looks like in action.

Endnotes

[1]Marsh, H., *Binding Chaos: Mass Collaboration on a Global Scale*, CreateSpace Independent Publishing Platform/Amazon, 2013.
[2]See Schuman, M., "Why Wages Aren't Growing," Bloomberg BusinessWeek September 21, 2017: https://www.bloomberg.com/news/articles/2017-09-21/why-wages-aren-t-growing.
[3]See Emmanuel, D., "A Bad Work Environment Can Be Bad for Your Health," CNN, August 22, 2017: https://www.cnn.com/2017/08/22/health/bad-work-environment-studies/index.html. Based on RAND Corporation study findings, Emmanuel reports that about three-fourths of American workers today experience excessive physical and emotional stress at their workplace, with half facing present or potentially dangerous working conditions and large numbers of women facing systemic workplace discrimination and sexual abuse.
[4]See "U.S. Home Prices Surge, Outpacing Wage Growth," *Los Angeles Times*, 26 December 2017: http://www.latimes.com/business/la-fi-home-prices-20171226-story.html, Soergel, A., "Even Americans Can't Afford the American Dream," *US News & World Report*, February 3, 2016: https://www.usnews.com/news/blogs/data-mine/2016/02/03/even-americans-cant-afford-the-american-dream and Imbert, F., "Cost of Living Is Increasingly Out of Reach for Low-Wage Workers," CNBC, August 31, 2015: https://www.cnbc.com/2015/08/31/cost-of-living-is-increasingly-out-of-reach-for-low-wage-workers.html.

[5]See El Issa, E., "2017 American Household Credit Card Debt Study," Nerdwallet, January 2018: https://www.nerdwallet.com/blog/average-credit-card-debt-household/. Nerdwallet's survey shows nearly a 5 percent increase in the number of US households with credit card debt over the past several years, with 43.9% of all households in December 2016, compared with 38.1% in December 2013. Nerdwallet's survey also found that "the average US household with revolving credit card debt carried a balance of $6,081 as of June 2017."

[6]See Cox, J., "What 'Are So Many of Them Doing'? 95 Million Not in Labor Force," CNBC, December 2, 2016: https://www.cnbc.com/2016/12/02/95-million-american-workers-not-in-us-labor-force.html and Cox, J., "US Unemployed Have Quit Looking for Jobs at a 'Frightening' Level: Survey," CNBC, June 8, 2016: https://www.cnbc.com/2016/06/08/us-unemployed-have-quit-looking-for-jobs-at-a-frightening-level-survey.html.

[7]See Smith, D. & Grad, S., "What's Behind the Dramatic Rise in L.A. County's Homeless Population," *Los Angeles Times*, 3 May 2017: http://www.latimes.com/local/lanow/la-me-homeless-rise-explainer-20170531-htmlstory.html.

[8]See Khazan, O., "The Link Between Opioids and Unemployment," *The Atlantic*, April 8, 2017at: https://www.theatlantic.com/health/archive/2017/04/joblessness-and-opioids/523281/.

[9]See Jayaraman, S., *Forked*, NY: Oxford University Press, 2016, p. 37.

[10]According to Blanco, O., "How America's Immigrant Workforce is Changing," CNN, May 26, 2017: http://money.cnn.com/2017/05/26/news/economy/immigration-snapshot/index.html, "Today, immigrants make up about 17 percent of the US labor force, and nearly one-quarter of those immigrants are undocumented. . . . Without the current rate of both legal and undocumented immigration . . . the total US workforce would shrink dramatically over the next 20 years."

[11]See Fu, L., "The Wealth Gap in the US is Worse than in Russia or Iran," *New York Times*, 1 August 2017: http://fortune.com/2017/08/01/wealth-gap-america/.

[12]See Sherman, E., "America Is the Richest, and Most Unequal, Country," *Fortune Magazine*, September 30, 2015: http://fortune.com/2015/09/30/america-wealth-inequality/.

[13]See "Wealth Inequality": https://inequality.org/facts/wealth-inequality/.

[14]See Leonhardt, D. & Quealy, K., "The American Middle Class Is No Longer the World's Richest," *New York Times* 22 April 2014: https://www.nytimes.com/2014/04/23/upshot/the-american-middle-class-is-no-longer-the- worlds-richest.html.

[15]See "Read the Letter," Responsible Wealth, United for a Fair Economy, 2017: http://www.responsiblewealth.org/read_the_letter.

[16]See Goldman, D., and J. Sahadi, "Only 13% of Business' Tax Cuts are Going to Workers, Survey Says," CNN Money, February 9, 2018: http://money.cnn.com/2018/02/09/news/companies/tax-cut-bonuses- buy-backs/index.html.

[17]See "Fact Checking Trump's Claim about the GOP 'Middle Class' Tax Cut," *Fortune Magazine*, November 6, 2017: http://fortune.com/2017/11/06/fact-checking-trumps-claims-about-the-gop-middle-class-tax-cut/.

[18]See Deneen, P. J., *Why Liberalism Failed*, 2018, New Haven: Yale University Press, 2018. Deneen asserts that advanced capitalism has begun to reach its natural limits, creating now counterproductive outcomes and diminished public confidence that are increasingly inclining towards the system's ultimate demise.

[19]See Fu, L., "The Wealth Gap in the U.S. is Worse than in Russia or Iran": http://fortune.com/2017/08/01/wealth-gap-america/.

[20]Pacitti, A., "The $27,000 Price Tag of Economic Stagnation and Political Polarization," Huffington Post, December 11, 2017: https://www.huffingtonpost.com/entry/the-27000-price-tag-of-economic-stagnation-and- political_us_5a2e9777e4b04e0bc8f3b6c1.

[21]See http://www.ips-dc.org/report-the-road-to-zero-wealth/.

[22]Turner, A., et al., *The Business Case for Racial Equity*, W. K. Kellogg Foundation, October 24, 2013: https://www.wkkf.org/resource-directory/resource/2013/10/the-business-case-for-racial-equity.

[23]See, "Cashing In on Renters," Working Partnerships USA/Silicon Valley Rising, 2017: http://wpusa.org/Publication/CashingInOnRenters.pdf.

[24]"The Average Payday Loan Borrower Spends More Than Half the Year in Debt to Lender": https://consumerist.com/2013/04/26/the-average-payday-loan-borrower-spends-more-than-half-the-year-in- debt-to-lender/.

[25]See Bastien, A., *Ending the Debt Trap: Strategies to Stop the Abuse of Court-Imposed Fines and Fees*, PolicyLink, March 2017. http://www.policylink.org/ sites/default/files/ending-the-debt-trap-03-28-17.pdf.

[26]Liese, D., "Edward Balleisen on the Long History of Fraud in America," Princeton University Press January 11, 2017: http://blog.press.princeton.edu/2017/01/11/edward-balleisen-on-the-long-history-of-fraud-in-america/. According to Balleisen, fraud has always been an element of American economic exchange; however, fraudulent corporate behavior has become more commonplace since the 1970s, often outpacing the capacity of public regulators to quickly correct it.

[27]See Grant, K.B., "$36 billion Might Be a Low Estimate for this Growing Fraud," CNBC/Personal Finance August 28, 2017: https://www.cnbc.com/2017/08/25/elder-financial-fraud-is-36-billion-and-growing.html.

[28]Picchi, A., "Here's the No. 1 Consumer Complaint in America," CBS News/MoneyWatch, July 27, 2017: https://www.cbsnews.com/news/heres-the-no-1-consumer-complaint-in-america/.

[29]Atiyeh, C., "Everything You Need to Know about the VW Diesel-Emissions Scandal," Car & Driver Magazine, October 24, 2017.

[30]Levine, Marianne, "Behind the Minimum Wage Fight, a Sweeping Failure to Enforce the Law," *Politico*, February 18, 2018: https://www.politico.com/story/2018/02/18/minimum-wage-not-enforced-investigation-409644.

[31]"Behind the Minimum Wage Fight, a Sweeping Failure to Enforce the Law."

[32]"Behind the Minimum Wage Fight, a Sweeping Failure to Enforce the Law."

[33]See Johnson, S., "Trumponomics Is Failing on Growth," Project Syndicate (The World's Opinion Page), January 31, 2018: https://www.project-syndicate.org/commentary/trump-us-economic-growth-2017-by-simon-johnson- 2018-01 and Lawler, J., "Trump Adviser Predicts 4 Percent Growth Next Year With Tax Cuts in Place," December 8, 2017, Washington Examiner at: http://www.washingtonexaminer.com/trump-adviser-predicts-4-percent-growth- next-year-with-tax-cuts-in-place/article/2642955.

[34]See Vlastelica, R., "Trouble Ahead? What 4 Recession Indicators Say about the Economy," MarketWatch, January 2, 2018: https://www.marketwatch.com/story/trouble-ahead-what-4-recession-indicators-say-about-the-economy-2017-12-28, as well as "Economic Check-In: Clouds on the Horizon," (featuring an interview with Lisa Emsbo-Mattingly, Fidelity's director of asset allocation research), August 11, 2017, Fidelity Viewpoints at: https://www.fidelity.com/viewpoints/market-and-economic-insights/economic-outlook-august-2017.

[35]See Gaudiano, A. M., "The Stock Market's New 'Wall of Worry' Is Built on Inflation and Rate Fears," MarketWatch, February 19, 2018: https://www.marketwatch.com/story/the-stock-markets-new-wall-of-worry-is-built-on-inflation-and-rate-fears-2018-02-17 and McQueeny, R., "Stock Market Today, March 14: Dow Slumps on Trade War Woes," Zacks, March 14, 2018: https://www.zacks.com/stock/news/295669/stock-market-today- march-14-dow-slumps-on-trade-war-woes.

[36]Flynn, Andrea, Dorian T. Warren, Felicia J. Wong and, Susan R. Holmberg, *The Hidden Rules of Race: Barriers to An Inclusive Economy,* NY: Cambridge University Press, 2017.

[37]*Binding Chaos: Mass Collaboration on a Global Scale*, CreateSpace Independent Publishing Platform/Amazon, 2013.

[38]See Capra, F., *The Tao of Physics*, Boulder: Shambhala Publications, 1974; *The Turning Point*, NY: Bantam Books, 1982; and *The Web of Life*, NY: Anchor Books/Doubleday, 1986.

[39]Reich, R. B., "The Next American Frontier," *The Atlantic* (March 1983): 43-58: https://www.theatlantic.com/past/docs/issues/83mar/reich.htm, as well as Reich, R. B., *The Next American Frontier*, NY: Times Books, 1983, pp. 140-141.

[40]For a current overview of the nature and depth of these disturbing trends, see "Rate of Environmental Damage Increasing across the Planet but Still Time to Reverse Worst Impacts," United Nations Sustainable Development Goals, United Nations, May 19, 2016: http://www.un.org/sustainabledevelopment/blog/2016/05/rate-of-environmental-damage-increasing-across- planet-but-still-time-to-reverse-worst-impacts/.

[41]See Rifkin, J., *The End of Work: The Decline of the Global Labor Force and the Dawn of the Post-Market Era*," NY: Tarcher/Putnam, 1995.

[42]*The End of Work*, p. xv.

[43]See Amadeo, K., "How Outsourcing Jobs Affects the U.S. Economy," The Balance, March 30, 2017: https://www.thebalance.com/how-outsourcing-jobs-affects-the-u-s-economy-3306279.

[44]See Archer, S., "A Fund Betting on Robots and AI is Crushing It—and It's Targeting Millennial Investors (BOTZ)," Business Insider, August 16, 2017: http://markets.businessinsider.com/news/stocks/robots-and-artificial- intelligence-etf-is-crushing-it-and-replicating-its-returns-is-easy-2017-8-1002262492.

[45]See Waters, R. & Bradshaw, T., "Rise of the Robots is Sparking an Investment Boom," *Financial Times*, May 2, 2016: https://www.ft.com/content/5a352264-0e26-11e6-ad80-67655613c2d6.

[46]Telephone interview with Annette Bernhardt, director of the Low-Wage Work Program at the UC Berkeley Labor Center and a senior researcher at the UC Berkeley Institute for Research on Labor and Employment, March 22, 2018.

[47]Petroff, A., "US Workers Face Higher Risk of Being Replaced by Robots. Here's Why," CNN/Money, March 24, 2017: http://money.cnn.com/2017/03/24/technology/robots-jobs-us-workers-uk/index.html and Heath, N., "Why AI Could Destroy More Jobs than It Creates, and How to Save Them," TechRepublic, (circa 2013): https://www. techrepublic.com/article/ai-is-destroying-more-jobs-than-it-creates-what-it-means-and-how-we-can-stop-it/.

[48]Manyika, J., et al., *Executive Summary: Jobs Lost, Jobs Gained: Workforce Transitions in a Time of Automation*, McKinsey Global Institute, McKinsey & Company, December 2017: https://www.mckinsey.com/~/media/McKinsey/Global%20Themes/Future%20of%20Organiza-

tions/What%20the% 20future%20of%20work%20will%20mean%20for% 20jobs%20skills%20and%20wages/MGI-Jobs-Lost-Jobs-Gained- Executive-summary-December-6-2017.ashx.

[49]See Hilger, N., "How Has U.S. Intergenerational Mobility Changed Since 1940?," World Economic Forum Agenda, July 20, 2015: https:// www.weforum.org/agenda/2015/07/how-has-us-intergenerational-mobility- changed-since-1940/. According to Hilger, the "post-1940 gains in intergenerational mobility were economically large. Back-of-the-envelope calculations suggest that the educational gains of poor children implied by the increase in relative intergenerational mobility may have raised aggregate annual earnings growth over the 1940–1980 period by 0.125–0.25 percentage points. These gains are reminiscent of the gains in allocative efficiency from reductions in occupational barriers facing women and minorities after 1960."

[50]This widely repeated quotation has been attributed to multiple sources ranging from the late civil rights icon Dr. Martin Luther King, Jr. to Nation of Islam principal Louis Farrakhan.

[51]"America's Monopoly Problem: How Big Business Jammed the Wheels of Innovation," October 2016: https://www.theatlantic.com/ magazine/archive/2016/10/americas-monopoly-problem/497549/.

[52]See Hawken, P., the Ecology of Commerce, NY: HarperCollins/Business.

[53]See Fullerton, J., Regenerative Capitalism: How Universal Principles and Patterns Will Shape Our New Economy, Capital Institute, April 2015: http://capitalinstitute.org/wp-content/uploads/2015/04/2015Exec Summary4-14-15.pdf.

[54]See Rifkin, J., The Zero Marginal Cost Society: The Internet of Things, The Collaborative Commons, and The Eclipse of Capitalism, NY: St. Martin's Press, 2014.

[55]Loh, P. & Jimenez, S., Solidarity Rising in Massachusetts: How a Solidarity Economy Movement Is Emerging in Low-Income Communities of Color, Boston: Solidarity Economy Initiative, 2017.

CHAPTER 5
New Pathways Towards a Sustainable Social Economy

I think this is a moment of a lot of possibilities, and openings.
. . . [We] are going to create a new economy, an economy
[where] everyone works, everyone counts and everyone contributes.

—Ai-jen Poo

The only practical and intelligent response to the vagaries of
hyper-capitalism, recounted in the prior chapter, is to rethink the
essential organizing foundations of our current economy, and all of
the informing policy logic and machinery that has supported it over
recent decades. We will not very likely find our way to the solutions
and outcomes concerned activists and observers seek by merely pursuing some modified or mitigated version of the path we are presently on. On the contrary, if people and nature are to have any real hope
of surviving the twenty-first century, we will need to substantially
redefine what economic success means and establish a whole new
framework of policy and practice in support of a far more equitable
and sustainable approach. To those ends, in turn, we will have to
organize and fight hard for fundamental policy changes that accelerate and encourage, rather than forestall and foreclose, the advancement of new and better ways to produce goods and services, protect
the planet, compensate workers and share prosperity.

It is challenging for most of us to imagine what economic activity might look like in a wholly-revised political economic context.
Some will logically worry whether the kind of change that is advo-

cated here can actually work. But, gratefully, there is an emerging body of new economic innovation and modelling that is already demonstrating highly positive results and possibilities for more widespread application. We need only follow the pathway leading logically from this work to find our best way forward. The focus of this chapter is thus to bring to the surface some of the leading exemplars in this emerging space with an eye to encouraging their replication and scaling in ways that can help ensure a far more sustainable and just economy. At the end of the day, it is as the leading domestic-worker advocate Ai-jen Poo has wisely asserted: we need to create an economy where everyone works, everyone counts and everyone contributes.

We are dramatically far away from such a goal in today's political economy, and we're getting farther and farther away with each passing year. We must do better, and we can. There is an emerging generation of new wealth- and value-producing enterprises on the horizon that are poised to establish a better pathway forward, from recent major developments in social-responsibility investments to green-economy innovations and evolving social-enterprise breakthroughs. But in order to fully benefit from these positive developments, progressive leaders and activists must fight to ensure that supportive policies are put in place soon to accelerate their replication, scaling and success. It is essential that we start from the strengths and assets we already have at our command in the following models to pursue the pathway forward that we need to be on.

Prosperity: New Models of Business for the Common Good

In 2017, Pedram Shojai, known to many as the Urban Monk, produced and hosted an important feature-length film entitled "Prosperity."[1] The film features various private companies that are emerging as leaders in their respective industries as a result of their commitment to environmental and social responsibility: including CookFox Architecture, Guayaki, Seventh Generation, Thrive Markets and Whole Foods. Recognizing, as this book does as well, that our current economic regime is increasingly over-inclined to value money and privilege over people, the environment and quality of life, Shojai raises important questions about our current way of doing things and about the growing costs of privileging money and things over life itself and enduring communal values. In a promotional trailer for the film "Prosperity," Shojai shares the following penetrating observations:

> The word 'currency' implies flow. Flow of what? Wealth? Possessions? Security? Power? How much of our precious lives do we spend pursuing . . . money? How many heartbeats do we trade for this stuff? . . . Money is useful as a medium of exchange and we all need it to live in the modern world. But our notion of prosperity has become too narrow: simply an accumulation of wealth. . . . All at what cost? Our health? Our environment? Our families? Our happiness?[2]

Indeed, there are many important questions like these to be asked about our current predicament; that is, that the very nature of our political economy is working for fewer and fewer people and creating more and more political and environmental challenges for the future. Companies like those featured in Shojai's film are helping in important respects to show us a better way forward through the fusing of environmental stewardship, social problem solving and profit-making. In the process, these and other environmentally and socially conscious companies are increasingly providing their workers with a living wage, quality working conditions and meaningful benefits.[3]

Various associations of socially and environmentally responsible businesses, such as the Social Venture Network, Business for Social Responsibility, B-the-Change and the Business Alliance for Local Living Economies (BALLE), have emerged over recent years as institutional vehicles for promoting and supporting this approach to commerce on a regional, national and global scale. At the same time, vital new activist and field organizing networks have formed as well to hold larger corporations and businesses more accountable to social and environmental responsibility aims, such as the California-based Greenlining Institute and the Boston-based United for a Fair Economy. Through conferences, public information and viral sharing efforts, direct technical assistance to forward-looking businesses and communities, networks like these are helping to change the possibilities and incentives for profit- making entities to shape a better world.

Progressive leaders and activists who are committed to the common good need to join and support these efforts much more vigorously in our quest for environmental and social advancement. By advocating aggressively for more businesses to operate at the highest (rather than the lowest) possible levels of attention to our issues, we can help to usher in a new age of business and commercial conduct that is attentive to the needs of humanity and the planet while also being profitable. There are many allied arenas in which we must become more active to achieve these outcomes, covering topical concerns ranging from tax and regulatory policy to local and regional planning and corporate governance. And there are now a growing number of opportunities we should support to promote corporate models and practices that better serve humanity and the environment. These include efforts to elevate new models in sustainable production and allied business ethics, worker ownership and living wage compensation opportunities, employee benefits, workplace culture, consumer responsiveness and product and service safety across all businesses and industries. By extension, the work ahead of us also involves the growing need to move businesses more intentionally to advance workers' growth, economic opportunity and physical security, as well as family benefits, such as paid family leave for emergencies and subsidized child care. It also involves advocating for meaningful corporate engagement in community problem-solving and philanthropy. Among the most powerful of emerging frameworks around which to build going forward are those related to developing far-reaching green economy business alternatives, scaling social- and worker-owned enterprises, and advancing collective impact models that guide capital more intentionally to positive and profitable social and environmental returns.

Building Towards a Green Economy

One of the most important transitions presently taking shape in our contemporary economy is the slow but steady recognition that global climate change is indeed very real and threatening, and that business and corporate enterprises that advance their work with an eye to environmental responsibility can both do well and do good in this evolving context. At the heart of the matter is the opportunity and the need to build towards a Green Economy that can at once remediate growing social, economic and environmental woes by converting our presently exploitative and extractive system of production and resource deployment to one more supportive of humanity and resource sustainability. An especially important call to action to accelerate the modern economy's development along these lines was offered by social justice advocate Van Jones in his book *The Green Collar Economy* (2008). Jones makes the case for change in the following compelling terms:

The world economy and the polar ice caps are both melting down. The global recession is bowling over investments and battering down job prospects. The impacts of global warming are imperiling our forests, our farmland, and our future. There is no place to hide—from either the economic crisis or the ecological threat. Here and all around the world, humanity faces an unprecedented double danger on a massive scale.

The solution is challenging but straight forward: we must create a new 'green collar economy'—one that will create good, productive jobs while restoring the health of our planet's living systems. By taking bold action, we can turn these two terrifying breakdowns into a single, comprehensive breakthrough.[4]

Today, evidence is mounting that private businesses and venture capitalists are indeed moving in a better direction, quietly reallocating their investments to burgeoning new opportunities in the emerging Green Economy. Little by little, this is having a favorable impact. According to recent reporting by CNN, for example, as of 2017, new jobs in the solar energy industry are being produced at nearly twenty times the growth rate of the overall economy.[5] Moreover, according to the Natural Resources Defense Council, US jobs in the clean energy space have recently surpassed the total number of employment opportunities in the conventional fossil fuel industry.[6] And a 2016 Booz Allen study of the green building sector conducted for the US

Green Building Council showed that green construction jobs now make up more than one-third of the entire US construction sector, accounting for nearly $200 billion in annual labor earnings.[7]

These are not small and unimportant developments. On the contrary, they reflect real and significant movement towards the more socially and environmentally responsible economy all progressives seek. But notwithstanding their promise and even the fairly significant pace of movement towards more responsible production models of late, the sad reality is that without more active and supportive public policy and accelerated investment in this space, we are simply not currently moving fast enough in the right direction for it to finally make the difference we need it to. Writing recently in *Rolling Stone Magazine*, environmental activist Bill McKibben sought to impress the timeliness of action that must be taken:

If we don't win very quickly on climate change, then we will never win. That's the core truth about global warming. It's what makes it different from every other problem our political systems have faced. [Unlike other issues], the problem with climate change [is] it won't stand still. . . .

There are plenty of tipping points: The Amazon, for instance, appears to be drying out and starting to burn as temperatures rise and drought deepens, and without a giant rainforest in South America, the world would function very differently. In the North Atlantic, "we're ahead of schedule with the slowdown and potential collapse" of the giant conveyor belt that circulates warm water toward the North Pole, keeping Western Europe temperate. It's tipping points like these that make climate change such a distinct problem: If we don't act quickly, and on a global scale, then the problem will literally become insoluble.[8]

The reality is that we do not have the luxury of waiting for a more sustainable and conscientious business model for our times. We must change and we must do so immediately. Fortuitously, it is both technologically and practically feasible to make this shift happen over the coming several decades. According to McKibben and other experts, the know-how, the platforms and the financing mechanisms needed to convert to a largely self-sustaining economy exist. What is still lacking is the political will to force the change we need through our various public and economic policies. Progressive leaders and activists of all kinds need to come together around aggressive organizing and mobilizations intended to force such change during the coming months and years. Because it is no lie to assert that the very future and survival of our respective families and communities fundamentally depend on our doing so.

Given that the American economy is dominated by private enterprise, the first order of change that has to occur must focus on the corporate and small business sectors.[9] It is essential that progressives push forward aggressively and collectively to compel businesses and corporations to help stem (and ultimately reverse) the current threat of global environmental catastrophe. To encourage more aggressive course correction in the traditional private economy, activists, consumers and shareholders need to put greatly expanded pressure on major corporations, forcing them to make their production processes more socially and environmentally friendly. Tax and regulatory reforms must be designed to discernibly reward corporations and businesses that demonstrate sustainability leadership, while subjecting those that don't to increased cost and competitive pressures.

But beyond these growing imperatives for progressive community organizing and activism in the traditional private economy, there is also pressing need for those who seek greater environmental responsibility from corporations to actively support and help scale emerging alternative business and investment models, like those made increasingly possible by progressive social entrepreneurs and social venture investors. Through the efforts of such pioneering change agents, it is possible to envision forthcoming breakthroughs leading to more eco-friendly production, socially responsible investment and good jobs. The more successful we can make these efforts, in turn, the faster we will likely see larger players in the economy begin to adopt and scale resulting innovations from the social sector in order to remain competitive, control costs and avoid public backlash for bad corporate citizenship. We can make all of this happen, if we are unwaveringly committed to doing so over the coming years.

Encouraging Worker-Owned and Social Enterprise

Among the most promising vehicles we can look to as a means of advancing environmentally and socially responsible business and industry are worker-owned and social enterprises. Worker-owned enterprises, such as cooperatives, and social enterprises that profit share with their employees are not new, per se, but until recently in America such enterprises have been relatively exceptional and overlooked by most conventional investors and the business media. Now they appear to be increasingly in vogue, given the multiple bottom line benefits (economic, environmental and social) that they are producing. In 2015, *The Atlantic* surveyed worker ownership in the United States, making the following observations:

> Nationally, there are 300 "democratic" workplaces collectively employing more than 3,500 people. . . .
>
> There are many different types of cooperatives. There are consumer cooperatives (such as New York City's Park Slope Cooperative); producer cooperatives (such as Florida's Natural Growers); multi-stakeholder cooperatives, which are democratically governed by workers, consumers, and producers, or some combination thereof; and there are worker cooperatives like Red Rabbit [an Austin, TX donut shop], which are equally owned and democratically governed by workers.[10]

While the present scale of this emerging field of economic activity—about $400 million in annual revenues, with some 8,000 workers employed in 2018[11]—remains small, the rate of increase has been highly impressive over the past few years. If companies that offer Employee Stock Ownership Plans (ESOPs), such as Costco, are also included in the mix, the number of US businesses using varying forms of worker equity participation now exceeds 10,000 and the number of workers implicated surpasses 14 million.[12] Owing to this trajectory and the promise of still more substantial development to come, the US

Census Bureau recently approved the inclusion of a new question set in its periodic field surveys to track the growth and development of worker-owned enterprises.

Worker-owned enterprises are set to expand significantly—possibly exponentially—in future years, fueled by the efforts of major cities and states looking for new ways to bolster local employment, promote neighborhood revitalization and augment tax revenues in a time of growing economic uncertainty. To those ends, Boston has included the development of worker cooperatives as an important goal in its long-range municipal plan to 2030. And New York City has recently committed more than $2 million in new public funding to develop and network its growing community of worker-owned enterprises. In 2015, California, which boasts the nation's largest state economy and number of active cooperative enterprises, enacted important new legislation to streamline the legal framework for establishing additional co-ops in its jurisdiction.

The essential driver underlying the recent spike in interest in cooperative enterprise is the growing desire among common people for expanded job security in uncertain times, more environmentally and socially responsible consumption and an alternative to recent economic concentration and dislocation. As it turns out, this form of enterprise by its nature singularly addresses such concerns by tending to increase employees' control over their economic fate, support local economic and community dynamism and other benefits to the larger society. As a result, given the failures of the current political economy across the planet, cooperative enterprises are likely to benefit.

Michelle Chen, writing in *The Nation*, has underscored the need for expansion of this form of enterprise:

> In an increasingly precarious economy, advocates push worker ownership as a pathway to restore equity and control to labor. Co-ops can boost career mobility and seed homegrown job opportunities, while communities benefit from an ownership structure that keeps capital reinvested locally, not exploited or outsourced to faceless corporate chains.[13]

While worker-owned enterprises, and especially those with a discernible environmental and/or social mission—remain exceptional in the US economic landscape, they are increasingly active in such industries as recycling, organics and home health care. The following are leading examples of worker-owned enterprises in each of these sectors. Looking ahead to the future, their proven successes should be amplified by both forward-looking investors and consumers, as well as replicated wherever possible across our national economy.

Recycling: Recology

Recology is a San Francisco-based waste management company that employs about 3,000 workers across a large swath of the western United States on revenues of nearly $1 billion annually. The firm's headquarters oversees more than 45 operating companies that provide integrated services to nearly 750,000 residential customers and more than 100,000 commercial customers in California, Oregon and Washington. Recology, which is 100 percent employee-owned, consciously strives to establish itself as a sustainable alternative to traditional waste management practices that depend on toxic, gas-emitting landfills to process and store trash. By comparison, Recology favors a closed-loop ecosystem, which is designed to ensure that no activity creates additional impact on the environment or resource depletion. Thus, rather than focusing on transferring garbage from a given neighborhood to a municipal landfill (where much reusable material is lost and increased environmental pollution is guaranteed), Recology focuses instead on sorting trash items for mass recycling. As it does so, it helps to reduce the carbon footprint required to meet expanding consumer and societal needs.

Recology's corporate goal of "Zero Waste" is to eliminate waste as we know it altogether. It uses various smart technologies and strategic alliances to advance its work and mission, including Optical Sorting (which tracks with and separates various recycling contents using infrared sensor technology), Negative ASP Composting (which uses biofilters to enhance and expedite compost processing), methane-based gas conversion to electricity (which draws on state-of-the-art landfill gas capture technology) and back-end collaborations with select business and government partners who purchase the company's recycled products and electricity. In addition, Recology uses products that it gleans from its recycling process—such as paints, cork and glass—to support its own internal building maintenance and operations; and it also partners with community artists and residents across its service geographies to employ portions of its products in public works and exhibitions, and to advance civic education on issues related to energy renewability and environmental sustainability. Recently, the company has been investing significantly in new fleets of trucks and street sweepers that are run on biodiesel in a more efficient and environmentally friendly way than conventional analogs.

As a result of its commitment to "Zero Waste," Recology has recently achieved the highest landfill diversion rate in the country through a collaboration with the City of San Francisco, which in 2009 created a Mandatory Recycling and Composting Ordinance. Recology is also presently active as a leading waste management partner to various other western cities and towns, including among others Santa Rosa, Portland and Seattle. But Recology has also spread to various rural communities and small towns in its three-state service area. In addition, the company has developed numerous eco-friendly, waste-recycled custom compost and landscape products for sale to organic farmers, gardeners and landscape professionals. Finally, it has developed a consulting service that assists farmers and other growers, who have found that the compost produced by Recology offers a viable alternative to using synthetic fertilizers.

The recent decision by China to cease allowing all new imports of foreign recyclable and solid waste materials beginning in 2017 has temporarily shaken the US waste management industry, which until now has been able to rely on a solid demand for its products and technologies from the fast-growing Asian market. The immediate effect of China's new approach is expected to risk a significant and decisive setback for the US recycling industry. According to Christine Cole, writing in *Scientific American*,

> The impact of this will be far-reaching. China is the dominant market for recycled plastic. There are concerns that much of

the waste that China currently imports, especially the lower grade materials, will have nowhere else to go. [. . .] Last year, the US exported 1.42m tons of scrap plastics, worth an estimated US$495m to China.[14]

The precise effects China's decision will have on American recycling firms like Recology or the overall US recycling industry are not yet fully clear, but one upside of this sudden—and certain to be painful— industry shift is an emerging focus on possible ways to significantly grow US domestic market demand for recycled materials and products. That is to say that, instead of seeking foreign export alternatives to China for our vast and growing societal waste, perhaps the better course would be to aggressively develop our domestic market for recyclables and allied products and services. Over time, doing so could serve as a boon to US employment, especially in such fields as structural and landscape engineering, agriculture, manufacturing, transportation, communications and energy. Recycled plastic can be processed into chemicals, as well as fuels for transportation and aviation, and into food packaging, among many other products.

Moving in this direction could be a game changer in America, considering how much waste we produce as a nation and how little capacity the world has to manage it all. If more environmentally and socially responsible, worker-owned companies like Recology could be supported through facilitating local, state and national policy incentives, new demand could be created to employ potentially hundreds of thousands if not millions of American workers in good and rewarding jobs that pay well, offer meaningful benefits and better serve the common good. And, as importantly, both as a nation and as a world we could make substantial headway addressing and ultimately reversing the growing dangers currently posed by over-production and toxic waste dumping and mismanagement.

Recology's success is attributed in large measure to its employee-driven leadership and cooperative ownership model. Because Recology is 100 percent employee-owned, its workers have a heightened sense of commitment to the company, its goals and customer satisfaction. The very success of the company and its employees is because of its responsiveness to the local communities and regions it serves, not to shareholders, and many company managers and employees are deeply invested in those communities.

Organics: Evergreen Cooperatives

One of the most interesting and promising models in worker-owned enterprise is the Evergreen Cooperative Initiative (ECI), which in recent years has developed highly innovative, job-generating social enterprises in organics and community-based weatherization and laundry services; it also operates a stand-alone for-profit business consulting service. Launched in 2008 by a group of leading Cleveland-based institutions — including the Cleveland Foundation, the Cleveland Clinic, University Hospitals, Case Western Reserve University and the municipal government — ECI seeks to create living-wage jobs in six low-income neighborhoods that have a median household income below $18,500, in an area known as Greater University Circle. A supporting Evergreen Cooperative Development Fund has been created to serve as a capital investment vehicle to fuel these and allied activities undertaken by ECI, with contributing investors and advisors now including the Cleveland Foundation, Shorebank Enterprise Cleveland, the Ohio Employee Ownership Center at Kent State University, the Democracy Collaborative of the University of Maryland, and the National Development Council.

ECI was developed to create an economic breakthrough in Cleveland. Rather than promoting a trickle-down strategy, it focuses on economic inclusion and building a local economy from the ground up. Rather than offering public subsidies to induce corporations to bring what are often low-wage jobs into the city, the ECI strategy calls for catalyzing new businesses that are owned by their employees. Rather than concentrate on workforce training for employment opportunities that are largely unavailable to low-skill and low-income workers, the Evergreen Cooperative Initiative first creates the jobs and then recruits and trains local residents to fill them. ECI pays its worker-owner employees a living wage and provides extensive supports to facilitate their career development. All of this stems from ECI's informing vision to encourage community wealth-building that increases asset ownership among needy individuals and communities, strengthens the municipal tax base, prevents financial resources from "leaking out" of the area and ensures local economic stability and vitality.

At the heart of ECI's agenda are the following four mission-driven aims:

- Promote, coordinate and expand economic opportunity for low-income individuals through a growing network of green, community-based enterprises
- Promote community stabilization and revitalization of the divested neighborhoods of Greater University Circle and similar areas of Cleveland, Ohio
- Promote public understanding of cooperative principles and how cooperatives and other community wealth-building models function
- Encourage and enable cities and other areas throughout Ohio and the United States to implement their own local programs, inspired by Evergreen's mission, vision, strategy and principles

By combining strong management, market development strategy and public-private partnerships, ECI has shown significant early success, demonstrating the potential synergies of combining environmental and social responsibility with profit-making. After early growing pains to establish the model's viability, ECI has made great strides over the past decade to prove its efficiency and potential successful replication in other communities. A recent report in *US News & World Report* stated:

With strong leadership, additional capital and solid execution, Evergreen has reached solid ground. Two of the three businesses—Evergreen Cooperative Laundry and Evergreen Energy Solutions (a retrofitting business)—are now profitable. The third business, Green City Growers, provides hydroponically grown gourmet produce, and it is on track to break even this year. The company now employs about 120 people, many of whom would otherwise have a hard time finding work. Revenue streams are more diversified: At this point only about 15 percent of revenue comes from the original anchor institutions.[15]

Such success would be noteworthy under any circumstances, but Evergreen is additionally distinguished by the fact that its primary employee-owners are community residents, many of whom have come to ECI with limited skills and work experience. In fact, as of late 2015, nearly 40 percent of ECI's worker-owners were ex-offenders with criminal records that have otherwise hindered their recent employment prospects. The substantial success ECI has had in recruiting, training, employing and advancing such employees has been nothing short of paradigm shattering. Indeed, the Initiative has established an important new model for healing neglected post-industrial economies in the American heartland. In addition, ECI is also part of a larger experiment in alternative wealth-building and wealth-sharing models being considered by stakeholders in the enterprise. The Greater University Circle Initiative, an important component of ECI's work, is a unique partnership between the public sector, Northeast Ohio's philanthropic community and University Circle's anchor institutions. Launched in 2005, it leverages the $3 billion of annual purchasing power of the community's leading anchor institutions to help catalyze and build community-based businesses that create green jobs and ultimately enhance the economic stability of nearby low-wealth communities.

ECI's efforts in organics production and distribution have been an important part of this story. Servicing a wide variety of local businesses, schools and grocers, the Initiative subsidiary Green City Growers (GCG) offers a wide variety of organic products, including basil, butter lettuce, mixed greens and water cress among other offerings. GCG's harvests are produced, moreover, without any pesticides or other harmful growing agents, on an around the clock basis in a state-of-the-art hydroponic greenhouse that enables uninterrupted, year-round production. Each year, GCG's facility and staffing enable the production of 3 million heads of lettuce and 300,000 pounds of organic herbs for both local and regional consumption. The GCG greenhouse sits on a 10-acre inner-city site that was once a center of urban blight. With 3.25 acres of nonstop greenhouse production, supported by the latest energy efficiency technology, it now serves as a vibrant anchor for the surrounding neighborhood and a place of productive full-time employment for thirty local community residents.

GCG is a leader in environment-friendly technology. For instance, conventional production of one head of iceberg lettuce requires on average 40 gallons of water, but GCG can produce the same head of lettuce with only about 1 gallon, owing to its state-of-the-art irrigation system. GCG is able to capture 85 percent of the rainwater and snowmelt from the building's roof as the principal water source used to grow its greens. In addition, at GCG's greenhouse, a high-tech automated system controls exposure to natural light, allowing plants to thrive year-round even during gray Cleveland winters. Such profound efficiencies portend not only major scalable breakthroughs for GCG's ultimate competitiveness, but also for agricultural production generally in times of growing concern about climate change and persistent drought in many parts of the nation and world. And, last but not least, by all accounts, the combination of conditions that undergirds GCG's organic output results in a superior product. According to testimonials from leading area consumers, GCG's produce is both tastier and has discernibly longer shelf lives compared to traditional products.

Given the Evergreen Cooperative Initiative's impressive results to date, and the emerging profitability of its worker-owned organics enterprise and allied business units, it seems vital and timely for progressive leaders and activists everywhere to be seeking enhanced ways to advocate and support the replication and scaling of this work on a broad national level. The combination of being able to hire local, traditionally-hard-to-place workers for living wages while producing needed goods and services in environmentally and socially responsible ways, with back-end profit sharing opportunities for the workers involved, is beyond timely. Every community in the United States should be undertaking comparably creative efforts for the benefit of their people and the environment. So much more could be gained to ensure expanded next-generation integrity, dynamism and prosperity-sharing across the American economy. It really should be every forward-looking American's priority to learn more about the ECI approach and to fight for ways to adapt it to their own local and regional circumstances.

Home Care: Cooperative Home Healthcare Associates

Cooperative Home Care Associates (CHCA) is a nationally recognized, New York-based, worker-owned home care agency located in the Bronx. CHCA was founded in 1985 to provide quality home care to clients requiring assistance owing to serious physical and chronic conditions. CHCA started with twelve home health aides providing care to people who are elderly, chronically ill or living with disabilities. Today, CHCA, a certified B-Corporation, is the largest worker cooperative in the United States, employing large numbers of African American women and Latinas in the poorest urban county in the United States. CHCA's local focus makes its bottom line results particularly impressive. According to Fast Company, CHCA's revenues in 2015 were in the range of $60 million; and the organization has been profitable in all but three of its now more than thirty years of operation.[16]

In 2000, CHCA created Independence Care System (ICS), a multibillion-dollar managed-care company that contracts with the City of New York to assist chronically sick and disabled adults. According to journalist Laura Flanders, "With ICS, CHCA filled an unmet need while also creating its own primary customer to fuel the co-op's growth. ICS is [now] responsible for 60 percent of CHCA's business, and the co-op has grown from 500 workers in the late 1990s to 2,300 today."[17] CHCA's reach also extends deeply into health-care job training. With Paraprofessional Healthcare Institute (PHI), a nonprofit founded by CHCA in 1992, CHCA provides free training for 600 low-income and unemployed women annually and serves as a significant driver of employment in the Bronx.

The home healthcare industry has been the focus of growing attention in recent years, owing mainly to concerns about uneven quality of care (including evidence that about 20 percent of clients are physically or otherwise abused by home-care providers), and low industry standards for pay and skills development. According to former Fast Company staff writer Jay Cassano,

A quarter of the workers who do this labor live in households below the federal poverty line and half only do the job part-time. These workers are overwhelmingly female (90%), people of color (56%), and lacking formal education (58% have at most a high school diploma or GED). Despite being health care workers, one in three did not have health insurance as of 2014.[18]

Among the largest problems facing the home healthcare industry are persistent low skill levels and pay, as well as insecure hours and working conditions. CHCA has addressed these concerns in multiple ways. First, by training and then guaranteeing ownership shares to workers who have paid $1,000 over time on flexible terms to invest in the enterprise CHCA incentivizes its employees to achieve ownership status and to co-share responsibility for the organization's continuing success. As of 2014, half of all of CHCA's employees were worker-owners. Many comprising the other half were training and saving to achieve that status. Second, CHCA offers its employees family health insurance, as well as membership in the Service Employees International Union Local 1199, which establishes collective bargaining rights for covered workers. Third, CHCA ensures its senior worker-owners a minimum of thirty hours of work per week and profit-sharing based on company performance, which substantially enhances CHCA employees' economic security. Fourth, and finally, CHCA offers its employees allied benefits that substantially help to increase employee commitment, quality and longevity compared to industry norms. These include, for example, annual dividends based on CHCA's profitability, the right to serve on CHCA's board of directors and vote in elections, and free tax preparation to help worker-owners obtain Earned Income Tax Credits.

Among the benefits to CHCA that result from these policies is far better worker retention: only 15% turnover, compared to the industry average of 40%. With expanded worker retention and ownership opportunities, and by extension heightened employee job satisfaction, the quality of healthcare provided also exceeds industry norms. Bryan Welch, CEO and Publisher of B the Change Media, has written that,

CHCA is proving the business case for employee engagement through ownership and shared responsibility. Health care workers at CHCA make about $17 an hour including benefits. They receive twice the legally required amount of training. "Case managers" help new employees find child care and, when necessary, secure the right to work from immigration authorities. After training, workers get a peer mentor who helps them navigate the myriad tasks associated with providing for the complex needs of their clients in their homes.[19]

CHCA's track record of investing heavily in its people's economic opportunities and capacities to serve has resulted in evident organizational success, as well as improvements in the nature and quality of care afforded to its many clients. While CHCA's success is surely the product of somewhat unique circumstances and experiences gleaned over more than three decades of practice, it is not unfathomable to imagine its core business model being highly replicable in other parts of the nation that would benefit from similar results.

Progressive advocates of all sorts who care about community health and vitality, economic empowerment and social change should all be uniting to endorse the CHCA model of care and its replication and adaptation in still other cities and regions of the country. Given the nation's rapidly-aging population and the expectation of significantly elongated life expectancies, home health care is presently considered to be the US economy's fastest growing sector, with a rate of nearly 5% per year through 2024, which equates to some 750,000 jobs.[20] There is no reason why a substantial share of these new jobs could not be successfully organized in other cities around the kinds of corporate ownership strategies and values employed by CHCA. Indeed, every workplace in America could be vastly improved in quality, social impact and worker compensation if CHCA's model were to be more widely embraced in the American economy of the future.

Advancing Allied Models of Social Enterprise

In addition to supporting the expansion of worker-owned enterprises with strong environmental and social missions, progressive

Americans need to support opportunities to implement other forms of social enterprise that are showing promise in various communities and industries across the United States. From innovations in the food and retail spaces and the emerging cannabis industry to activities in community economic development and social-investment financing, the social enterprise field is rapidly developing new approaches to environmental and social responsibility, community engagement and development, and related public problem-solving. Like the successful worker-owned enterprises examined above, allied social enterprises have a vitally important role to play in helping to usher in the next American economy—one that will be far more responsive to environmental, economic, political and social justice concerns. The following are some examples of successful social enterprises and field support efforts that warrant increased attention and endorsement in progressive circles.

Food Service: Restaurant Opportunities Centers United

Great potential for future community building and economic revitalization resides in the food industry. So much of people's health and social well-being flows from our relationship to the food we eat; and many poor people and communities across our nation fundamentally lack access both to decent food at affordable prices and employment opportunities in food service.[21] Restaurant workers, a large proportion of whom are immigrants and women, are among the most undercompensated and abused employees in our national economy.[22] Many restaurant workers live at or below the federal poverty line and face significant workplace discrimination, pay theft, economic dislocation and physical abuse from employers in many different kinds of food service establishments.

One of the most exciting and promising of emerging social enterprise models that addresses these issues is being developed by Restaurant Opportunities Centers United (ROC), a national labor-based alliance of some 30,000 restaurant workers, restaurant owners and consumers. Through public reporting and advocacy on restaurant-industry practices, applied modelling and training efforts in restaurant work and management, as well as innovations in social media-based watch-dogging, ROC is slowly but surely changing restaurant standards for the better. Through its efforts to raise the bar on persistent industry concerns related to food sourcing and production processes, hiring and career advancement, worker safety and benefits, and compensation and tipping, ROC has radically changed the conversation impacting restaurant consumer education and preferences

The Restaurant Opportunities Center of New York was initially founded in New York City by Fekkak Mamdouh and Saru Jayaraman after September 11th, 2001 to provide support to people working in restaurants who were displaced as a result of the World Trade Center tragedy. In collaboration with leading New York area restaurant professionals, ROC spearheaded the successful development of COLORS restaurant in New York's Greenwich Village to support healthy and affordable dining alternatives, and the hiring and career advancement of multicultural food service personnel negatively affected by the 911 terrorist attack on the City. Based on its successful start in New York City, many who worked in restaurants in several other cities approached ROC about initiating chapters in their locations. The organization has responded and thus currently supports active chapters in New York, Massachusetts, Michigan, Illinois, Washington, California, Louisiana, Washington DC and Pennsylvania.

COLORS restaurants have evolved as frontline laboratories for progressive grassroots change in America. Each operation shares essential properties: part restaurant, part training facility, part worker-owned cooperative incubator. COLORS customers enjoy worldly ambiance and quality global cuisine made of fresh local and seasonal ingredients sourced from producers who practice sustainable agriculture, support fair trade and ensure employees get paid sustainable wages. A COLORS Hospitality Opportunities for Workers Institute (CHOW) works to equip lower- to middle-range restaurant workers with the knowledge and skills required to advance in the industry. Each year, through CHOW, ROC trains more than 1,000 future restaurant employees nationwide and achieves an average placement rate of 60-75 percent, in each instance with a living wage level. Program participants learn specialized industry skills related to meal service, wine selection, food safety, culinary arts and bartending.

Through ROC's "One Fair Wage" campaign and associated efforts, workers, employers and consumers are mobilizing for higher wages, and race and gender equity through what it calls "high road" employment and operational practices: fair compensation, meaningful employee benefits and expanded opportunities for civic engagement, training and upward mobility. The "One Fair Wage" effort seeks an end to the presently bifurcated minimum wage system that guarantees all workers an hourly compensation of $7.25 throughout the nation, with the exception of restaurant and agricultural workers. Presently, the effective minimum wage rate for restaurant workers is $2.13 per hour.[23] Employers who hire agricultural workers are also largely exempted from paying the federal minimum wage, with resulting farm laborer compensation often falling well below that level. As a result of these realities, many restaurant and agricultural workers live in poverty. By seeking to raise the minimum wage for food and restaurant workers to the current federal standard for all other workers, ROC seeks to balance the playing field that has left so many in the food production and restaurant service sector in or near poverty.

ROC has also sought to partner with forward-looking restauranteurs to eliminate tipping by simply building living-wage compensation for their employees into their general pricing (as is done in Europe and most other parts of the world). Through its Restaurants Advancing Industry Standards in Employment (RAISE) program, a peer learning and industry activism effort, ROC has established partnerships with some 200 food service establishments dedicated to advocating for and applying sustainable business practices for the benefit of employees and consumers alike. In addition, building on these efforts, the organization has recently developed a Diner's Guide to ethical eating and an allied new computer app that enables restaurant-goers to comment on the business ethics, quality and operational practices of participating commercial food establishments, in the style of Yelp! and Angie's List. ROC's creative use of social media to educate and activate consumers has begun to incentivize more policymakers and restaurant owners in various states to support "high road" employment and business decisions.

Owing to continuing, glaring disparities between the status of workers of color and white workers employed in food service, ROC has also effectively advocated for greater industry mobility for people of color. It has co-produced with Race Forward and the Center for Social Inclusion a Racial Equity Tool Kit that restaurant owners and managers can utilize as they develop training and promotion programs. And, most recently, it has partnered with one of the nation's most dynamic criminal justice reform organizations, the Oakland, CA-based Ella Baker Center, to form a highly ambitious and innovative new community advocacy and training center entitled Restore Oakland. Restore Oakland will bring together community leaders and nonprofits from across the city to collaborate on everything from housing rights and healing, to jobs and conflict resolution, to business incubation and workers' rights. ROC United and the Ella Baker Center are pursuing this timely, game-changing effort in close collaboration with various local change and social justice organizations, such as Designing Justice + Designing Spaces, Community Works West, Causa Justa/Just Cause, Restorative Justice for Oakland Youth (RJOY) and La Cocina.

The proposed complex that will house Restore Oakland sits in the Fruitvale District of East Oakland, a perennially-challenged area of the city that has historically lacked equitable housing, employment and services. The $17 million-project, to be opened in early 2019, will offer a wide variety of programs and opportunities to neighborhood residents who experience one of the highest rates of incarceration in the Bay Area and unemployment rates that are three times the Alameda County average. The offerings to be prioritized by Restore Oakland will include: job-training and placement, business incubation, restorative justice and community and economic power-building. As it gains traction and demonstrates impact as a vehicle for addressing persistent local poverty and the recovery of chronically unemployed, formerly incarcerated and otherwise structurally disadvantaged workers, Restore Oakland is likely to create an additional groundswell of interest in replicating the program within ROC's expanding array of national relationships. Indeed, the social enterprise model that ROC is developing with the Ella Baker Center is one that makes good sense to reproduce in other parts of the nation. It is programs like this that offer great potential for the food service industry and social enterprise. Accordingly, it should be the business of all progressive leaders and activists enthusiastically to support these developments.

Cannabis: Harborside Health Center

For at least fifty years now, American society and culture have been at loggerheads over the appropriate legal status, regulation and allowable use of cannabis, the psychoactive drug in marijuana. Various states have now legalized the use of cannabis either for health or recreation in contravention of prevailing federal law. Yet, in still much of the nation, vast law enforcement and judicial resources continue to be allocated to cannabis-related offenses. Leading national advocacy organizations, such as the ACLU and the Drug Policy Alliance have documented and challenged glaring racial disparities applicable between people of color versus whites apprehended, arrested and criminalized for marijuana-related offenses. The social and economic costs of policing and incarceration are many and profound. As a society, we have experienced a growing disconnect between the general public and policymakers regarding the appropriateness of our current approach to cannabis regulation. Presently, a large majority of Americans support the legalization of marijuana for medical therapy; moreover, a significant majority also supports outright legalization of the drug. The debate over marijuana has had—and continues to have— considerable built-in volatility relative to public opinion and public policy.

Nevertheless, in a growing number of states, the movement towards marijuana legalization has been building, with western states in particular taking real legal and policy leadership in this direction. Since 2012, Alaska, California, Colorado, Nevada, Oregon and Washington have legalized marijuana for general recreational use by adult consumers. In addition, even more states have authorized marijuana to treat diseases and health issues. Market analysts have reported that, even with current federal prohibitions in force, legal marijuana sales approached $10 billion in the U.S. during 2017, representing a 33 percent revenue increase over the prior year, 2016.[24] They also predict a roughly 30 percent expansion in the market through 2021, when annual industry revenues are expected to approach $25 billion.[25]

Indicative of rapidly increasing public and official state-level acceptance of cannabis as a legitimate medical and social consumer product have been a growing number of marijuana dispensaries for the legal use and sale of cannabis-based products. In such cities as Denver, Los Angles, Seattle and and Washington, DC, it is now entirely possible for adults to shop for and consume marijuana and related products without state law-enforcement interference. In these places and others, highly credible, efficient and responsible dispensaries provide for the safe and satisfying consumption of marijuana. Typically, these operations feature inviting store designs, a growing array of product lines and helpful, professional and informed service staffs.

The leading enterprise in this space is Harborside Health Center, the pioneering Oakland, CA-based cannabis dispensary and wellness center founded and headed by Steve DeAngelo, author of *The Cannabis Manifesto* (2015). Harborside, which has recently expanded to San José and plans for further expansion to other California venues, is the largest and most respected cannabis dispensary in the country today. In 2016, the organization posted revenues of $30 million from its Oakland flagship store alone. Harborside combines the sale of a vast array of cannabis product lines with hard-hitting public advocacy and intellectual leadership for the growing national field of cannabis entrepreneurs, professionals and consumers.

Harborside operates as a nonprofit social enterprise that is dedicated to building "a world that lives by the values cannabis teaches us." These values focus on twelve dichotomies that are represented in all of its corporate service and advocacy efforts: kindness over cruelty, creativity over conformity, freedom over tyranny, change over the status quo, generosity over greed, reason over superstition, knowledge over ignorance, diversity over exclusion, sustainability over disposability, wellness over intoxication, truth over lies; and love over hate. These corporate values put into relief that what DeAngelo and others like him across the nation are proposing is not merely the advancement of an interesting new business model or money-making opportunity, but rather a fundamental shift in how people relate to themselves, to one another, to the larger society and ultimately to the natural world. All of this has profound political and economic implications.

Modeling humane business practices, Harborside pays its employees a living wage and also offers them medical, dental and vision insurance, an employer-matched 401k program, an Employee Assistance Program, FSA/Commuter Benefits, paid time off and a generous employee discount. Harborside is also committed to equal employment opportunity and does not discriminate on any legally recognized basis. In addition, Harborside sponsors special education and outreach programs, as well as discounts for seniors and veterans in their efforts to treat the many painful conditions they often face. It also has a program to provide weekly care packages to qualifying medical patients who are unable to afford their medicine.

In 2017, Debra Borchardt, a leading cannabis industry analyst, reported that legal marijuana companies and organizations will produce more jobs than the nation's manufacturing sector by 2020:

. . . by 2020 the legal cannabis market will create more than a quarter of a million jobs. This is more than the expected jobs from manufacturing, utilities or even government jobs, according to the Bureau of Labor Statistics. . . . by 2024 manufacturing jobs are expected to decline by 814,000, utilities will lose 47,000 jobs and government jobs will decline by 383,000. (*Forbes*, 27 February 2017)

Despite the obvious benefits of safe, legal and responsible marijuana use, a powerfully situated minority of conservative politicians in America staunchly opposes the nation's move towards officially authorized commercial exchanges and consumption of cannabis. One of the only logical explanations for conservative political resistance to marijuana's broader normalization throughout the American economy is the presumed competition the new industry's success might pose for the alcohol and pharmaceutical industries. Over recent years, big profits from these sources have lined the campaign coffers of elected officials who have in turn played the biggest role in suppressing the marijuana industry's prospects for success. Another reason for opposition among conservatives—perhaps a holdover from times past—is the moral concern that legalizing cannabis will only ensure its early, negative and ultimately destructive use by young people, despite considerable evidence that, even with legalization in many places now, there is no data to support such concerns.

Harborside Health Center and others like it are challenging the status quo in fundamental ways and gradually succeeding despite the many obstacles being posed by those whose philosophical, political and economic interests they threaten. This is because, when all is said and done, the public's broad and growing endorsement of cannabis as a helpful and healing medicine has forever overtaken the capacity of right-wing moralizers, politicians and law enforcement agencies to reverse the course of history. For so many reasons, during the years to come, cannabis culture in America will surely become an even more integral aspect of our national culture. And this is as it should be. One day in the future, people will look upon marijuana the way they now look upon any other item of legal purchase and use. And the expansive benefits of cannabis—an age-old, proven, natural medicine—will carry the day.

In the meantime, as the industry is developing and evolving, it presents essential opportunities to promote more broadly the heightened brand of environmentally and socially responsible enterprise and community-building that organizations like Harborside Health Center make possible. These entities offer vast new opportunities and potential for economic development and wealth-building, especially in low- and moderate-income communities that have struggled to attract investment. These include opportunities for good jobs at livable wages for workers lacking employment alternatives, expanded health and healing potential benefitting consumers and the capacity to revitalize poor, rural and urban communities across the nation.

Community Economic Development: Thunder Valley CDC

Innovative and impactful social enterprise opportunities that advance environmental and social justice, upward mobility and community building in low-income rural areas are badly needed but still rare. Given the persistence of rural poverty across the nation and the downward trend in economic activity benefiting such communities over recent decades,[26] this is something that must soon change. The greatest challenges are to be found in the nation's Native American rural communities. One of the great exceptions to this sad state of affairs is the visionary work being advanced by the Thunder Valley Community Development Corporation (Thunder Valley CDC) in one of the nation's most impoverished places: the Lakota Indian Reservation at Pine Ridge, South Dakota, where almost half of all residents—44.2 percent—live in poverty and only half of the adults are employed.

The Thunder Valley CDC is the product of a long tradition of community reinvestment innovation led by the Ford Foundation in the 1960s to support the formation of organizations like the Bedford-Stuyvesant Restoration Corporation (BSRC) in Brooklyn, which established an important template for national and regional community revitalization through public- and private-sector partnerships, among other strategies. Over the years, community development corporations like BSRC have paved the way for low income community improvements across the nation, including projects to expand affordable housing, job-training, business development, youth development and civic engagement, focusing especially on socially and economically disadvantaged populations. They have financed and scaled these efforts through funding from multiple public and private sources. And they have developed allied social enterprises intended to advance their core objectives to alleviate poverty and its negative impacts on people, communities and society.

Developing from this lineage of community change efforts, while also innovating approaches, Thunder Valley CDC has assembled an impressive array of private and public supporters, including the Bush Foundation, Northwest Area Foundation and the Surdna Foundation, as well as such public entities as the US Departments of Agriculture, Health and Human Services and Housing and Urban Development. With major support from sources like these, the organization has developed one of the most ambitious and exciting comprehensive community redevelopment projects to be undertaken in the long history of the national CDC movement—a decade-long effort to create thirty single-family homes, forty-eight apartment units and ten artist studios, a community center, a public market, a geothermal greenhouse, a youth shelter; and powwow grounds; it has also built the infrastructure to support the development in the form of roads, sewers, electricity and broadband.[27]

Among the project's additional distinctions is its fundamental commitment to community engagement in the entire array of planning and implementation of the Thunder Valley project and its related commitment to sustainable economic principles. A recent report on Thunder Valley CDC's work and approach by the Doris Duke Charitable Foundation offers the following observations on the distinctive nature of the corporation's work:

> [T]he basic idea behind this work is the concert of Thunder Valley CDC's ecosystem of opportunity, currently a set of seven initiatives that are seen as interdependent and managed holistically to improve the lives of Lakota youth and families. The ecosystem includes community development, social enterprise, Lakota language, food sovereignty, youth leadership, sustainable housing and workforce development. All of these initiatives are a result of priorities local residents identified when creating the Oglala Lakota Regional Plan in 2012. One of Thunder Valley CDC's very first projects upon its founding in 2007 was in fact a community mapping event with about 30-40 participants visualizing on one large whiteboard their current conception of life at Pine Ridge and, on a second board, their idea of the future. Thunder Valley CDC organized the exercise to develop a vision for Pine Ridge that was drawn up not by one or two individuals but by a larger, more representative sample of the community.[28]

A noteworthy aspect of this work is the corporation's goal to reduce the community's baseline energy use by 60 percent and create some 250 green building jobs for Reservation residents. As reported by the Robert Rauschenberg Foundation,

> [Thunder Valley] CDC is building a new zero-carbon, zero waste facility with 100 percent energy generation, 100 percent

water reuse, and a sustainable food production complex, that will also provide affordable housing and job opportunities on the reservation. Affordable housing and job opportunities on Pine Ridge means that residents do not have to commute hundreds of miles to earn poverty wages, which itself has an impact on the area's carbon footprint. Using the Lakota belief that 'we are all related' in order to bridge the gap of indigenous beliefs with architects, engineers, planners, artists and designers Thunder Valley CDC . . . can yield an international model for addressing climate change while building pathways out of poverty for the world's most struggling communities.[29]

In summary, Thunder Valley CDC has fundamentally changed the equation in Indian Country regarding what true community development can look like. Instead of fostering programs to prepare reservation residents for jobs and lives in far away and culturally foreign cities and towns, Thunder Valley CDC goes in the other direction: it seeks to encourage a doubling down on investments in the local community that enable residents to remain on the reservation, living and working in sustainable and culturally-reinforcing ways.

News of Thunder Valley CDC's success has spread throughout Indian Country and brought numerous requests for assistance in duplicating its model. The demand has been so great, in fact, that the corporation has established a new enterprise, NDN Collective, which will enable Thunder Valley CDC to help other communities replicate or adapt its model to suit their varying needs. The idea of extending the benefits of the Thunder Valley CDC model to other communities, both within and beyond the US Native American community is exciting and timely. At a time when recent federal policy has redoubled support for extractive oil drilling on the nearby sacred lands of the Standing Rock Sioux and elsewhere, Thunder Valley's alternative approach to community and regional economic development stands in stark contrast to the views of conventional authorities. The Thunder Valley approach is the way of the future and must be considered the new standard for progressive leaders and activists across America. By supporting true community-driven design, renewable energy innovations, sustainable agriculture, indigenous micro-enterprise and communal live-work arrangements, in the years to come the needs of modern people can be better aligned with nature. As a result, all of humanity and the planet can be made more healthy and whole. These are the essential qualities of the Thunder Valley CDC model, which are firmly steeped in notions of a regenerative economy, one that both serves humanity and supports the Earth's essential ecosystems.[30]

Financing and Scaling: REDF

While social enterprises are essential in advancing more progressive forms of economic exchange in struggling and disadvantaged communities, such efforts simply cannot succeed and scale up without strategic infusions of start-up and expansion capital, informed technical assistance and supportive public policy promotion. Indeed, social enterprise as an emerging sector in the US economy requires robust intermediary support in each of these areas to thrive and evolve as a growth center of more socially equitable and environmentally friendly economic activity, alternative business capitalization and jobs.

During recent years, numerous social venture capitalization funds and technical advisory organizations, as well as field support organizations have emerged to address the expanding need for investment and support across the national social enterprise field. In fact, the growth of organizations and funds active in this space has been remarkable, even over the past four years. According to Anne Field, writing in *Forbes*,

> [Social responsibility investment] assets have expanded to $8.72 trillion in the US, a 33% increase from 2014. That's a significant portion of total assets under management. The research, first conducted in 1995, studies US asset managers and institutional investors using one or more sustainable investment strategies. Asset managers, including 477 institutional investors, 300 money managers and 1,043 community investing financial institutions, consider environmental, social or cor-

porate governance (ESG) criteria across $8.19 trillion in assets, up 69% from two years ago.[31]

Leading players in this rapidly expanding space now include large global and national entities, such as the London-based Bridges Fund Management (with total assets of nearly $1 billion), San Francisco-based RSF Finance (whose combined assets stand at about $120 million), and the New York-based Nonprofit Finance Fund (whose socially and environmentally focused loan expenditures now exceed $100 million annually). But the field is also increasingly seeing the rapid emergence of important smaller and boutique finance and technical assistance providers, such as Kapor Capital (whose work focuses on seed capitalizing social mission-oriented tech companies) and the Impact America Fund (which concentrates investments on social purpose businesses run by minority entrepreneurs in low-income neighborhoods).

One of the most interesting of the emerging leaders in this area, however, is San Francisco-based REDF. REDF was formed in 1997 as the Roberts Enterprise Development Fund by George Roberts, a founding partner of KKR, which is a leading global finance firm that manages investments across multiple asset classes, including private equity, energy, infrastructure, real estate, credit and hedge funds. Roberts launched REDF to expand job development programs for those in society who face the greatest difficulties getting and holding onto a job, including people with histories of homelessness, incarceration, mental illness and addiction. His goal was visionary: invest in social enterprises that create jobs for traditionally hard-to-employ people and reinvest the earnings in skills development, training and services for such employees and others like them. Roberts intended for REDF to operate as a "venture philanthropy" that could both help finance as well as build the capacities of nonprofit social enterprises in the San Francisco Bay Area. REDF thus provided grants and other financial assistance to a select portfolio of entrepreneurial nonprofits with revenue-generating and job-creating business units. Along with that capital, it offered extensive business supports and mentorship. The socially conscious businesses REDF initially supported focused on the expansion of both productivity and jobs for people in need, including gardening and janitorial services, recovery-centered retail outlets and reuse/recycling enterprises. Applying the standard principles of private equity venture funding in the social investment context proved to be a transformative impulse.

Reviews of seven social enterprises supported by REDF show that, on average, every $1 these social enterprises have spent has returned nearly $2.25 in benefits to society. Moreover, evaluation of REDF's field impact further reveals that after only one year of work experience in a social enterprise, the income of people employed by REDF-supported entities increased more than 250 percent, while income from government benefits dropped from 71 percent to 24 percent and housing stability tripled.[32] Aside from the evident material value benefiting workers and communities, REDF's work helps to advance family stabilization, self-sufficiency, hope and other important and long-held national values.

REDF's early successes in the Bay Area led to its designation as a national leader in social innovation by the Obama White House in 2011. The designation resulted in a hefty $7.5 million matching federal grant to help REDF expand its model over a five-year period spanning 2011-2015. It was the largest award ever made by the federal Social Innovation Fund (SIF). The award helped REDF extend its reach for the first time beyond the Bay Area into other parts of California, especially Southern California and the West. In 2016, it received an additional $7 million SIF matching grant to extend the model nationally. Presently, building on these impressive developments, REDF is advancing an ambitious, five-year $75 million fund raising campaign to help advance a next stage of innovation in US social enterprise through the year 2020. Through the campaign, the organization seeks to help 50,000 of the nation's hardest-to-employ workers move into the workforce. Already, through a broad combination of private and public investors, it has secured $50 million towards its goal and helped 16,000 people within its key beneficiary populations to secure employment.

Since its inception, REDF has supported nearly 150 diverse social enterprises with seed and growth capital through direct financing and specialized advisory services, and leveraged some $450 million in social enterprise-generated revenue in the process. The enterprise partners that work most closely with REDF include some of the nation's most innovative and inspiring social ventures, such as Goodwill Industries (Silicon Valley), the Center for Employment Opportunities (New York), Chrysalis (Los Angeles), Farestart (Seattle), Juma Ventures (San Francisco) and Cara (Chicago). Almost all of REDF's beneficial investment activity and job generation has occurred at the grassroots level, moreover, which is an important factor in contemporary economic development, given the growing pressure on local economies from the expanding concentration of capital and jobs in larger national chain distributors and employers.

REDF's successes to date are full of actionable policy implications. They suggest real potential to expand the employment base for far greater numbers of traditionally hard-to-employ Americans, if as a nation we are prepared to make sufficient expanded social investments in the work of groups like REDF. Among the elements of REDF's success has been its emphasis on combining smart financing to help the nation's most innovative and impactful social enterprises to increase their impact and expansion with supportive business training and education programs, strategic technical assistance, field-enhancing research and public policy advocacy intended to enhance social enterprise successes through more facilitative legislation and public sector partnership support. In these respects, REDF has assembled important knowledge and know-how based on its extensive experience over twenty years; and one of its great strengths over the years has been its readiness to share with others in ways that help to build the social enterprise field, its leadership and best practices. It has supported vital field leadership development through a fellows program for graduate students aspiring to social investment careers, as well as more seasoned practitioner-focused leadership and cross-learning opportunities through an Accelerator Program. It has also supported strategic studies and publications on the outcomes of its work, in addition to advancing policy and advocating for more evidence-based solutions to the problems of chronic unemployment.

Most recently, as another means to expand field learning and exchange on social investment, REDF has introduced an interactive, online suite of information, training and problem-solving content entitled the REDFworkshop. The REDFworkshop connects and informs an engaged network of social enterprise stakeholders and encourages sharing best practices, discussing challenges and building new partnerships. Since its inception in 2015, the REDFworkshop has distinguished itself as one of the social enterprise field's essential "go-to" sources for field-related information and learning. The site offers guided and interactive tools for start-up social enterprises, video interviews with diverse stakeholders, discussion boards, an interactive dashboard and other features.

Considering the many structural problems that are increasingly threatening to diminish the US job market in future years, along with the remarkable success REDF has experienced in supporting social enterprises, one wonders why greater numbers of political and business leaders are not clamoring for more of what this fund offers. REDF's model affords progressive leaders and activists committed to fundamental reforms in workforce development with a ready and proven framework that can be replicated and scaled with huge social and economic advantages. Given all that is at stake, it is vital that we more actively align to champion and support such efforts in workforce and social innovation during the coming months and years.

Financial Asset Building and Capital Investments

In addition to supporting the further normalization, development and scaling of leading worker-owned enterprises and social enterprise organizations as logical tools for building US economic, environmental and social responsibility, it is a matter of the highest priority for progressive Americans to explore innovations in asset-building and asset-management. So much of what determines what can happen today in America, and what can happen tomorrow, ultimately depends on the accumulation and control of financial assets. Without forward-thinking people and institutions leading and innovating in this critically important domain, it is hard to imagine how progressive interests can possibly lead us to better opportunities and outcomes for people, families, communities and the natural world. The following are especially promising developments in new thinking and practice related to asset-building and capital investments that can help us move towards an economy in which everyone works, everyone counts and everyone contributes.

Baby Bonds and Children's Savings Accounts

One of the greatest challenges facing our nation is the growing divide in wealth that so characterizes our times, especially as relates to race and ethnicity. According to Deutsche Bank, nearly one-third of American households now have $0 in wealth, the worst situation since the U.S. government began tracking household wealth levels in the early 1960s.[33] Families of color have struggled especially hard to try to build assets in recent years, especially following the highly disproportionate incidence of foreclosures during the mortgage market meltdown that created the Great Recession.[34] As reported in a mid-2017 report in *The Washington Post*, the negative effects of the Great Recession were particularly harsh for African Americans and Latinos compared to whites, even when accounting for comparable levels of education:

> While net worth for all racial groups fell by about 30 percent during the Great Recession, black and Hispanic families experienced an additional 20 percent decline between 2010 and 2013 at a time when wealth stabilized for white families. . . . Between 2013 and 2016 . . . the wealth gap between black and white families grew by 16 percent . . . and by 14 percent between Hispanics and whites. In 2016, white families had a median net worth of $171,000, compared with $17,600 for blacks and $20,700 for Hispanics.[35]

Largely as a result of these and other factors, the median net worth of white households is presently 10 times that of African American households. The racial wealth divide in America is hardly new, but it has been increasing dramatically.[36]

With such large and growing gaps in financial assets taking shape across the nation, the prospect of improved equal opportunity and upward mobility for households of color is significantly being constrained, particularly in an economy that is centrally based on the accumulation and control of capital. What can be done to alter the balance of wealth in our economy so that we close this racial wealth gap and expand the flow of capital in a way that benefits many more Americans? The political tenor of our times makes clear that to resort to major wealth transfers—especially along racial lines—is highly unlikely for the foreseeable future, either through expanded taxation of the wealthy or legislated reparations payments to African American and other minority populations aggrieved by the nation's long history of formal racial oppression.

One possible strategy, however, is being researched by William A. ("Sandy") Darity, Jr. of Duke University and Darrick Hamilton of the New School in New York City, who have developed the concept of publicly-supported Baby Bonds to lift up poor and working-class Americans through a universal asset-building program.[37] Darity's and Hamilton's proposal is to adopt a major new national policy that would guarantee every new child born in the United States a variable investment sum to be invested over the course of the recipient's first eighteen years of life in private equity market vehicles equivalent to an IRA, from between $500 on the low end to perhaps as much as $50,000 on the high end. The amount received in each instance would depend on the recipient's parents' household income and wealth holdings. As recently reported by *The Washington Post*,

> Under the proposal, kids of incredibly rich parents such as Bill and Melinda Gates or Beyoncé and Jay-Z would get the lowest amount, $500, while babies born into extremely poor families would get the highest amount, $50,000. There would be a sliding scale to determine how much each baby would receive based on the parents' wealth. A typical middle-class baby would receive around $20,000.[38]

With the accumulated resources earned from these investments, beneficiaries would be able to cash in their holdings after reaching legal adulthood only for certain designated asset-building purposes, such as paying for a college education or certified skills training, buying a first home or starting a business. Owing to the distribution of assets based on household economic status, lower income beneficiaries would benefit disproportionately from this policy innovation; but through their enhanced investment possibilities, others would additionally benefit, and substantially. One of the biggest winners would be private financial services corporations and banks, whose asset-management and lending professionals would oversee fund investments and resulting spikes in demand for home-mortgage and business financing. The larger economy would gain as well from expanded consumer purchasing power that would result from the ultimate recirculation of Baby Bond assets across the nation.

A similar program was piloted in the United Kingdom at much lower initial investment levels (between 250 and 1,000 British pounds) from 2002 to 2010, but the program was discontinued following the Great Recession, owing to financial pressures on the nation's diminished treasury. And during the 2016 US election cycle, the Baby Bonds concept was endorsed by Democratic Party presidential nominee Hillary Clinton, who officially endorsed the idea of giving all babies born in the United States $5,000 to be used for college or buying a home.

The Baby Bonds concept employs the logic of targeted universalism that has been promoted by john a. powell in his book *Racing to Justice*. Basically, powell affirms the need to adopt

> strategies that are both targeted and universal. A targeted universal strategy is inclusive of both dominant and marginalized groups, but pays particular attention to the situation of the marginalized group. . . . Targeted universalism rejects a blanket approach that is likely to be indifferent to the reality that different groups are situated differently relative to the institutions and resources of society.[39]

Some progressives have advocated for a Universal Basic Income to promote expanded economic security in America, but the estimated costs would be quite high, compared to Baby Bonds. According to recent reporting in *The Washington Post*:

Universal basic income and Baby Bonds are both ways of lev-
eling the playing field, but the key difference is Baby Bonds
are cheaper, because the money goes out only once to an individual, not year after year. In the United States, a universal
basic income would probably cost over $1 trillion a year, com-
pared with an estimated $80 billion a year for Baby Bonds.[40]

Another proposal, family-financed Children's Savings Accounts
(CSAs), are more generic and less prescriptive than Baby Bonds and
have been around for the past couple of decades,[41] having been
endorsed by important financial empowerment organizations, such as
Prosperity Now (formerly the Corporation for Enterprise Development). These accounts benefit from public and private incentives,
such as the federally supported 529 educational saving plans and no
or very low monthly service fees, and have served as an important
incentive for families to save as well as educate their children about
the long term importance of saving and finance.[42] But for very poor
and cash-strapped families, it has been difficult to take full advantage
of these benefits owing precisely to their limited household resources.

Given that capital accumulation and asset control are increasingly vital aspects of survival in contemporary America, it is more essential than ever for leading progressive thinkers and activists to rally
around compelling policy proposals like those mentioned above.
Unless and until there are active measures put in place to accelerate
the opportunities for low-income families to build capital, it is likely
economic inequality will grow and, right along with it, even more
entrenched political and social conflict.

Investing for the Common Good

Last but not least, in order to encourage a more responsive and sustainable economy for the future, one that operates first and foremost in
service to people and the natural world, it is crucially important for
progressive leaders and activists to more aggressively support innovations in investment and capital management. Our advocates must target private equity and banking institutions, government agencies, pension funds, foundations and nonprofits and major corporations to align

around the more strategic and collective deployment of the investment resources that we control individually for the common good.

Recent years have witnessed the appearance of socially and environmentally responsible impact investing, as well as triple bottom-line performance measures that co-value economic, environmental and social returns on investment.[43] In the process, a vast array of new social and environmental responsibility investment leaders have emerged under the umbrella of leading trade groups, such as the Forum for Sustainable and Responsible Investment (US SIF), with financial assets under management now exceeding $8 trillion.[44]

For the past several decades, shareholder activism in the public equity investment space has been an important aspect of progressive organizing. Such activism has its roots in the effective pressures applied during the 1970s and 1980s on universities and corporations that supported apartheid or were doing business with South Africa. It also traces to consumer activism through such organisms as the Interfaith Center for Corporate Responsibility (ICCR), the Coalition for Environmentally Responsible Economies (CERES) and the Sisters of St. Francis of Philadelphia.[45]

Building on this rich history of shareholder activism for change, today's progressive leaders and institutions need to redouble the use of collective-impact strategies and mission-related investing to help shape better outcomes for our economy, society and world. Leading private foundations, such as the Heron, Ford, Kresge and the David and Lucile Packard foundations are among a growing group of significantly-endowed institutions that have taken the lead in this space, along with supporting nonprofit finance, technical support and advocacy groups such as the Nonprofit Finance Fund, Mission Investor's Exchange, Opportunity Finance Network, Global Impact Investors Network, US SIF, Confluence Philanthropy, and others.

Recent evidence suggests that there is increasing parity relative to Return on Investment (ROI) between conventional and alternative market plays. In a growing number of instances, in fact, alternative investment vehicles featuring environmental, social and governance (ESG) screens outperform conventional investments, in some instances by as much as an 18% higher return.[46] According to Confluence Philanthropy (CP), there are many ways that more purposeful investors can help to support improved social and environmental outcomes through innovation, collective action and advocacy. Examples of mission-related investing practices for philanthropic organizations identified by the organization include:

- Holding cash deposits at community-owned banks and lending institutions
- Leveraging ownership in the market through proxy-voting and shareholder engagement
- Structuring program-related investments that provide loans with primarily charitable intent to non-profits and for-profit institutions
- Making equity investments in screened public and privately held companies that seek to maximize market rates of return with high impact
- Structuring angel or venture capital investments in early stage companies promising social/environmental as well as financial return[47]

In all of these ways, private social-purpose organizations, like foundations, social enterprises, community banking institutions and social-service nonprofits can achieve much more in their work by amassing and deploying their investment dollars together for the common good. That is to say, they can do more of this work individually in ways that are certainly meaningful, but much more importantly, they can do it at a grander level of scale by consciously joining forces to make an even larger contribution to the better world we all seek. With more aggressive urging and partnership from progressive leaders and activists, these important institutions can help to guide more needed resources towards communities and ecosystems that are bearing the weight of the world's declining industrial order and, in the process, produce far more responsible and sustainable outcomes in the future.

By collectively advancing this work, forward-looking investors can help to model the behavior we hope for and seek from more conventional investing institutions. They can use the power of their aggregated capital to encourage greater corporate reinvestment in low income communities, more creative efforts to employ and help build the assets of struggling workers and their families and more green investments that generate well-paid jobs for working and middle-class Americans. By combining forces in these ways, we can encourage more responsive business development that enhances local economic dynamism through small business and expanded social enterprise activity that mitigates the expanding footprint of increasingly unresponsive corporate chains. As the superiority and multiple benefits of these new approaches to institutional investing take hold, leading field innovators can lift up a framework of proven outcomes that in turn can help to drive still more socially and environmentally responsible investment in mainstream capital markets.

Building a Sustainable Social Economy

The examples featured here, lifting up what is in play and emerging as next-generation models for a socially and environmentally responsible economy, demonstrate the kinds of leadership, innovation and purpose that will be increasingly required to save humanity and the planet. We simply have to find the methods and the means to rapidly accelerate the scaling and replication of models like these, if we are to survive the present century as a species and as a planet. We must move from a fundamentally materialistic and transactional economy to one in which every individual has an opportunity to work, to count and to contribute. We must make every aspect of our production process sustainable and respectful of the integrity of the natural world and local communities alike. In this book, we consider the meeting point of all these essential goals a Sustainable Social Economy. The good works highlighted here fundamentally embody the essence of such an economy and offer critically important lessons to all of us about how best to accelerate its greater centrality in our national policy and practice. What has to come now is our joining together in a far more concerted and intentional way than ever as a progressive community to actively will this new economy into being. For when all is said and done, there can be no more important task at hand and no more timely endeavor.

Endnotes

[1]See "Prosperity: The Roadmap," a film by Pedram Shojai and Mark van Wijk, September 29, 2017: https://well.org/.

[2]See "Prosperity-Documentary Feature Film" (promo reel) https://www.indiegogo.com/projects/prosperity-documentary-feature-film#/.

[3]On account of their approach to socially and environmentally responsible business, such firms have been widely recognized. For example, Guayaki, the maker of Yerba Mate beverage products, has received multiple awards for "Most Democratic Workplace" from Atlanta-based WorldBlu (a workplace culture and quality promotion organization). See NFM Staff, "Natural Foods Merchandiser/Company News," New Hope Network, June 27, 2008: http://www.newhope.com/news/company-news-37 and also the Guayaki: http://guayaki.com/about/987/Guayaki-Social-and-Environmental-Awards.html. Whole Foods, the major grocery chain, has been touted by Fortune magazine as a leading retail employer for various aspects of its work culture and employee benefits. See Tkcazyk, C., "Five Reasons Why It's Great to Work at Whole Foods,", *Fortune Magazine* May 18, 2011: http://fortune.com/2011/05/18/5-reasons-why-its-great-to-work-at-whole-foods/.

[4]Jones, V., *The Green Collar Economy: How One Solution Can Fix Our Two Biggest Problems*, NY: HarperCollins, 2008, p. 1.

[5]Egan, M., "Solar Energy Jobs Growing 17 Times Faster than US Economy," CNN/Money, May 25, 2017: http://money.cnn.com/2017/05/24/news/economy/solar-jobs-us-coal/index.html.

[6]Ettenson, L., "U.S. Clean Energy Jobs Surpass Fossil Fuel Employment," NRDC, February 1, 2017, : https://www.nrdc.org/experts/lara-ettenson/us-clean-energy-jobs-surpass-fossil-fuel-employment.

[7]Shutters, C., "New Study Finds Green Construction Is Major US Economic Driver," US Green Building Council, September 15, 2016: https://www.usgbc.org/articles/new-study-finds-green-construction-major-us-economic-driver.

[8]McKibben, B., "Winning Slowly is the Same as Losing," *Rolling Stone Magazine*, December 1, 2017: https://www.rollingstone.com/politics/news/bill-mckibben-winning-slowly-is-the-same-as-losing-w512967.

[9]About 90 percent of all US employment is in the private sector, with small businesses being especially represented in the mix. See "Frequently Asked Questions," Office of Advocacy, Small Business Administration, September 2012,: https://www.sba.gov/sites/default/files/FAQ_Sept_2012.pdf.

[10]Semuels, A., "Getting Rid of the Bosses," *The Atlantic*, July 8, 2015: https://www.theatlantic.com/business/archive/2015/07/no-bosses-worker-owned-cooperatives/397007/.

[11]US Federation of Worker Cooperatives: https://usworker.coop/what-is-a-worker-cooperative/.

[12]"ESOP (Employee Stock Ownership Plan) Facts," National Center for Employee Ownership: https://www.esop.org/ and Riley, T., "How Worker-Owned Companies Work," Moyers&Co., March 22, 2013: http://billmoyers.com/2013/03/22/how-worker-owned-companies-work/.

[13]"Worker Cooperatives Are More Productive than Normal Companies," *The Nation*, March 28, 2016: https://www.thenation.com/article/worker-cooperatives-are-more-productive-than-normal-companies/

[14]"China Bans Foreign Waste—but What Will Happen to the World's Recycling?" *Scientific American*, October 21, 2017: https://www.scientificamerican.com/article/china-bans-foreign-waste-but-what-will-happen-to-the- worlds-recycling/.

[15]Brodwin, D., "A Cleveland Success Story," *US News & World Report*, July 21, 2016: https://www.usnews.com/opinion/articles/2016-07-21/evergreen-cooperative-is-a-cleveland-jobs-success-story.

[16]See Cassano, J., "Inside America's Largest Worker-Run Business," Fast Company September 8, 2015,: https://www.fastcompany.com/3049930/inside-americas-largest-worker-run-business.

[17]See Flanders, L., "How America's Largest Worker Owned Co-Op Lifts People Out of Poverty," *Yes! Magazine*, August 14, 2014: http://www.yesmagazine.org/about.

[18]Cassano, J., "Inside America's Largest Worker-Run Business."

[19]Welch, B., "Simply the Best: CHCA's Employee-Ownership Model," *Medium*, September 6, 2016: https://medium.com/@bthechangemedia/simply-the-best-chcas-employee-ownership-model-97b8300c6afa.

[20]See "Home Healthcare: Fastest-Growing Industry Faces Workforce Challenges," American Mobile Nurses: https://www.amnhealthcare.com/home-health-industry-growth/.

[21]For background on contemporary food justice issues, see Food First, a longstanding advocacy organization dedicated to increasing food justice in the United States and abroad: https://foodfirst.org/about-us/our-work/.

[22]See Jayaraman, S., *Behind the Kitchen Door*, Ithaca, NY: Cornell University Press, 2014: https://books.google.com/books/about/ Behind_the_Kitchen_Door.html?id=ITBKDwAAQBAJ&printsec=frontcover &source=kp_read_button#v=onepage&q&f=false.

[23]See Doyle, A., "What You Need to Know About Minimum Wages for Workers Who Receive Tips," *The Balance*, January 2, 2018: https://www.thebalance.com/minimum-wage-for-workers-who-receive-tips-206 2119.

[24]See Berke, J., "The Legal Marijuana Market Is Exploding—It'll Hit Almost $10 Billion Sales in This Year," BusinessInsider, December 8, 2017: http://www.businessinsider.com/legal-weed-market-to-hit-10-billion-in-sales- report-says-2017-12.

[25]Berke, J., "The Legal Marijuana Market Is Exploding."

[26]Muro, M. & Whiton, J., "Geographic Gaps Are Widening while US Economic Growth Increases," Brookings Institution: https://www.brookings.edu/blog/the-avenue/2018/01/22/uneven-growth/.

[27]Peak, C., "It's About More than Just a Pipeline," NationSwell, February 15, 2017: http://nationswell.com/nick- tilsen-standing-rock-thunder-valley-community-development/ and, also, Grozdanic, L., "Wind and Solar-Powered Thunder Valley Regenerative Community Rises in South Dakota," Inhabitat, El Segundo, CA at: https://inhabitat.com/wind-and-solar-powered-eco-community-to-house-4000-members-of-the-oglala-lakota- nation/thunder-valley-regenerative-plan-by-bnim-1/.

[28]"Grantee Spotlight," Doris Duke Charitable Foundation: http://www.ddcf.org/grants/grantee-spotlight/thunder-valley-cdc/.

[29]"Thunder Valley CDC," Robert Rauschenberg Foundation: https://www.rauschenbergfoundation.org/grants/climate-change/thunder-valley-cdc.

[30]See Fullerton, J. & Lovins, H., "Creating A 'Regenerative Economy' to Transform Global Finance Into a Force for Good," FastCompany, October 29, 2013: https://www.fastcompany.com/3020653/creating-a-regenerative- economy-to-transform-global-finance-into-a-force-for-good.

[31]Field, A., "More Evidence of Impact Investing Growth—And What It Means for Social Entrepreneurs," Forbes, January 31, 2017: https://www.forbes.com/sites/annefield/2017/01/31/more-evidence-impact-investing-growth-and-what-it-means-for-social-entrepeneurs/ #1591b35e7b7f.

[32]See REDF's website report on "Our Impact": http://redf.org/impact/

[33]Hooper, Peter, et al, "US Income and Wealth Inequality," Deutsche Bank, January 2018: https://www.db.com/newsroom_news/Inequality_Jan2018.pdf

[34]Long, H., "There's a Serious Proposal to Give Babies Born in the United States $20,000 (or More)," January 8, 2018, The Washington Post at: https://www.washingtonpost.com/news/wonk/wp/2018/01/08/theres-a-serious-proposal-to-give-every-baby-born-in-america-20000-or-more/?utm_term=.2968eac30139. Ibid. In mid-2015, *The Atlantic* reported black family wealth being about 13 times below the level of

white family wealth. See White, G. B., "The Recession's Racial Slant," June 24, 2015, *The Atlantic*: https://www.theatlantic.com/business/ archive/2015/06/black-recession-housing-race/396725/. See also, Jan, T., "White Families Have Nearly 10 Times the Net Worth of Black Families. And the Gap is Growing," September 28, 2017, The Washington Post at: https://www.washingtonpost.com/news/wonk/wp/2017/09/28/ black-and-hispanic-families-are-making-more-money-but-they-still-lag-far-behind-whites/?utm_term=.c70a9b26358f.

[35]Jan. T., "White Families Have Nearly 10 Times the Net Worth of Black Families. And the Gap is Growing": https://www.washingtonpost.com/ news/wonk/wp/2017/09/28/black-and-hispanic-families-are-making-more-money-but-they-still-lag-far-behind-whites/?utm_term=.c70a9b 26358f.

[36]See Oliver, M. E., and T. M. Shapiro, *Black Wealth, White Wealth*, NY: Routledge, New York, 2006: https://books.google.com/books?id=4ksJuX 02DNwC&printsec=frontcover&source=gbs_ge_summary_r&cad=0#v= onepage&q&f=false.

[37]See again Long, H., "There's a Serious Proposal to Give Babies Born in the United States $20,000 (or More)."

[38]See again Jan. T., "White Families Have Nearly 10 Times the Net Worth . . . "

[39]powell, j. a., *Racing Towards Justice*, Bloomington, IN: Indiana University Press, 2012, pp. 23-24.

[40]See, again, Long, H., "There's a Serious Proposal to Give Babies Born in the United States $20,000 (or More)."

[41]See Cramer, R. et al., "Children's Savings Accounts," New America Foundation's Asset Building Program, June 2014: https://static.new america.org/attachments/1657-childrens-savings- accounts/CSAEviden ceImplicationsFINAL6_14.pdf.

[42]See Youth Banking Resource Center, Federal Deposit Insurance Corporation (FDIC), January 5, 2018: https://www.fdic.gov/consumers/ assistance/protection/depaccounts/youthsavings/index.html, as well as "Ready, Set, Save: Teach Your Kids Smart Money Habits," 2018, USAA, San Antonio, TX at: https://www.usaa.com/inet/wc/youth_ first_start_savings_main?0&akredirect=true.

[43]See the Forum for Sustainable & Responsible Investment's informative: https://www.ussif.org/sribasics, as well as "Triple Bottom Line," *The Economist*, November 17, 2009: https://www.economist.com/node/143 01663.

[44]See Field, A., "More Evidence of Impact Investing Growth—And What It Means For Social Entrepreneurs," *Forbes*, January 31, 2017: https://www.forbes.com/sites/annefield/2017/01/31/more-evidence-

impact-investing-growth-and-what-it-means-for-social-entrepeneurs/ #1591b35e7b7f. See, also, Benjamin, J., "Socially Responsible Investing Is Coming of Age," *Investment News*, March 6, 2016: http://www.investmentnews.com/article/20160306/FREE/160309960/socially-responsible-investing-is-coming-of-age.

[45]The Interfaith Center on Corporate Responsibility pioneered the use of shareholder advocacy to press companies on environmental, social and governance issues. See http://www.iccr.org/about-iccr. For background information on CERES, see Wapner, P., *Environmental Activism and Civic Politics*, Albany: State University of New York Press, 1996, p. 130. CERES, a coalition of fourteen leading environmental activist organizations, advanced the Valdez Principles for responsible corporate conduct in the aftermath of the 1989 Exxon Valdez Oil Spill. For more about the Sisters of St. Francis of Philadelphia's shareholder activism see MacDonald, J. G., "The Power of Nun: Taking a Lead Role in Shareholder Activism," *The Christian Science Monitor*, February 27, 2006: https://www.csmonitor.com/2006/0227/p14s01-wmgn.html. See, also, Silk L. & Vogel, D., *Ethics & Profits: The Crisis of Confidence in American Business*, 1976, Simon & Shuster, New York.

[46]See "Socially Responsible Investing: Earn Better Returns from Good Companies," *Forbes* August 16, 2017: https://www.forbes.com/sites/moneyshow/2017/08/16/socially-responsible-investing-earn-better-returns-from- good-companies/#4341c71a623d.

[47]Confluence Philanthropy's informative corporate website at: http://www.confluencephilanthropy.org/What-Is-Mission/Impact-Investing.

CHAPTER 6
Democratic Renewal, Shared Prosperity and a New Social Contract for Twenty-first-Century America

> Never doubt that a small group of thoughtful, committed peo-
> ple can change the world. Indeed, it is the only thing that ever
> has.
>
> —Margaret Mead

The essential focal points and purposes of this book are, first, to
advocate for a different way forward for American democracy and
economy; second, to identify organizing, leadership and problem-
solving models that are emerging to help shape a better future along
these lines; and, third, to encourage a broader unification of progressive efforts to advance the kind of democratic action and economic
empowerment we need. Prior chapters here have accordingly sought
to identify and lift up selected examples of what could be progressive
America's next stage platforms and standards for civic and economic
advancement. While the visionaries and practitioners driving these
new and better ways forward are presently relatively few in number,
their innovations are extremely significant. More and more practitioners and thinkers are lining up behind these new ways of envision-
ing and acting in our times.

The present volume has highlighted only a handful of the many
exciting examples of this sort that are currently active. That is to say
that, while still in formation, there exists on the horizon growing possibilities to improve human and planetary conditions in response to

regressive and dangerous policies that conservative and neoliberal forces have instituted to the great detriment of so many people and the natural environment. Normalizing, accelerating and scaling this emerging body of progressive initiative and innovation for broader application across our nation and world is what must come next. As this work progresses, the need evolves with it to establish new frameworks and societal agreements to govern human and institutional relations. Given the highly unsatisfactory and unsustainable nature of present efforts in public policy and wealth creation, it is beyond vital that we establish a new and different pathway forward.

The Power of a Small Group of Committed People

As the cultural anthropologist Margaret Mead once famously observed, it is generally small committed groups of ordinary people that, by coming together and challenging conventional wisdom, significantly change the course of history. Indeed, real change tends to come from the bottom of society and is driven by those who are most directly affected by misplaced policies and practices. This has been true in the United States since its founding, from breaking away from English royal governance to abolishing slavery and extending suffrage to women to instituting labor rights to our present movements for economic democracy, disability rights, gender equality, immigrant rights, racial justice and violence prevention. Typically, the protagonists of our most successful social movements have been poor people, women and the young. It is still the case today that the change we need in America and the world is more likely to emerge from the surging movements of common men, women and young people than from the White House, the Halls of Congress or the Supreme Court. Evidence to support this assertion is all around us. Virtually all of the important social movements that have emerged in recent years to achieve real impact on the key issues of the day started with small, largely unknown groups of deeply committed grassroots people.

Whether they be marriage-equality advocates, or pioneers in cannabis legalization or social enterprise, or living-wage proponents, or stewards of sustainability and indigenous land rights, or Dreamers, or champions of black lives, or women and girls finding solidarity and solace through the #MeToo movement, or young people saying #Never Again to mass gun violence—in each instance, the growing voices for change that have emerged began in whispers, off the radar and beyond the bright lights of television cameras. But, happily, in turn, each of these organic, grassroots movements has emerged to create a whole new conversation in society that would have been impossible to imagine only a few short years ago. If more effectively unified and harmonized in their efforts, the collective power of these progressive movements can establish the most potent force for change in our nation in more than a generation.

Getting Back to Basics

We need to revisit basic assumptions about our current political and economic practices, and our corresponding responsibilities to one another, to others around the globe and to the natural environment. We need to do this first and foremost by reactivating dormant aspects of our political democracy using new approaches and technologies that engage people in progressive policy-making. We also need to rethink the essential purposes and rules of our economic system, and introduce new economic incentives so that our economy meets the quality-of-life and survival needs of real people, families, communities and natural ecosystems. In short, we need to establish a new social contract for the twenty-first century, one that better serves all of humanity and planetary life.

The Price of Change

These are large and sweeping aims, to be sure. And there is no guarantee that the things progressives would most like to see happen next in these areas will somehow magically come to pass. If we want the nation and the world to track more closely with our progressive vision and values, we will have to work and fight very hard for it. That has been the case for progressive people since the beginning of history. And, looking ahead, even in the best-case scenario, the change we need and seek will require formidable—even unprecedented—commitment and mobilization. Such change is not unattainable by any stretch of the imagination. In fact, it is entirely within our reach if we are smart, disciplined and aggressive in our collective efforts for a widespread democratic and economic reform agenda. But, to forge the kind of change that is needed will require new approaches and attitudes concerning leadership, partnership and collaboration.

In the future that awaits us, we will have to do much more together than apart. We will have to learn new consensus-building and resource-sharing skills. And, in the process, we will have to deepen our trust and common bonds with other progressives and their organizations. Much of what is required to make this happen will not come without pain or cost because of how we have become used to operating—often in misplaced competition or in disconnected silos. Progressive leaders and anchor institutions need to come together to advance tactical and time-sensitive collaborations in the short term, but also to promote and scale far more strategic and permanent joint endeavors that dramatically amplify the progressive community's power and impact in the future. This in turn will mean reorienting our progressive leaders' and institutions' essential sensibilities about working across issue sets, constituencies and assets in ways that mitigate and overcome past impediments to partnership and reform. It will mean setting aside egos and internecine conflicts and divides in ways that help us better to align and harmonize our efforts for the common good. It will mean accommodating a new ethic of collective action and advancement, rather than prioritizing more individuated and contingent efforts, as we have during recent years. In many instances, it will mean having to learn a whole new way of doing business.

Daring to Go Big

In the next phases of the journey, it is essential that progressive leaders and people think big about the kinds of changes we want to see in the coming years. We need to direct our focus to making our collective impact worthy of the substantial opportunities and challenges we face in this work. These are not times for dabbling on the margins or making incremental improvements in the ways we conduct our public business or allocate scarce public resources. On the contrary, given that no less than the integrity of our nation and the fate of the world are at stake, we need to move forward in bold and significant ways. If we fail to act now and decisively, America's democratic traditions and institutions, as well as our economic leadership and vitality, will continue to erode.

In that unhappy scenario, we would likely see rapid additional decline in our domestic and global security, as well as in the overall quality of life for people across much of the world. We would also see continuing, rapid diminishment of our environment and natural-resource base. And we would almost certainly see the more widespread global decline of the best of western democratic values. What else do we need to know to conclude that the kind of change our politics and economy require to avoid these stark possibilities is not one of degree, but rather one of kind?

Redefining What Success Means

We need to face this new reality by building a vision of a better way forward that can genuinely excite a large number of people by promoting more mutually reinforcing actions across the field of progressive change networks. There are important precedents for this in our history. During the progressive era of the early twentieth century, for example, intellectuals, labor leaders, educators, social workers and others organized successfully to demand new national education and labor standards, as well as new political rights for women. During the Great Depression, responding to the will and needs of millions of poor workers and families, forward-looking national leaders supported massive new investments in social insurance and public works programs. And during the Great Society years, moved by mass protests and marches involving millions of disaffected Americans, the nation's political leaders advanced critically important civil rights legislation and new national outlays for novel and important consumer and environmental protections. During earlier periods of our national journey, the leaders of the times encouraged Americans to invest jointly in civic and community-building campaigns. In moments of great collective need for our nation,

Americans have always risen to the occasion. The past century is replete with examples of this. From the mobilization of millions of otherwise unemployed artists and workers in Depression-era employment and service programs to the massive paper, tin and rubber recycling drives organized to advance the allied cause during WWII, to the robust call to action so many young Americans answered at the height of the Cold War following the formation of the Peace Corps, past successful mobilizations like these helped to shape our national identity and transform our society and world.

As we come to understand our shared aims and responsibilities, we must strive similarly to achieve levels of impact and change that are much more than incidental and fleeting. In this coming chapter of national policy and investment prioritization, progressives will face both the opportunity, as well as the need to strike an even more intentional and collective chord in defense of humanity and nature. In this context, we will be called to redefine what success means in our political and economic lives, focusing much more than ever on what is best for people and the planet rather than privilege and profit. Through greater power- and prosperity sharing, we can realize a more inclusive civic culture and a more sustainable economy that positively engages and serves far more Americans than is presently the case. In the process, we can do much to remedy the gross excesses of today's political and economic systems, and their increasingly degrading impact on people and the natural world, thus helping significantly to improve the long term prospects for human and global survival. But it will take a high degree of intentionality, a radically new orientation to the purposes of our economy and much work to make this happen.

Developing New and Better Metrics

Supporting, scaling and sustaining robust public and private initiatives that help solve our greatest human and ecological challenges must establish new standards of ambition and success for our economy and its systems of compensation and exchange. Presently, our leaders and institutions are grossly inhibited in these connections by their reliance on success and impact measures that reflect our system's increasingly misplaced emphasis on materialism and financial asset accumulation at the expense of other aspects of human and environmental consideration. Indeed our present focus on data derived from standard reporting metrics, such as the Gross Domestic Product (GDP), the Consumer Price Index (CPI) and the S&P 500, informs us about the aggregate performance of our economy. But it tells us nothing about the relative distribution of our national assets, the corollary impacts of our expanding production footprint on public health and global sustainability, or the diminishing quality of life and public satisfaction that finally matches up with what our current economic models produce.

In recent years, recognizing the limits of such standard measures, numerous efforts have emerged to establish alternative metrics for policy decision-makers that consider more of the total impact of economic investment on affected people, communities and ecosystems. These alternative measures provide a more rounded view of the economy's qualitative performance relative to people and communities, fairness and equity, and environmental sustainability. Among others, such alternative measures include:

—*The Gini coefficient*, a widely used measure of economic inequality within select nations in the world.
—*The United Nations Human Development Index*, a composite statistic of life expectancy, education and per capita income to rank countries into various tiers of human development.
—*The World Happiness Index*, a nation-by-nation measure of the levels of population contentment and quality of life.
—*The Genuine Progress Indicator*, a measure used by the State of Maryland to enhance the accuracy of its economic performance data by including such indicators as inequality, non-market benefits and environmental concerns.
—*The Self-Sufficiency Standard*, a comprehensive alternative to the Federal Poverty Guidelines, based on measures and appli-

cations developed by University of Washington and MIT researchers.

Looking ahead, as progressive leaders and grassroots advocates seek to redirect our economy to more socially and economically equitable ends, it is vitally important that our major public institutions and their leaders adopt more holistic metrics, such as those referenced above, to better guide institutional policy and investment. At the end of the day, if our systems of measuring societal success focus only on the material and the monetary, much is bound to be lost. The growing importance of money over all other human values that we see overtaking our public culture, institutions and relationships speaks to this point and raises profound questions that every American should reflect on at this pivotal moment in our history.

When more and more people are being left out of the equation, and more and more of our natural world is being sacrificed in the name of development and profit for only a very select few, can we really say we are succeeding? By the same token, when record profits produce unprecedented poverty and income inequality, social dislocation and conflict, and growing ecological crises, can we ever truly be assuaged by an upward bump in our nation's GDP, an unusually low CPI or a raging stock market index? The answer is a resounding no. Accordingly, in the future, we need to standardize new measures of systemic performance that make our economics and related democratic decision-making far more accountable to human and environmental considerations. In short, we need to ensure that our formal systems of measuring economic progress put the needs of people and the planet first, well ahead of privilege and profit.

A Working Framework for the Future

As we work collectively towards a new social contract, one that better meets the human and ecological imperatives of our times, we need to build a supporting framework to successfully operationalize it. This will involve consolidating the sort of large and compelling vision that can drive generational, if not multi-generational transformation. It will also involve establishing more formal systems and structures for strategically integrating and aligning progressive America's anchor organizations and leaders, and, wherever possible, their associated policy priorities, organizing campaigns and capacity-building efforts. A final key aspect of this work will involve amassing and optimally allocating new financial resources to fuel a successful progressive change agenda for the twenty-first century.

When progressive Americans, through our hard work and heightened sense of urgency, are able to harness these factors—a winning agenda, a stronger harmonization of advocacy and movement-building efforts and a better allocation of financial resources to advance this work—the change we seek will be both possible and palpable. But it will take all of us rowing in the same direction, bringing our unique and discreet contributions to the fore in ways that add up to more than the component parts of our respective efforts. The model projects and initiatives in democratic revitalization and economic justice highlighted here reflect strong working examples on which to build the agenda that progressive Americans need. What they require to evolve as new standards in the next stage of the American journey is the broader field-wide endorsement and coordination of progressive activists across the land, as well as supportive policy and capital investments by a more activist and engaged federal government and social-investment community.

Seven Next Stage Steps to the Future We All Want

There is much work to be done to address the debacle produced by hyper-capitalism along with its supporting and misguided policies afflicting common people and the natural environment. Achieving the level of change we need is going to require decades of progressive investment and action to overcome the drag our current approach has imposed on our democratic institutions, economy and environment. But there is a clear path to change, if progressive leaders and activists are able to join hearts and hands to act in a purposeful and disciplined way over the coming years. There are seven imperatives that are especially vital for next-generation progressive action and leadership.

These are the over-arching priorities and investments around which we must unify in order for us all to move forward together in new and better ways. Together these imperatives establish the roadmap for next generation progressive wins and, ultimately, a fundamental reshaping of our democracy and economy in ways that are more in keeping with both our nation's foundational promises and evolving needs.

1. Fight for and Secure New Guaranteed Federal Rights to Basic Social Goods

No matter how much we tell our governmental leaders we want fundamental change, we remain largely unheard and things get worse. And no matter how hard we work and try to do all "the right things," it is becoming more and more impossible to achieve our dreams, let alone anything like financial security or a reasonably comfortable retirement. If we are to exert pressure on government, it is imperative that we secure essential public goods as newly guaranteed federal rights. In particular, it is most vital for progressive leaders and change agents to advocate aggressively in the years to come for major constitutional reforms and/or national legislation establishing, at a minimum, the following new federal guarantees: 1) quality, cost-free education (building on publicly-supported early childcare and pre-school learning), 2) living-wage employment, 3) single-payer health care coverage and 4) safe, affordable housing. There are certainly other areas of concern around which one could also propose the establishment of new federal rights designed to expand access to essential social and economic goods. Among these are race- and gender-based income equality for comparable work, meaningful access to safe and nutritious food and enhanced public transit and disability-community accommodations. In America's evolving economy and culture, the absence of fair and meaningful access to these essential things is effectively a death blow.

Except in extremely rare cases, no one lacking these basics is going to have anything like an equal opportunity or a reasonable hope of economic security or a quality living standard in the future ahead. Instead, they will be resigned to a life of second-class status or even worse. In too many cases, the only realistic prospects for the most vulnerable people living in the absence of new basic federal guarantees like those enumerated above will be more poverty, crime, drug addiction, homelessness and early death. Merely accepting this as the new normal would constitute a material breach of our nation's longstanding commitments to fairness and egalitarianism. Without expanding public protections and investments that empower our people with the essential tools they need to participate and contribute meaningfully in our evolving society and economy, there can be no more claim that ours is a land of real and equal opportunity; and neither can there be any further pretense that our nation is committed to "liberty and justice for all," as invoked in the American Pledge of Allegiance.

Americans who are unable to keep up with the accelerating churn of our hyper-capitalistic economy will cost taxpayers more and more money and require more and more government intervention in the years to come—burdening our already stretched and deficit-driven public sector. Continuing in this direction can only inspire still additional public expenditures to manage resulting increases in poverty, social dislocation and political unrest. Consequently, one of the most important organizing and advocacy goals progressive leaders and activists must support in this time of resistance is establishing new social and economic guarantees and investments.

Such efforts will no doubt be met with staunch and incredulous right-wing rejection, and arguments that they are unconstitutional, antithetical to the free market and liberal-democratic traditions, and otherwise ill-conceived. Conservatives and neoliberals will argue that the proposal at hand is inherently socialistic, inflationary and generally unworkable. During the height of the Great Depression in the 1930s, similar arguments were made against the Roosevelt Administration's pursuit of more aggressive federal initiatives to encourage national cohesion and spur economic recovery; and important programs advanced by FDR for these purposes—including those embedded in the National Industrial Recovery Act and the Agricultural Adjustment Act—were ultimately rejected as unconstitutional by the US Supreme Court.[1] But other key elements and agencies of Roosevelt's New Deal—the Social

Security Administration, the Works Progress Administration and the National Labor Relations Board, among them—survived to help our nation regain its essential social, political and economic footing.

Predictable and tired contemporary objections against enhanced federal rights and spending should not discourage the efforts of progressive activists. Indeed, without the added income security and ultimate social cost-savings a move to expand such federal guarantees would enable, it is difficult to imagine how America's middle and working classes, and especially younger Americans just entering the workforce, could possibly participate in the society and the economy of the future in ways that are meaningful and enduring.[2]

2. Advance New Measures of Societal Well-Being

Earlier discussion here underscores the need for a refinement and standardization of the various emerging alternative measures of national progress we have seen over recent years, to account for the built-in limitations of current measures, such as the GDP and CPI, which focus exclusively on material economic variables. These emerging alternatives are increasingly needed to expose policymakers and the general public to far more nuanced and accurate information about the efficacy and impact of various public-policy and investment decisions that bear on the economy's performance and its relative benefits to diverse groups. The new metrics we need to support, like many of those described earlier, must account for the human and environmental impacts of production and growth that traditional measures do not.

Recently, leading nonprofit institutions have begun to research precisely how to quantify these values as part of our measures of economic growth and social impact. One such effort dating back to 2013 is that of the Insight Center for Community Economic Development, in Oakland, which has sought to develop a more unified system of accounts in the social and economic performance measurement field with support from the Michigan-based Kresge Foundation.[3] With proper care, these efforts can expand and be built on by experts and interested progressive leaders during the coming years in ways that ultimately inform the introduction of some unified alternative measure, or at least some amalgamated index of leading alternative indicators, that can provide public policy leaders with a more accurate and socially and environmentally friendly measure of the real-life impacts of national investment, economic activity and growth. Unless and until we develop such new national measures of balanced economic performance, much of our transactional activity and public policy will continue to camouflage the real costs of production that are currently being subsidized by all of us—mostly unwittingly—through the externality costs embedded in our existing production system.

3. Promote a More Unifying Civic Culture

One of the most important things progressive leaders and activists can do in the next stages of our work is to advocate strongly for efforts to resuscitate our nation's democracy and civic culture through expanded investment in constructive public dialog, community participation in public problem-solving and the arts. Over the past 40 years, through major reductions in public funding for school-based community engagement projects, civic education and creative culture, we have foreclosed opportunities for too many Americans to better unite around our common issues and humanity. And, in doing so, we have dangerously diminished our sense of mutual understanding and collective purpose as Americans. It is hard to imagine the center holding much longer, given how uninformed, divided and rancorous community relations have become across our society. In response, progressive Americans need to advocate aggressively to ensure that future public budgets at all levels of government reflect greater attention to the important shared benefits that result from increased investments in improved human relations, civic-education and engagement initiatives, democracy-building efforts and creative culture projects.

Leading Social Investors Are Helping to Model the Way Forward

During recent years, important private social investment leaders, such as the Ford Foundation and Agnes Gund, W. K. Kellogg Foundation and Weingart Foundation, among others, have shown real leadership in connection with supporting civic-minded arts and culture projects and/or concentrating their institutional and program resources to address growing divides related to racial and economic equity. Social investment leadership efforts and initiatives like these should encourage still other private sector leaders to work towards eliminating persistent and growing social and economic divides. In the coming years, if we are to do better as a nation, far greater numbers of public and private sector leaders will have to align their support around such efforts.

Investing in Civic Culture, Engagement and the Arts is Good for Our Economy, as Well as Our Democracy

As Richard Florida, author of *The Rise of the Creative Class*, has observed, many of today's most talented and coveted workers are principally engaged in creative pursuits. These are both traditional creatives, such as visual artists and actors, as well as new economy professionals in areas such as technology and digital design. Increasingly, workers of the Creative Class—who are typically far better compensated than service workers—drive regional development by virtue of the places where they choose to live, work and spend.[4] More and more, these are places that are culturally tolerant, diverse and dynamic. The nation's emerging Creative Class is thus highly inclined to reject such conventional magnets as tax breaks, transportation hubs and other efficiencies, tending instead to be drawn to locations and workplaces that offer diversity and cultural amenities, access to green spaces and a strong sense of community. Increased investment across America that would enhance the availability of such amenities would likely produce multiple benefits, including better community relations, increased access to arts and cultural offerings and expanded prospects for regional economic success and prosperity-sharing.

Recently, research has shown that a diverse population is among the factors that produce robust growth within economic regions; these include minority middle-class and immigrant inhabitants. Such factors depend in turn on public policy and the extent of private investment that supports broader diversity and inclusion in the development of regional dynamism. According to Chris Benner and Manuel Pastor, leading investigators in this area:

> Linking regional prosperity and regional equity has great appeal—after all, who would not like it if all good things came together? But the interesting thing is that this is not merely a question of wishing for the best: statistical research is suggesting that doing good and doing well can go hand in hand.[5]

Overall, Benner's and Pastor's findings are in direct contrast to standard conservative tenets that argue the economy works best, both for growth and prosperity-sharing, when it is most unregulated. As Benner and Pastor see it, "Counting just on growth is not likely to lead to 'just growth'—a set of outcomes that include economic expansion and social equity but also an inclusive conversation about how best to achieve inclusion."[6] Rather, it is precisely more active, intentional and inclusive public policy and investment that increasingly builds our strongest regional economies.

Given the above set of observations, progressive leaders and activists would do well in the next stages of our journey to organize heavily in local and regional public and private funding settings, to seek enhanced budgetary resources for proven and promising efforts in civic education, community building and reinvestment, human relations and cultural arts. Where formal community consultation and reviews in connection with such funding decisions are not available in the form of public oversight boards or independent arts or human relations commissions, progressive advocates at the grassroots and regional levels should collaborate with local officials to change their governing policies in ways that allow and encourage the formation of such bodies. And, in instances where they face official reluctance or refusal to do so, local and regional activists should aggressively organize to demand change. By focusing on these things and ultimately succeeding, we can help to create a more informed, unified and progressive framework for expanding the nation's social cohesion, civic participation and economic vitality.

4. Organize and Invest to Resuscitate Our Waning Democratic Systems

There is a growing number of new progressive policy proposals and frameworks presently in play that, if scaled and applied more broadly across the land, would bolster our nation's democratic systems. From highly participatory new voting methods to civic and political leadership development models, and from campaign finance law reforms to the broader application of information technologies, we have the tools to improve our nation's diminishing levels of voter and civic engagement. But these innovations cannot be normalized without continued widespread organizing and advocacy. That is to say that it is principally up to progressive leaders and activists to demand such reforms and innovations. In the process, we must focus on coming together in unprecedented alliances and collaborations that involve sharing resources and pursuing joint advocacy efforts that are more integrated, strategic and sustainable. It is especially essential that leading progressive change agents work hard together to better combine resources and leverage the work of our institutions and networks in a more permanent, rather than merely tactical way.

We need to take direct action together and build the alliances of our strongest entities in varying fields to create a much broader collective impact. In this context, formal alliances of the following anchor organizing networks should be forged: ADAPT, Black Lives Matter, Jobs with Justice, MoveOn.org, National People's Action, the National Domestic Workers Alliance, #NeverAgain, the PICO National Network, 350.org, United We Dream, the Water is Life Movement, and leading regional immigrant and refugee rights coalitions, such as the Illinois Coalition for Immigrant and Refugee Rights and the Coalition for Humane Immigrant Rights of Los Angeles. In addition, we need to redouble our support for essential intermediary and advocacy organizations that offer important field building convenings, as well as financial, policy and technical support for ground-level organizing and advocacy campaigns. Such organizations include the Center for Community Change, Ella Baker Center, the Emerald Cities Collaborative, Green for All, the Greenlining Institute, Indivisible, Midwest Academy, Movement Strategy Center, the National Immigration Law Center, PolicyLink, the Women's March, United for a Fair Economy, Urban Habitat and Working Partnerships USA.

Support Next-Generation Leadership

Given the nation's evolving demography and culture, it is essential that progressive leaders and activists invest heavily in the formation and preparation of the next generation's multicultural political and civic leaders. More and more of these leaders will—and should—be women and people of color, young Americans, Americans with disabilities, LGBTQ Americans, people of limited economic means, environmental justice advocates and people whose lives have been shaped by the built-in inequities of the US criminal justice and immigration control systems. To help us move in these essential directions, it is additionally imperative that progressives combine forces to compel American public schools to reintroduce quality civics education in their standard curricula; and public and private institutions alike should ensure greater, rather than diminished, investments in public art and community service programs, especially for our youth, through vastly expanded funding support.

When our nation's increasingly diverse voices and views are more meaningfully factored into policy-making and community-building, our society will naturally begin to evolve in a more harmonious, productive and winning direction for all. To advance this important democracy-enhancing work, progressive activists need especially to align with and more fully support key emerging groups that are building our next generation leadership. These include Americans for Indian Opportunity, API Vote, Black Lives Matter, Higher Heights for America, New American Leaders, the New Leaders Council, United We Dream and the Women's Policy Institute of California. To fully appreciate why advancing this work is so vital today, one need only consider the recent power and eloquence that has emerged in recent years through the actions and voices of young Americans organizing for criminal law and law enforcement reform, violence prevention, environmental justice and immigrant and worker rights.

Amplify Our Collective Efforts to Combat Anti-Democratic Practices

Progressive Americans must align more aggressively to challenge fundamentally anti-democratic practices, such as political gerrymandering, particularly by conservative politicians seeking to make it almost impossible for progressive and racial-minority candidates to win in districts across the nation. More and more, progressive forces need to push for independent redistricting commissions such as those now operating effectively in Arizona and California, to ensure better alternatives to the redrawing of political boundaries by partisan office holders who have a stake in maintaining the status quo. Presently, some nine other states are considering such reforms.[7] Leading national organizations, such as the ACLU, the Brennan Center, Indivisible and MoveOn.org are at the forefront of progressive community education and organizing efforts to combat systematic gerrymandering, and should be actively supported by the broader progressive movement in their continuing efforts.

Join Forces to Demand and Secure Fundamental Reforms in Criminal Law and Policing

In order to enhance the nation's democratic integrity, we must reform criminal law and practice in ways that are far more equitable along racial and class divides. Today in America, some 6 million mostly poor Americans, a disproportionate share of whom are people of color, are incarcerated in or on parole from local, state and federal penal institutions that strip them of opportunities to vote or otherwise contribute to civic and economic life. In states like Florida, Iowa, and Kentucky, convicted felons are ineligible to vote even after they have served their prison terms and been released. The problem is exacerbated by the increasing reliance on private prison contractors as a public cost saving measure; this creates perverse incentives to maximize the number and length of incarcerations in order to optimize their profits. Justice is further distorted when it comes to racial minorities, who suffer a grossly disproportionate number of false convictions. Recent data reveal that, with respect to most police interactions, white Americans tend still to be treated far more leniently than people of color at each stage of the process, from apprehension to pre-trial detention, and that courts similarly favor whites over Americans of color in both their propensity to convict and to mete out more severe sentences.[8]

Recent years have seen important and timely new efforts emerge to address these and other disturbing aspects of US criminal law and justice that diminish our nation's democratic vitality and fairness. Going forward, it is vitally important that progressive leaders and activists redouble our efforts to demand a fundamentally more equitable focus across our legal system, especially in relation to the application of criminal law policies and practices affecting people of color at both the state and federal levels. Progressive groups and their leaders need to work with anchor rights and justice organizations such as the ACLU, the Alliance for Boys and Men of Color, Ella Baker Center, Barrios Unidos, Black Lives Matter, the Brennan Center, the Color of Change, the Equal Justice Initiative, the National Compadres Network and the Sentencing Project. We must assist these organizations in converting their ideas and proposals into American law and policy. Additional public-policy reforms are needed to stem the use of excessive police force in communities of color. Without these interventions, we are fundamentally denying people of color active engagement in and benefits from the best of our democratic way of life. We need to ensure that everywhere across the nation law enforcement professionals are trained and incentivized to seek alternatives to killing persons suspected or apprehended for violations of the law, that working body cams become the norm for all law enforcement officers and that independent citizen review bodies are established universally as the primary means of investigating and deciphering the legal disposition of police officers involved in the shooting of any individual.

Coalesce to Achieve Smarter and More Humane Immigration Policy

We need to pursue massive reform of our current immigration law and policies. Presently, some 11 million people, most of them from Latin American, Asian, African and Middle Eastern nations, are living, working and contributing to our economy and culture in important ways. In the overwhelming number of cases, these foreign-born individuals have become contributing and valued members of our work places, schools, communities and places of worship. But because of draconian laws and policies anchored in the misplaced prejudice and cultural anxiety of many white Americans and conservative politicians, even longstanding immigrants who have proven their devotion to this nation have been relegated to a shadow, second-class status in our contemporary legal system.

Growing anti-immigrant sentiment and policy over recent years has borne down heavily on affected immigrant families and communities. The most recent implementation of senseless refugee policy has resulted in the intentional incarceration and separation of families seeking international legal protection from persecution and violence in their homelands; it is a sure sign that America—a nation built by immigrants and staunch opposition to the political persecution of religious and ethnic minorities—is losing its soul. Immigration authorities are mandated to raid more and more homes, schools and businesses, and deport large numbers of immigrants, often in violation of due process. Even the foreign-born children of immigrants who were brought to the United States as children and who have grown up knowing no other country than America—the so-called Dreamers—have been subjected to regulations and controls that diminish their safety and security, despite considerable evidence of their many productive contributions to our nation as students, workers and community builders. The time has come to rectify the practical and moral blight that our current immigration system imposes on individuals, families and communities.

There is no real way to maintain our cultural dynamism and global competitiveness if we do not quickly advance superior immigration policy. Besides its inconsistency and inhumanity, our current immigration policy ultimately discourages accessibility to foreign talent and capital that would benefit our nation, not to mention the intense need for labor to sustain our lifestyle as the current worker population ages and leaves the workforce. We need to rethink and humanize our laws and policies by establishing a clear and accessible pathway to citizenship for Dreamers and other longstanding undocumented Americans who have shown themselves to be more than responsible participants in our civic culture and economy. To help drive our policy proposals and reforms, we need to look for guidance from such leading organizations as Asian Americans Advancing Justice, the National Immigration Law Center, United We Dream, Unidos US, and the various regional coalitions for immigrant and refugee rights.

Aggressively Contest Foreign and Other Illegal Meddling in Our Elections

Finally, in the face of revelations that Russian governmental operatives were unduly involved in influencing our presidential race in 2016, it is imperative that progressives from every part of the nation unite collectively to advocate for public investment in election security measures that can better ensure the effective and trustworthy functioning of American voting systems. In the absence of such measures, any and all domestic improvements we secure to enhance the fairness and responsiveness of our democracy will be potentially compromised and even negated by continuing outside interference from hostile foreign sources—or nefarious domestic actors—whose interests are antithetical to those of progressives. And, to the extent evidence emerges that US (or foreign) politicians, government officials or private citizens were complicit, they should be exposed for corrupting our democratic institutions and made to feel the full weight of the law.

5. Embrace Restorative Justice and Economics

The increase in economic exclusion during times of declining opportunity has pushed so many millions of people into extreme poverty, homelessness, mental illness and crime. Our families, communities and our larger society have lost more than just the talent and potential social contributions of those we have effectively thrown overboard. By losing them, we have lost connection with one another and with ourselves. Today, mental and allied health challenges are particularly on the rise across America, with notable and disturbing incidents of drug addiction, suicide and violence affecting more and more of our communities. The expanding national opioid crisis reveals much of the problem, as does the growing incidence of mass shootings. Indeed, today in America, nearly 45 million people or 20 percent of the population are struggling with mental health challenges; in 2016, national expenditures to treat mental illness in America totaled more than $200 billion, constituting our nation's leading cost center for medical health conditions.[9]

Among children and teens, depression and suicide are especially growing problems. The Centers for Disease Control and Prevention recently found that fully 1 in 5 American children ages 3 through 17 —about 15 million—have a diagnosable mental, emotional or behavioral disorder in any given year.[10] The problems appear to be especially pertinent to increasing numbers of young women and girls, whose recent incidents of severe depression and suicide have become particularly pronounced. Indeed, the suicide rate for teen girls in America reached an historic national high in 2015, and a Johns Hopkins University report from 2016 showed significant increases in the rate of adolescent and young adult depression since 2008.[11]

In many communities of color, moreover, especially among young men and boys, gang affiliation, illicit drug use and violence remain significant problems, which are facilitated in turn by inter-generational poverty and exclusion from the economy and mainstream society. Racially-biased school discipline and expulsion policies, over-policing and surveillance in minority-dominant communities, unequal and unjust applications of criminal law, and draconian sentencing protocols all add to the cycle of violence and incarceration. Mental health issues and trauma, thus, are understandably prevalent among American boys and young men of color. Yet, outside of a small handful of nonprofit advocates and agencies, little is available for these young people in the form of community assistance or support. As a result, ironically for boys and young men of color engaged in gang and allied criminal activity, their counter-cultural affiliation is the lone space in which they are able to achieve a sense of stability, identity and belonging. It is difficult for most people living outside of these realities to comprehend how this could be so. But it is, and given the lived experience of such young men and boys, their inclinations in these directions, however self-destructive, senseless or confusing from the vantage point of the larger society, are in fact logical.[12] The resulting costs to all of us are significant and growing. Indeed recent research shows that the direct costs of blindly discarding these young men is expanding at each turn with now $80 billion being spent annually by US taxpayers to warehouse criminal offenders, a highly disproportionate share of whom are young men and boys of color.[13]

Recalibrating Our Focus as a Society

One of the many explanations for these disturbing trends—perhaps the most important one—is that, notwithstanding historic stock market values and levels of wealth generation in America, more and more people in our society are feeling fundamentally unhappy, vulnerable and left out. For too many, our society and economy are simply moving too fast, our historical opportunity structures are closing, our culture is becoming harder and more unforgiving, and our leaders and institutions are becoming less and less responsive to public will and needs. In this context, although many, if not most, Americans are working harder and longer than ever, they are actually less and less financially and otherwise secure. In addition, for most people, in the hustle to survive there is less and less time for family, community, faith, recreation and recovery. For most, there is only a growing workload, an expanding debt burden and higher and higher stress levels to show for all of our so-called "progress" as a country.

If America is to advance, we need to ramp up substantially our collective efforts as a society to re-humanize our economy, our various systems of public engagement and support, and our associated public policies. We need to promote new efforts in restorative justice and economics that are designed to help people to achieve their greatest potentialities, rather than accelerate our current approaches which clearly work to hold back growing numbers of people along with their families and communities. In the process, we need to reprogram our society's strategic thinking and resource expenditures in less punitive and exclusive directions; and we need to work instead to invest in supportive and responsive ways that lift people up. This is not just the right thing to do; it is the smart and essential thing to do if we are to regain our nation's moral, democratic and economic leadership in the decades to come.

Embracing Restorative Justice

Restorative justice efforts take many forms and traverse many fields, ranging from law enforcement and judicial administration to public health and education, and from employment and social enterprise to civic culture and the creative arts.[14] By developing affirmative alternatives to ultimately unproductive punitive public policy, restorative justice strategies strive to humanize our ways of seeking recompense, reconciliation and criminal rehabilitation in the aftermath of criminal violations and their attendant traumas. A central restorative-justice principle calls for perpetrators to atone for their legal and moral violations in ways that are ultimately redeeming for themselves, their victims and kin, and the larger society. In all but the most heinous of criminal cases, restorative justice imposes punishments that are less geared to conventional incarceration and punitive sentencing, as we know it today and, rather, focuses more on learning, healing and accountability to the larger community through meaningful public service and reconciliation agreements with victims and/or victims' survivors. The notion and evolving practice of restorative justice is not only supported by social innovators and progressive justice advocates, but also by a growing number of researchers and scientists who support its formal application in our judicial system. For example, the University of Wisconsin's School of Medicine and Public Health recently reported that restorative justice approaches reduce juvenile- and adult-offender recidivism while increasing victims' and survivors' satisfaction with the criminal law system.[15]

Rethinking the Essential Purposes and Framework of Our National Economy

The most important thing progressive Americans can do to meet the present imperatives before us is to double down on our demands for systemic policy reforms designed to set our economy on a substantially different and better course. One of the most effective ways we can do this is to aggressively support the building of a sustainable social economy, one that is based on energy renewability and environmental responsibility, as well as broader economic justice and prosperity-sharing that can help to resuscitate our working and middle classes. To begin, we can move in this direction through major changes in our tax system, our regulatory machinery and federal and state policy to aggressively reorder economic investments and rewards to promote fundamentally more sustainable industry and enterprise. We can also fight even harder for more secure and well compensated jobs for average American workers. But even beyond these efforts to make our economy more responsive and responsible to people and nature, we need to envision and work for an American economy that over the long term produces far greater social and environmental equity, fairness, prosperity-sharing, collective purpose and responsibility. As the political philosopher John Rawls recommended, we need to advance a new theory of justice to govern our national priorities.[16] That is, we need to invoke a new creed in our public and private decision-making that mandates the state, as well as private institutions, to take actions that are in service to society's most needy people, humanity at large and the natural world. When we position the needs and well-being of society's most vulnerable people and the planet at the center of all major policy and private pursuits, we will achieve new levels of societal cohesion, mutual accountability, and success.

Promoting and Scaling Socially Responsible Enterprise

To address these and related considerations as we move ahead, we need to support the broad national scaling of successful, socially responsible enterprises that address our most pressing human and environmental needs, while also employing large numbers of Americans at living wages and with favorable benefits. Large private corporations that support this pathway through their business investments, alliances and procurement should be more favorably treated under our federal and state tax laws than those that do not. On the other hand, US corporations that actively work in other directions and are shown to have a pattern of grossly abusive conduct in relation to their workers and community health and safety should face real consequences for their misdeeds. Whenever and wherever possible, chronically irresponsible producers and employers should be subject to nationalization and resale to more responsible private investment and management groups.

Where foreign firms are implicated in these ways, they should be denied further access to our territory, our markets and our consumers. In the worst cases of corporate misconduct, whatever their geographical source, violating board members and executives should be subject to significant fines and prison terms. All of these changes in approach would require significant and sustained public organizing to produce enabling legislation and regulations designed to vastly increase corporate accountability when business conduct violates the law. Progressive leaders and activists should take the lead in helping to forge these efforts intended to make our economy far more responsive to human and environmental needs during the years to come.

Gearing Policy Support to Main Street, Rather than Wall Street

It should be the priority of all progressive community leaders and activists to advocate for greater public and private sector support of local economies that effectively encourage small-to-mid-sized and independently owned businesses to thrive. The more we can build our local and regional economies around Main Street versus Wall Street, the more likely we will be to rebuild the kind of social capital, community reinvestment and environmental stewardship that has waned so substantially across America during recent decades. And, by extension, the more conscious we can be in our efforts to promote "buy local," "hire local" and "invest local" campaigns, the more likely we will be able to maximize the assets our communities can keep and grow, rather than merely sending off all the profits they generate to some far away corporate headquarters in another nation or state.[17]

6. Promote Socially and Environmentally Responsible Collective-Impact Investing

A particularly promising strategy for encouraging more sustainable and socially beneficial enterprise is to harness collective-impact investing. Collective-impact efforts have been the focus of a growing cohort of social and environmental investment managers during the past decade, especially at larger private foundations and nonprofits seeking to advance their program and advocacy aims.[18] Generally, such efforts have been borne out of the recognition that isolated, singular efforts, no matter how deliberately pursued and resourced, are simply less effective than more inclusive efforts that engage multiple stakeholders in comprehensive, rather than piecemeal, responses to the issues. This is especially the case in instances where the issues of concern are highly complex and otherwise seemingly intractable.[19]

Investing for More Than Financial Profit

Impact investing acknowledges the power of directing traditional market investment to profit-generating deals and holdings that fundamentally support social and/or environmental benefits.[20] There has been significant growth in the formation of private equity funds investing in companies and social enterprises whose goods and/or services show a positive return on investment as well as positive impact on important social and environmental challenges. According to Jay Coen Gilbert,

A 2017 survey conducted by the Global Impact Investing Network (the GIIN, pronounced like the drink, is a de facto trade association for this emerging marketplace) found that in 2016, more than 200 self-identified impact investors . . . made nearly 8,000 investments. These investments totaled $22.1 billion and focused on creating a positive impact on society or the environment in addition to a positive return for investors. The GIIN projects that dollar amount will grow by more than 20 percent to $25.9 billion this year. And that growth doesn't include new funds in formation.[21]

While the scale of B Corporation and related social and environmental responsibility investment activity is presently very small as a proportion of the overall size of American and global capital markets, it is less and less inconsequential with each passing year. Indeed, the growth trajectory of this field has led large funds to commit talent and resources to impact investing, including Goldman Sachs and Bain Capital. In fact, various sources place the field's footprint at a far high dollar volume–with possibly as much as $114 billion presently under management.[22] And, looking at the broadest definition of investors considering social and environmental factors, some estimates go as high as $3.31 trillion in US-domiciled assets held by 443 institutional investors, 272 money managers and 1,043 community investment institutions applying various environmental, social and governance (ESG) criteria in their investment analyses and portfolio selection.[23]

Among the major philanthropic institutions helping to fuel impact investing, through social and environmental investment screening, program-related investments, micro-lending and other forms of mission-related investing, are the Heron Foundation, the Kresge Foundation and the David and Lucile Packard Foundation, as well as allied nonprofit anchor intermediaries such as the Nonprofit Finance Fund and Mission Investors Exchange. During recent years, leading institutions and networks like these have begun to demonstrate the early potentialities of alternative investment vehicles.[24] Independent social-venture capitalists, like Jay Coen Gilbert, have also stepped into the mix with new field innovations such as B Corporations, as well as pooled investment funds specializing in scaling socially and environmentally friendly firms and social enterprises.[25] Such vehicles seek both to make profits and actively to help improve the circumstances of average people, communities and the environment.

We Need a "Massive, Radical Change" in Investment Practices

Recent leadership and collaborative efforts in both collective impact and impact investing have come from major global and national social investment institutions in joint ventures intended to achieve real impacts on complex public problems. In Detroit, for example, the Ford Foundation and the Kresge Foundation have recently partnered with a coalition of public and private investors to help increase the ability of low-income families to purchase and renovate once-vacant homes through a mix of grants, loans and loan guarantees. Such collaborative efforts could—indeed should—be in play in every part of the nation, both in large cities, like Detroit, as well as in smaller cities and towns and rural communities all across America.

In a 2017 Ted Talk, Nancy Roob, president of the Edna McConnell Clark Foundation, advocated for "a massive, radical change in the way funders invest," arguing that we need to create a new normal whereby "dozens, if not hundreds, of funders join together so that funding flows more rationally and robustly to leaders with proven strategies for solving big social problems."[26] Roob's comments were concentrated on the ways private funders and donors make conventional charitable grants. But the essential wisdom of her call for a more unified social investment strategy, involving multiple players joining forces to advance and scale proven and successful local and regional innovations, could also apply to the ways in which significant social investors deploy their endowment capital and private equity assets.

Imagine the vast potential for change if the nation's leading philanthropies and nonprofits worked more intentionally and strategically to align not only their charitable efforts, but also their capital investments towards more socially and environmentally responsible ends. With combined assets in the hundreds of billions of dollars, participating social-investment and nonprofit leaders could have a far more significant impact on communities as well as the larger capital markets in which their dollars would be collectively infused. Through the expanded reach of both their good deeds and their market influence, a more united universe of agents for social change could produce unprecedented benefits for low- and moderate-income urban and rural communities alike, that are presently not possible. They could vastly scale socially responsible businesses and promising social-enterprise models that produce significant public and environmental value, pay living wages, offer meaningful employee benefits and pension plans, and train and activate workers who are otherwise not able to secure employment in the conventional marketplace.

Moreover, by concentrating on investments driven to minority- and women-owned firms, social enterprises that employ traditionally hard-to-place workers (such as Americans with disabilities, young people, ex-offenders and the mentally ill), and green economy leaders, charitable organizations participating in more intentional social and environmental responsibility investments of this sort could help profoundly to transform the landscape of the American economy and society. In many cases, this work would likely lead to profitable new investment and allied employment opportunities for conventional investors and workers as well. Indeed, in the future, socially and environmentally responsible enterprises could become the new normal for how America conducts business, optimizes human resources and better protects the planet.

For guidance on how progressive leaders can benefit from and help to shape this evolving work for greater social and environmental good, we need to look to anchor social investment and finance organizations, such as FSG and the Aspen Institute Forum for Community Solutions, as well as supportive intermediary organizations, such as the Global Impact Investing Network (GIIN), the Nonprofit Finance Fund, Social Venture Network and Business for Social Responsibility. But to fully harness the benefits of this expanding field, we especially need to look to leading entities that are creatively innovating in the space at the community and enterprise levels. These include the Boston Impact Initiative Fund, Bronze VC, ConnectUP!MN, REDF, Propel Capital and Transform Finance.[27]

7. Integrate and Align Progressive Advocacy Efforts

Important voices in the progressive community have begun to converge around the idea that we need to do a better job of harmonizing and joining our respective efforts in organizing, policy advocacy, leadership development and community investment across our various constituencies, issue areas and geographies. It is time to make this among our top priorities in all aspects of what we do now. As Linda Sarsour, executive director of the Arab-American Association of New York and co-founder of Mpower Change, states in a timely new documentary film entitled "Waking the Sleeping Giant: The Making of a Political Revolution,"

> We've been doing environmental justice, racial justice, immigrant rights; everyone's been doing their own separate mobilizations, separate set of priorities. [But what we need is] a

real political revolution that's multiracial, multi-ethnic, multi-everything. . . .When you are organizing, the most basic thing you need to do is look around the table and think to yourself "who's not here? Whose voice is not at the table? And once we start doing that for each other, then our organizing becomes more intersectional, and believe it or not, we expand the table and we expand and build more power."[28]

By unifying our efforts to advance a shared, comprehensive agenda on the issues of greatest concern to all of us, by strategically aligning our collective voices and resources, and by modeling the behavior we seek in our national leaders and institutions, we can maximize our impact for the greater good. Through efforts of this sort, ideally, progressive leaders and institutions can examine ways to raise the bar on our own practices related to multicultural inclusion, access and representation, as well as employment, investment and environmental responsibility.

If we are honest with ourselves, even within our own ranks, we know there is much work to do in each of these areas. That work has to start today. To these ends, we should be working together more intentionally to establish new norms and standards for our own conduct that can help to model for others what is possible in ways that make change more viral and real for less progressive leaders and organizations. By committing ourselves in our respective works to expanded intergroup dialog and partnership, more inclusive hiring and engagement practices, living wage employment and good jobs, socially and environmentally conscientious practice and procurement, and collective impact-investing, progressive leaders across America can substantially change the direction of our nation towards more harmonic, beneficial and just outcomes. Many of our leading organizations and networks are moving in this direction, but their efforts need to be met by the work of many others still. At the end of the day, in order for us to achieve the vision of the future we all want, none of us can do it alone. We can only advance together, because we are finally one community. We need each other and all of the talent, all of the ideas, all of the passion and all of the hope that resides in us and our shared values. There is no other way to forge lasting change in society except by people of conscience coming together to get the job done. There never has been. And there never will be.

Endnotes

[1]See Leuchtenburg, W. E., "When Franklin Roosevelt Clashed with the Supreme Court and Lost," Smithsonian Institution, May 2005: https://www.smithsonianmag.com/history/when-franklin-roosevelt-clashed-with-the- supreme-court-and-lost-78497994/. Among the major battles FDR lost in the Supreme Court during 1935 and 1936, respectively, were his proposals to enact a National Industrial Recovery Act (to establish broader controls over industrial production and pricing policies) and an Agricultural Adjustment Act (to more aggressively support farm production and economies through public subsidies and other measures).

[2]On the matter of relative cost savings resulting from more proactive and preventive social investments in people and communities, consider the following article showing the considerable economies and better outcomes achieved through homelessness prevention strategies like those made possible by Permanent Supportive Housing (PSH): Snyder, K., "Ending Homelessness Today," National Alliance to End Homelessness, June 30, 2015: https://endhomelessness.org/study-data-show-that-housing-chronically-homeless-people-saves-money-lives/.

[3]See Céspedes Kent, A., et al., *Measuring Up: Aspirations for Economic Security in the 21st Century*, Insight Center for Community Economic Development, April 2013: https://gallery.mailchimp.com/bf2b 9b3cf3fdd8861943fca2f/files/Insight_MeasuringUp_FullReport_Web_ 01.pdf.

[4]See especially chapters 4 and 12 of *The Rise of the Creative Class*, NY: Basic Books, 2002.

[5]Benner, C., and M. Pastor, *Just Growth: Inclusion and Prosperity in America's Metropolitan Regions*, NY: Routledge, 2012, p. 2.

[6]Benner, C., and M. Pastor, *Just Growth*, p. 9.

[7]See Farmer, A., "Citizen-Led Efforts to Reform Redistricting in 2018," Brennan Center for Justice, February 7, 2018: https://www.brennancenter.org/analysis/current-citizen-efforts-reform-redistricting.

[8]Kahn, A., and C. Kirk, "What It's Like to be Black in the Criminal Justice System," Slate, August 9, 2016: http://www.slate.com/articles/news_ and_politics/crime/2015/08/racial_disparities_in_the_criminal_justice_sys te m_eight_charts_illustrating.html, as well as Kamalu, N.C., et al., "Racial Disparities in Sentencing: Implications for the Criminal Justice

System and the African American Community," *African Journal of Criminology and Justice Studies*, Vol. 4, No. 1 (June 2010): https://www.researchgate.net/publication/260386399_Racial_Disparities_in_Sentencing_Implications_for_the_Criminal_Justice_System_and_the_African_American_Community.

[9]See Flanagan, T., "America's Highest Healthcare Cost in 2016? Mental Health," Healthcare Recruiters International, September 5, 2016: http://www.hcrnetwork.com/americas-highest-healthcare-cost-2016-mental-health/.

[10]See, Snow, K., and McFadden, C., "Generation at Risk: America's Youngest Facing Mental Health Crisis," NBCNew, December 10, 2017: https://www.nbcnews.com/health/kids-health/generation-risk-america-s-youngest- facing-mental-health-crisis-n827836.

[11]Fox, M., "Depression Worsening in Teens, Especially Girls," NBC-News, November 14, 2016: https://www.nbcnews.com/better/wellness/depression-worsening-teens-especially-girls-n683716.

[12]For more on the many complex issues affecting gang-affiliated and otherwise at-risk boys and young men of color in America see De Jesús Acosta, F., and H. Ramos, eds., *Overcoming Disparity: Latino Young Men and Boys*, Houston: Arte Público Press, 2016; De Jesús Acosta, F., H. Ramos, eds., *Latino Young Men and Boys in Search of Justice: Testimonies*, Houston: Arte Público Press, 2015; and De Jesús Acosta, F., *The History of Barrios Unidos: Healing Community Violence*, Houston: Arte Público Press, 2007. See also the informative website of the Oakland-based Alliance for Boys and Men of Color: http://www.allianceforbmoc.org/.

[13]McLaughlin, M., et al., "The Economic Burden of Incarceration in the U.S.," Institute for Advancing Justice Research and Innovation, George Warren Brown School of Social Work, Washington University, St. Louis: https://advancingjustice.wustl.edu/SiteCollectionDocuments/The%20Economic%20Burden%20of%20Incarceration%20in%20the%20US.pdf. According to the authors, while the direct expenditures for inmate incarceration in America are now some $80 billion annually, the total cost to society is more in the range of $1 trillion.

[14]See Australia-based Restorative Practices International on the core aims and practices of restorative justice at: https://www.rpiassn.org/practice-areas/what-is-restorative-justice/.

[15]"Restorative Justice in the Criminal Justice System," March 24, 2017: http://whatworksforhealth.wisc.edu/program.php?t1=20&t2=113&t3=101&id=494.

[16]Rawls (1921-2002), author of the renowned study in political philosophy, *A Theory of Justice* (Cambridge: Harvard University Press, 1971,

1999), advanced the moral assertion that modern civilized societies must first and foremost serve the interests of their least privileged members to achieve true justice, fairness and legitimacy.

[17]December 22, 2017 phone interview with Deborah Frieze, Co-Principal, Boston Impact Initiative: http://bostonimpact.org/about/#bii-about-team.

[18]See the Collective Impact Forum, a collaborative project of multiple private funders and donors committed to collective-impact work: https://collectiveimpactforum.org. The Forum is sponsored by FSG and the Aspen Institute Forum for Community Solutions with partnership and funding of social investment leaders the Annie E. Casey Foundation, the Bill and Melinda Gates Foundation and the William and Flora Hewlett Foundation.

[19]See Kania, J. and M. Kramer, "Collective Impact," *Stanford Social Innovation Review* (Winter 2011): https://ssir.org/articles/entry/collective_impact.

[20]See Coen Gilbert, J., "Putting The Impact In Impact Investing: 28 Funds Building A Credible, Transparent Marketplace," *Forbes*, October 9, 2017: https://www.forbes.com/sites/jaycoengilbert/2017/10/09/putting-the- impact-in-impact-investing-28-funds-building-a-credible-transparent-marketplace/#5ff307313e5f.

[21]Coen Gilbert, J., "Putting The Impact In Impact Investing . . ."

[22]See Bouri, A., "Three Big Takeaways from the Latest Impact Investing Data," *Stanford Social Innovation Review* May 17, 2017: https://ssir.org/articles/entry/three_big_takeaways_from_the_latest_impact_investing_data.

[23]"Market Sizing: Just How Big Is Impact Investing?" bethechange July 22, 2016: https://bthechange.com/market-sizing-just-how-big-is-impact-investing-c4209f400849. In addition to these examples of the impact investment field's emerging scale, it should be noted that a series of significant social investor conferences that were convened by Correlation Consulting principal Georgette Wong from 2007 to 2012 under the banner of the "Take Action: Impact Investing Summit," brought together 125 pioneering socially and environmentally focused investors representing some $4.5 trillion in assets. See RSF Social Finance: http://rsf-socialfinance.org/person/georgette-wong/.

[24]Onek, M., "Philanthropic Pioneers: Foundations and the Rise of Impact Investing," *Stanford Social Innovation Review*, January 17, 2017: https://ssir.org/articles/entry/philanthropic_pioneers_foundations_and_the_rise_of_impact_investing.

[25]See "24 Financial Ventures Changing the World through Social Impact Investing," CauseArtist July 25, 2016: http://www.causeartist.com/changing-the-world-through-social-impact-investing/.

[26]See Roob, N., "In 10 Years: A New Normal for Philanthropy," Ted Talk February 9, 2017: http://www.emcf.org/about-us/staff/nancy-roob/nancy-roob-tedxpennsylvaniaavenue-talk/.

[27]For more information on these kinds of emerging social investment fund leaders, as well as general challenges and opportunities for the field, see Foxworth, R., "Wealth Inequality and the Fallacies of Impact Investing," Medium, February 18, 2018: https://medium.com/balle/wealth-inequality-and-the-fallacies-of-impact-investing- eea902924309.

[28]See Jacob Smith: http://www.jacobsmith.com/films.

Conclusion

The heresy of one age becomes the orthodoxy of the next.

—Helen Keller

By the time this book is published, the 2018 mid-term elections will already have occurred and we will have learned more about how temporary or long-term Trumpism will turn out to be. Even if the election turns out, as most expect it will, to be a net win for the Democratic Party and a relative rejection of extreme right-wing ideology and continued chaos in Washington, it will remain to be seen whether the outcome portends a meaningful, lasting move towards the fundamentally new and different policy directions advocated for here. Only time will tell, of course. Major changes are generally the result of extreme circumstances and mass shifts in thinking and perspective that ultimately establish wholly new social agreements and possibilities.

If Democratic Party representatives do succeed in wresting power from the conservatives serving in the congressional majority as of this writing, that is, a majority that serves as a largely unquestioning blank check for the wayward Trump presidency, it will prove to be a major missed opportunity if the prevailing Democrats simply revert thereafter to business as usual: namely, a lighter and somewhat "friendlier" form of conservatism and neoliberalism. A moderate shift in national leadership and direction would do nothing to meaningfully alter the course of our nation and world, and so would do nothing to save us from the fast-approaching trauma that is already baked into the DNA of our domestic and global political economy. Rather, staying on a slightly moderated version of the course we have been on for the past four decades would not change the future.

Such an unhappy eventuality is entirely unnecessary and avoidable, but it will not be forestalled without amplified public advocacy and organizing from progressives. Even if Democrats regain control of Congress in 2018 and eventually the White House in 2020, there is no guarantee that renewed Democratic Party leadership alone will solve the many daunting challenges we face. On the contrary, the past decades are filled with examples of Democratic Party leaders making poor choices on matters of utmost relevance to social, political, economic and environmental justice. To concretize the point, one need only consider the Party leadership's decisions leading to the draconian criminal justice "reforms" of the 1990s, its unquestioning support of US military policy in the Middle East since 2003, the vast number of family- and community-disrupting deportations of undocumented immigrants (many of them lacking criminal records) that began in 2008 under the Obama administration and the continuing absence of a real Democratic Party strategy on climate change.

All of this suggests that the significant transformation that needs to occur in the next phases of American and world history cannot depend on either of the major political parties or the politicians they produce; rather, the better future we all seek will have to rely on the ideas, hard work and demands of common people like you and other activists, and more collective efforts to hold the professional politicians, whatever their persuasion, accountable to something larger than business as usual. That is to say what will define the future of our nation and our planet must increasingly be informed by dedicated progressive leaders and activists through even more aggressive organizing and advocacy. For this is how the nation's founders intended for US democracy and economy to work: by the will and the hand of the American people. Over the coming several years, accordingly, progressive leaders and institutions will need to redouble both their individual and collective efforts to chart a new course for the future, a course that centers on people and the planet, rather than on privilege and profit.

By defeating conservative politicians at the ballot box in 2018 and 2020, progressive leaders and activists can help to set the stage for scaling and normalizing the kinds of values, perspectives and innovations described throughout this book. By coming together, as progressives have done so many times in the past to advance reforms that mark our nation's best accomplishments, we can help to create a far better future, both here at home and eventually across the rest of the world. And, by moving in these directions, we can resuscitate humanity's potential and the planet's prospects for revival and long-term survival.

To progressive leaders who are at the forefront of change in our politics, economy and society, many arguments presented here will be known or otherwise familiar. But many of these ideas, concepts and models are at the outer edges of conventional experience, awareness and comfort; so much of it may be easily discounted or disregarded in establishment circles and among less-informed observers as impractical, wishful or otherwise overly optimistic. But that is mainly because the notions and applications advocated for in these pages implicitly challenge prevailing thought, and by their very nature and existence they pose inconvenient truths that are difficult for all but the most visionary among us to take seriously, let alone comprehend. There is nothing new about this. As Helen Keller once remarked, it is typically the case that challenging new ideas are first considered heretical, only to become accepted and taken for granted. With the rise of new ideas comes a complementary decline in the currency and standing of what was once accepted fact and law.

We must organize and align all progressives to institute our ideas and practices as an essential imperative for the survival of our planet and its people. In doing so, we can collectively bend the trajectory of our national politics and economy in fundamentally more just and sustainable directions over the decades to come. In this transitional journey, ideas and innovations like those featured in this book can help to facilitate an epic change in course. Our hard work will at some point sooner than later help to replace our current, increasingly unresponsive systems of pay-to-play politics and hypercapitalism with something different and better. In this calculus, every one of us has a role and a responsibility. None of us is exempt. What we decide to do today will make the difference for better or for worse relative to what tomorrow brings. Will we decide to proceed as a nation committed to reviving our best traditions of opportunity, inclusion, innovation and democratic example? Or will we instead elect to fall further into the celebration of selfishness, greed, neo-fascism and conspicuous consumption that has brought us over recent years to our current lamentable state?

At the end of the day, these choices are ours to make and to see through. If we are unable or unwilling to join forces and fight for a new and better way forward, as advocated throughout this book, then the future of our nation and world can only continue to be a troubled, violent and ultimately failed race against the end of the world as we know it. But, if we are able to step up to our potential and succeed, the nation and the world we will leave behind to our progeny will be a far better and kinder one: a world, that is, that finally reflects the very best of what humanity and nature are capable of.

APPENDIX

ADVISORS

Eric Abrams
Chief Inclusion Officer, Stanford University Graduate
School of Education, Palo Alto, CA

Orson Aguilar
Executive Director, The Greenlining Institute, Oakland, CA

Antony Bugg-Levine
CEO, Nonprofit Finance Fund, New York, NY

Angela Glover Blackwell
Founder in Residence, PolicyLink, Oakland, CA

Chrissie Castro
Social Justice Activist and Weaver, Native Voice Network,
Los Angeles, CA

Diana Dorn Jones
Executive Director, United South Broadway Corporation,
Albuquerque, NM

Darrick Hamilton
Executive Director, Kirwan Institute for the Study of Race
and Ethnicity, The Ohio State University

Saru Jayaraman
Co-Director and Co-Founder, ROC United, Oakland, CA

Surina Khan
CEO, The Women's Foundation of California, Oakland, CA

Stewart Kwoh
CEO, Asian Americans Advancing Justice, Los Angeles, CA

Homero Leon, Jr.
Partner, Lucas & Leon Attorneys at Law, Atlanta, GA

Geraldine P. Mannion
Program Director, US Democracy and Special Opportunities Fund, Carnegie Corporation, New York, NY

Adrienne Mansanares
Chief Experience Officer, Planned Parenthood, Denver, CO

Robert L. McKay, Jr.
Principal, McKay Investments, San Diego, CA

Scott Nielsen
Director, Advocacy Programs, Arabella Advisors, Chicago, IL

Derecka Mehrens
Executive Director, Working Partnerships USA, San José, CA

Zachary Norris
Executive Director, Ella Baker Center, Oakland, CA

Sheryl Oring
Distinguished Humanities Scholar, University of North Carolina at Greensboro, NC

Felix W. Ortiz III
Founder, Chairman and CEO, Viridis Corporation, New York, NY

Star Paschal
Board Vice Chair, Equal Voice Action, Auburn, AL

Manuel Pastor
Director, Program for Environmental and Regional Equity, University of Southern California, Los Angeles, CA

Kathi Pugh
Private Attorney and Board Chair, Disability Rights Education and Defense Fund, Berkeley, CA

Mike Roberts
President, First Nation's Institute, Longmont, CO

Anthony D. Romero
Executive Director, American Civil Liberties Union, New York, NY

Felicia J. Wong
President and CEO, Roosevelt Institute, New York, NY

Georgette Wong
Founder and Principal, Correlation Consulting, East Sound, WA

Richard Woo
Executive Director, The Russell Family Foundation, Gig Harbor, WA

EXPERT INFORMANTS

Nwamaka Agbo
Next Economy Fellow, Movement Strategy Center, Oakland, CA

Alberto Altamirano
Founder and CEO, CityFlag, San Antonio, TX

Annette Bernhardt
Director, Low-Wage Work Program, UC Berkeley Labor
Center, Berkeley, CA

Maria Blanco
Executive Director, UC Immigrant Legal Services Center,
Davis, CA

Sayu Bhojwani
Founder and President, New American Leaders, New York,
NY

Angela Brown
Policy Director, CF LEADS, Accord, MA

Christopher M. Brown
Financial Policy Director, PolicyLink, Oakland, CA

Kenneth C. Burt
Former Political Director, California Federation of Teachers,
Sacramento, CA

Annette Case
Independent Policy Consultant, Seattle, WA

Sharon Cornu
Strategic Communications and Community Engagement
Consultant, Oakland, CA

Tom David
Philanthropic Consultant and Former Vice President, The
California Wellness Foundation, Menlo Park, CA

Tammy Dowley-Blackmon
Principal, TDB Consulting Group, Boston, MA

Dr. Louis Freedberg
Executive Director, EdSource, Oakland, CA

Deborah Frieze
Co-founder and Managing Partner, Boston Impact Initiative, Boston, MA

Gabe Gonzalez
Founder, Project RP, and Former Campaign Director, Center for Community Change, Chicago, IL

Laura Harris
Executive Director, Americans for Indian Opportunity (AIO), Albuquerque, NM

César Hernandez
Senior Organizer, Center for Community Change, Washington, DC

Mary Ignatius
Statewide Organizer, Parent Voices, San Francisco, CA

Carla Javits
President and CEO, REDF, San Francisco, CA

Amy Mall
Senior Policy Analyst, Land & Wildlife Program, Natural Resources Defense Council, Washington, DC

Ali Noorani
Executive Director, National Immigration Forum, Washington, DC

Torie Osborn
Senior Strategist, Office of Los Angeles County Supervisor Sheila Kuhl, Los Angeles, CA

Carl Palmer
Board President and Executive Director, Legacy Works Group, Santa Barbara, CA

Peter Pennekamp
Senior Fellow, Community Democracy Workshop, Seattle,
WA

Mark Philpart
Senior Director, PolicyLink & Principal Coordinator,
Alliance for Boys & Men of Color, Oakland, CA

Anna-Nanine S. Pond
Principal, Anna Pond Consulting, Brooklyn, NY

Laurel Prevetti
Local Government Professional, Los Gatos, CA

Anne E. Price
President, Insight Center for Community Economic
Development, Oakland, CA

C. M. Samala
Co-Founder & Managing Partner, Jump Canon, San Francisco,
CA

Dr. Gabriela Sandoval
Research Director, Addressing the Health Impacts of Utility
Shutoffs Project, The Utility Reform Network, San Francisco,
CA

Joseph (Joe) Scantlebury
Vice President for Program Strategy, W. K. Kellogg
Foundation, Battle Creek, MI

Brenda Shockley
Deputy Mayor, Economic Development, City of Los
Angeles, Los Angeles, CA

Jacob Smith
Independent Film Producer and Former Mayor, Golden, CO

Robb Smith
Independent Policy and Program Consultant, Oakland, CA

Katie Taylor
Senior Director, Housing and Wealth Building, National
Urban League, New York, NY

Philip Tegeler
President/Executive Director, Policy & Race Research
Action Council, Washington, DC

Calvin M. Williams III
Senior Associate, Movement Strategy Center, Oakland, CA